Industrial England
1776–1851

Development
of English Society

Series Editor:

Dorothy Marshall

Formerly Reader in History in the University of Wales

The series will sketch the ways in which English society, seen as an entity, has developed from the England of the Anglo-Saxons to the England of Elizabeth II. Each volume is a separate study of a period of significant change, as seen by a specialist on that period. Nevertheless it is hoped that, taken as a whole, the series will provide some answers to the question 'How did we get from there to here?'

Future titles will include

The Later Middle Ages to the Accession of Henry VI *by E. J. King*
From Revolution to Revolution 1688–1776 *by John Carswell*
The Making of Modern English Society from 1850 *by Janet Roebuck*

Industrial England
1776-1851

Dorothy Marshall

Formerly Reader in History in the University of Wales

Routledge & Kegan Paul

London

First published 1973
by Routledge & Kegan Paul Ltd
Broadway House, 68–74 Carter Lane,
London EC4V 5EL
Printed in Great Britain by
Western Printing Services Ltd, Bristol
© Dorothy Marshall 1973

ISBN 0 7100 7470 0

326330

Series Editor's Preface

It is a truism that 'of the making of books there is no end' but, at least with regard to the study of history, there are two cogent reasons why this should be so. One is that each decade sees the examination of more and more source material as the increasing flood of research continues to rise. This, in itself, can necessitate the revision of older views and older certainties in the light of new knowledge. But even if no new material were available there would still be a need for new books because every generation asks its own questions and demands its own answers that make, or at least attempt to make, sense to contemporaries. The nineteenth-century student of history was concerned mainly with the world of politics, with the growth of the constitutional monarchy and of religious and personal freedom. Then with the turn of the century men began to ask different questions, questions concerned with the industrial society in which they lived, and Archdeacon Cunningham produced his pioneering work *The Growth of English Industry and Commerce*. For the first decades of the twentieth century the emphasis was on economics rather than social developments, though to begin with there was no very clear distinction between them. As economic history became more technical there also emerged a growing interest on the part of the non-specialist public in the everyday life of their ancestors, and the success of G. M. Trevelyan's *Social History* demonstrated how widespread the appetite for this kind of information was. Meanwhile the growth of the welfare state incited more and more people to ask questions about the history of the society in which they lived. How, for instance, had the relationships between the various layers which comprised it altered over the centuries? How far was social structure determined by economic factors? To what extent did the distribution of wealth within a society determine its form of government, both national and local? To what extent were ways of thought and attitudes towards religion, social problems, changing as the structure of society changed? The questions are endless.

It would be presumptuous to suggest that this series on 'The

Development of English Society' can even begin to answer them. Its aim is the much more modest one of sketching out the major ways in which English society, seen as an entity, has developed from the England of the Anglo-Saxons to the England of Elizabeth II. Each volume is a separate study of a period of significant change, as seen by a specialist on that period. Because each period presents different problems there can be no uniform pattern of treatment. Each author must make his or her own selection of where to place the emphasis in each phase of development. Nevertheless it is hoped that, taken as a whole, the series will provide some answers to the question 'How did we get from there to here?' This series is not, therefore, intended for specialists or to add to the volume of existing research; it is designed primarily for students whose courses, one hopes, will be enriched by a greater understanding of the main trends and developments in English society. It is intended to be a background book, not a text book, and as such the series should appeal to that increasingly wide circle of readers who, while not wanting to be bombarded by too much detail and too many facts, are interested in tracing back to its roots English society as we know it today.

This particular volume deals with the years between 1776, when the rift between England and her American colonies flared into open rebellion, and 1851, when the Great Exhibition blazoned forth Britain's industrial prominence to the world. This period played a crucial part in the story of the development of English society because it provides a link between that society in its traditional and its modern form. In the following pages I have tried to disentangle a few of the more important threads that joined together these two very different Englands. Throughout I have used the word England in its more limited sense. This is not because I wish in any way to ignore the changes that were also taking place in Welsh or Scottish society during these years but because, though these countries exercised a considerable influence over what was taking place in England, what was true of English society was not at any given time necessarily true of her sister countries. I hope this volume will whet readers' appetites for deeper and wider reading on at least some aspects of Regency and early Victorian England. I have accordingly both provided suggestions for further reading and, as far as possible, incorporated in the text contemporary material which can be followed up in collections of documents readily available in any good library, in the hope that their accessibility will encourage readers to explore them more fully for themselves.

Finally, my grateful thanks are due both to Dr Janet Roebuck and to John Carswell who very kindly looked at part of my MS. and made helpful suggestions, to my old friend Ethel Tattersall Dodd, whose knowledge of my very individual spelling and punctuation goes back to our days together in the Upper IV, and who, despite this knowledge, gallantly undertook the task of both struggling with my typescript and correcting my proofs.

Contents

Figures

Certain facts and figures can show us, in a very concentrated and succinct form, the state of the nation and the condition of the people. These have been kept to a minimum and the four graphs listed here will be found highly informative.

Chapter 1   The Economic Framework

English society in the closing decades of the eighteenth century can be likened to a traveller whose journey had taken him through foot-hills, across valleys where rivers had varied from turbulent torrents to broad and gentle streams, and over mountain ranges. Sometimes his journey had been hard and exhausting, sometimes pleasant and easy. But though there had been variety, the type of terrain that he had had to face had always been familiar, plains and rivers, foothills and mountains. He could rely on past experience. There had always been time to draw breath and readjust his technique as he left the hills for the valleys or the plains for the mountains. Now he was approaching a new type of country. His past experience would be far from valueless but it would have to be adjusted to very different con-ditions. Instead of achieving one summit, only to find its fellow facing him, the rocks behind which he could shelter were growing smaller, the wind fresher and more challenging. As he topped the rise he saw before him a vast plateau over which the mists hung low, so that, peer as he might, if there were further peaks ahead he could not see them, let alone discern their shapes and sizes. As he tried to look ahead the landscape seemed to be dominated by strange and unfami-liar forms. Though in the later stages of his journey he had noted many small indications that the terrain was changing, he had not expected anything so revolutionary. Nor had he expected the force of the wind that seemed to be pushing him further and further away from his familiar past. It was exciting but it was confusing and frighten-ing too.

The changes that faced English society and made the England of 1851 very different from that of 1776 possessed all these qualities. Whether men welcomed or feared it, they were being blown towards a new society by an irresistible wind of progress. Probably most people were reasonably content with the England that they knew, because to them it seemed a more desirable country in which to live than that which their fathers had known. It was healthier, it was wealthier, it

1

seemed to have achieved political stability. The old landmarks had not yet been swept away, or dwarfed and smothered and replaced by novel ways of life and modes of thinking. England was still a 'green and pleasant land' untouched by 'dark, satanic mills'. The majority of its people lived in the country. Apart from agriculture, which absorbed much labour, and the crafts or professions that depended on it, most industry was located in rural areas. Except for London, which had grown enormously in the eighteenth century, most British cities and towns were small. Even by 1801 only fifteen had a population of over 20,000. There were a few large ports but London monopolized much of the country's seaborne trade, though Bristol still handled a great deal of traffic, being the chief port for the slave ships carrying their human cargoes between Africa and the Caribbean. Many smaller ports served the coastal trade which played a vital part in the national economy until the revolution in inland transport. But by 1786 Liverpool was believed to have a population of around 50,000 and was growing rapidly. Apart from the ports, most towns were still each the natural centre of some rural area, providing it with a market for its local produce or industry and supplying it with those things that its people needed for their everyday wants. Men still wore clothes made by the local tailor and shoes by the local shoemaker. Some towns, such as Exeter and Norwich, had long been commercial centres for the clothing industry, organizing production in the rural hinterland and providing facilities for buying raw materials and selling the finished goods. During the eighteenth century towns of this type, particularly when they served some expanding industry, had been on the increase. Both Manchester and Birmingham are examples of this kind of growth. However, the actual manufacture of most goods still took place in the houses of the workers. The family was the normal economic unit and the number of persons who worked on their employer's premises was small; so were the premises on which they worked. Breweries, iron foundries, brickyards all employed wage labour, as did many minor industries, but most industry took place in the home. This was the traditional pattern, however much its details might vary from district to district and from industry to industry. Very few people in 1776 could have visualized what the next fifty years would bring forth.

This is not the place for either a detailed examination of the causes of the Industrial Revolution or for a comprehensive analysis of its major changes. Nevertheless because these changes affected the pattern of social development in this country so drastically the links

between the two must be indicated. Three factors profoundly influence social developments; rapid changes in the size of a country's
population, an improvement or breakdown in transport, and changes
in the ways in which the majority of people earn their living. In the
closing decades of the eighteenth century and the opening decades of
the nineteenth there were dramatic changes in each of these. They are
not easy to disentangle, and the historian is perpetually faced with the
aged problem of the egg and the hen, which came first? The inter-
actions between these factors were so intricate and complex that the
attempt to isolate them, however necessary for the sake of clarity,
must inevitably cause some historical distortion. Population figures
are notoriously unreliable before the first official census in 1801, and
even that leaves much to be desired. But because population was a
vital ingredient in the relative strength of the European powers, and
therefore a matter on which England, *vis-à-vis* her great rival France,
was very sensitive, English contemporary writers on political economy, as the new science was called, have furnished modern historians
with estimates that are a mixture of such statistics as were available
and brilliant guesswork. It seems unlikely that anyone will now get
nearer to the truth. The starting-point for all such calculations is the
work of Gregory King, who reckoned that in 1687 the population of
England and Wales amounted to roughly five-and-a-half million.
The increase by the mid-eighteenth century was considerable and had
possibly reached a figure of between six-and-a-half and seven million.
What is certain is that by 1801 the crude figure was 8,872,000 and the
revised figure, when allowances had been made for omissions and
errors, was 9,168,000. By 1851 this figure had doubled. Within the
period covered by this volume, therefore, the population had increased
approximately twofold. It had taken from prehistoric times to 1801
for the population to reach a mere nine million. It took only fifty
years for it to double itself and, fifty years are well within the life-span
of a man. Why this tremendous population explosion took place when
it did is still a matter of argument between historians, one school
laying the greater stress on a fall in the death rate, particularly of that
of young children and childbearing women, as providing its main
impetus, the other stressing the effect of a rising birth rate due to
changing social patterns, such as earlier marriages and more economic
opportunities. The argument is complicated by the fact that this
increase was not confined to Britain. Sweden, whose statistics go back
to 1749, experienced a similar one. The population of France was
growing in the same way; so was that of Ireland. Whatever the

explanation, certain consequences followed. The mass of the people had always been inadequately housed; now the problem was intensified. Moreover, these increased numbers had to be clothed and fed. They had to be organized in such a way as to increase the national product unless once again poverty and disease were to do their work. If the increase were to be maintained then new economic resources had to be developed and transport improved. The fact that although after 1851 the rate of increase lessened, the population not only continued to grow but, it is generally agreed, managed to improve its standard of living, is proof that this was done. Nevertheless the strain on traditional society was immense. Had the country not adopted new methods in agriculture, in industry and in transport the disasters that Malthus prophesied as a result of an ever-growing population must have followed.

The most rapid rise in the birth rate between 1780 and 1820 not only increased the population materially, but also altered the composition of the age groups within it. Though the death rate was heavy, and was to rise again in the towns in the third and fourth decades of the century, it seems to have dropped below its eighteenth-century peak. The result was a greater proportion of children, teenagers and young adults in the population. On one occasion Edwin Chadwick was to complain that half the labour troubles and undisciplined behaviour of the urban workers was due to the large number of hotheads who had less sense of responsibility than their elders. The argument is suspect; the interesting point is that it was made. This disbalance in age groups produced other problems for society. At what age should this very youthful segment of the population be allowed to swell the labour force in order to provide itself with the means to live? Until it was able to do so, how was it to be fed and clothed? How could it best be inured to social discipline, instructed in religion and given the modicum of education that the new industrial techniques were beginning to demand? Behind these questions lay the yet more fundamental one, was the flood of young lives becoming too overwhelming? In the past statesmen had considered a large population to be an advantage. In the new circumstances was it a curse? If so, how could it be curbed?

This spectacular increase of population had mental and emotional as well as material repercussions. In the past the problem had been to keep people alive in the face of the ravages of plague, the constant menace of smallpox and typhus, and the periodic failure of the harvest. The possibilities of the new situation were presented to the thinking public by Malthus, who in his successive editions of his *Essay on Population* (1798, rev. ed. 1803) issued a grim warning to his fellow countrymen when he argued in convincing terms that, because food supplies increased only by arithmetical progression while population increased by geometrical progression, the consequence must be a welter of suffering unless something could be done to check the birth rate. His views were not original. But by presenting in one coherent whole the scattered observations of other men he won wide acceptance for them and conditioned the way in which men thought about the new social problems with which they were faced. This is not surprising. Men believe the evidence of their own eyes. Though the future was to prove Malthus wrong, at least in the short run and as far as Britain was concerned, when his contemporaries saw the population double in their own lifetime their fears are understandable.

A further problem arose from the fact that, in the towns at least, this population was no longer homogeneous. In comparison with Ireland, England was a rich country. As a consequence there had been throughout the eighteenth century a constant flow of Irish peasants to England to fill seasonal gaps in the labour force when additional help was needed with the harvest. Most of them had returned with their earnings to eke out the bare subsistence that was all the land shortage and lack of industry afforded to the Roman Catholic majority. Some, however, had remained in London, where an Irish colony in St Giles-in-the-Fields was of long standing. As the population of Ireland increased the need to emigrate increased with it. By the end of the century more and more Irish workers were coming, not just for the harvest, but looking for permanent, or at least semi-permanent, work in England. Some came in the Welsh colliers that carried coals to Ireland and returned with this human freight. Many came to Liverpool, to which after 1824 the new steam packet boats provided quick and easy transport. In comparison with the native increase the Irish influx was small, but from the social angle it was highly significant, because it introduced a new element into the expanding industrial towns, particularly those of Lancashire. If these immigrants fell sick or were unemployed, for however short a time, being without any other resources they were a constant cause of trouble and expense to the Poor Law authorities. Though they had no legal claim on the authorities, destitute immigrants could hardly be left to die openly in the streets, and they were in fact given casual relief and passes to return to Ireland. In the first year after the new Poor Law Act of 1834 an assistant commissioner reported that one-fifth of the population of Manchester was Irish. They were also unpopular for reasons very similar to those advanced against the coloured immigrants in the nineteen-sixties. Because for the most part they were unskilled and were competing for work in a labour market where there was no shortage of hands, they were prepared to accept employment at wages so low that no Englishman would accept them except under the compulsive threat of the workhouse. Moreover the Irish accentuated the desperate shortage of houses and by their habits created additional problems in the towns. In Ireland their living standards had been desperately low and their ideas of hygiene and sanitation primitive. Crowded into the worst possible quarters, existing on the wages of unskilled labour, wherever they congregated the area became a slum. English workers resented them because their competition brought down wages, respectable householders resented them because they believed that they put up the rates. Protestants disliked them because they were Roman Catholics, against whom popular prejudice was still strong. Few people were prepared to admit that the economic contribution that they made counterbalanced the strains that they brought to urban life in those areas where they settled most thickly. Yet without the manpower that they provided as builders' labourers, as navvies digging canals (the word 'navvy' comes from 'inland navigation') and later in making railways Britain could not have moved into her industrial future with the speed with which she did. Integrating a new element into the population is never easy and those who suffer in the process are apt to stress the debit and ignore the credit side in the nation's balance sheet.

If the increased population had not been accompanied by increased agricultural production (due at least as much to the enclosure of new land as to the use of better methods), by fundamental innovations in basic industries, and by a transformation in internal communications, all without too great a time lag, the barrier of limited resources might, as in the past, have checked what by the eighteen-twenties seemed an irresistible flood. That the economy was able to respond to its new opportunities meant, however, that new strains were put on the fabric of society by the changes that this response involved. Briefly, they transformed Britain from a bundle of regions into a geographical unity, and they turned the majority of her people into townsmen and industrial workers instead of country folk whose income in one way or another depended on the land. The fact that both these fundamental changes were taking place at the same time makes it difficult either to isolate them or to decide on priorities. In the past

Britain enjoyed little more than a political unity, and that only in the very general sense that Parliament represented the entire nation and legislated for it. Economic and social life, with some exceptions was largely regional. One should not exaggerate this static character of pre-industrial society. There had always been more personal mobility than is sometimes realized. Nevertheless until the closing decades of the eighteenth century travel had been physically exhausting, slow, and not to be undertaken lightly.

The art of road-making had to be relearned before the roads were tolerable for anything but the horseman and the horsewoman or the humble pedestrian. In winter, or after heavy rain, roads that crossed the clay belt were almost impassable. The fact that each parish was responsible for the roads meant that they were repaired in the most amateurish way. Many parts of the country had no signposts. Away from the main arteries of trade, which connected London, the bigger towns and the ports, it was often necessary to hire a local guide if the traveller did not wish to risk being lost in forests or on moors and commons. The use that could be made of rivers to supplement the inadequacies of the roads was limited. Not only were many parts of the country deficient in serviceable rivers, but navigation was frequently hindered by dams, by weirs, by shallows and by the difficulty of dragging heavy barges along the towpath where they could be used. The result was to divide the country into a series of economic and social regions, each with its own provincial capital, its own ports, its own industries and its own way of life. Exeter and Bristol dominated the west, Norwich and King's Lynn East Anglia, York the north-east, Liverpool and Manchester the north-west, and rising towns like Birmingham, or older ones like Nottingham and Coventry, the midlands. London merchants had links with them all, and their products, both manufactured and agricultural, gravitated to the London market, either for consumption there or for export. For most people these links were at second or third hand, or even non-existent. The clothes of the Devon clothier might be taken by packhorse to the metropolis, but the weaver rarely went further than the nearest market town. Unless he lived within walking distance, even a journey to Exeter or Bristol was an event. The man who had been as far as either would describe the marvels of the city to his fellow villagers as something very strange and wonderful. Conversely, the urban worker rarely went far beyond the fields that ringed the town, though exceptions must be made for those craftsmen whose work was often itinerant. Pedlars regularly penetrated the isolation of villages and scattered hamlets, drovers regularly brought animals on the hoof to London and the bigger towns. Yet even such men generally confined themselves to a limited district. It would be unusual to find a Yorkshire pedlar in Sussex, or a Lancashire one in Devon. Tramping craftsmen, too, had their regular beats.

Though to a lesser extent, the gentry also spent most of their lives in their own neighbourhoods. Only those with extensive estates and generous rent rolls, the type of country gentleman who represented a local borough, or, even more importantly, the county, passed some part of every year in London when Parliament was sitting. Usually he was accompanied by his wife and family. Sometimes he was rich enough to own a town house, but the more general practice was to rent one for the season, or even to take furnished rooms. The majority went less far afield for their urban pleasures. During the winter months, when the roads were at their worst and villages were cut off by seas of mud, floods or snow, the more affluent gentry found it pleasant and convenient to repair to the provincial capital. Cities like Norwich had a very active social life. If the county town were too distant then the lesser gentry congregated in the nearest town that had any pretensions to be a social centre, such as Preston, or went to some genteel spa like Bath. Here they could attend assemblies, patron-ize the local circulating library and make easy contact with their friends without the hazards of travelling some miles merely to dine with a neighbour. When roads were bad, and, except within the familiar radius of home, comparatively unknown, there was little inducement to go further afield than the nearest market town. Even visiting was generally confined to moonlit nights. This was true even in towns. In Birmingham the well-known Lunar Society, composed of scientists and men of letters, got its name from the fact that its meetings were arranged to coincide with the prospect of a moonlit night. This lack of easy communication with other areas led to an intensification of local feeling. Even national politics were based on the reality of local interests and rivalries. It was enough for one leading county family to be Whig for another to be Tory. Local traditions died hard. Local superstitions had an all but religious sanction. People from another town, in the country almost those from another parish, were 'foreigners' or 'off comes'. Dialect shaped the language of ordinary people and even the gentry thought it no disgrace to speak with a provincial accent.

This regionalism affected many aspects of the national life. As woods and forests were eaten up coal became a vital fuel, and coal was heavy to move. Indeed to do so, except by water, outside a ten-mile radius was rarely economic. The result was both a multiplicity of small pits and an effective check on the growth of large towns, unless these were also ports. Basic supplies of foodstuffs were also largely limited to what could be produced locally. The limit which bad transport placed on the growth of towns was extended to industry. Only towns that had access to raw materials in sufficient quantities, and that possessed facilities for marketing the finished goods, could hope to develop any large-scale manufactures. Woollen and cotton goods were comparatively easy to transport on packhorses. Bulky goods were a very different proposition. This meant that local needs were largely supplied by local craftsmen, though whether the goods that they were making were clothes, or furniture, or even the house itself, they often copied London designs. Since the arrival of the postal service news and fashions travelled with surprising rapidity even to the remoter regions. Even so, what was up-to-date fashion in York-shire was behind the times in London. This division of the nation into tightly knit communities had the further effect of creating a tradition of opposition to any interference from the central government that later was to affect profoundly the way in which social legislation was to be envisaged and enforced. Communities, whether they were corporations or parishes, had managed their own affairs for so long without outside interference that local traditions had grown up, either within the framework of undetailed legislation, or to supple-ment it. The result was a considerable diversity of practice in such matters as the routine of holding parish meetings or in administering the Poor Laws. This was partly because of a lack of knowledge as to what was done elsewhere. Communities were not only self-sufficient. They were self-satisfied: criticism was muted and innovation ham-pered.

The first major breakthrough came with the construction of a widespread network of canals. These had long been used in Holland and in France and it is not surprising, once there was a reasonable prospect of a good return on the heavy expenditure that building them would necessitate, that they should be introduced into England, though to read some accounts of the Duke of Bridgewater's experi-ment in linking his coalfield at Worsley with the profitable Manchester market one might suppose them to have been a British invention! The details do not concern us. The first canal boom came in the late sixties and early seventies of the eighteenth century, the second in the eighties and nineties. By the mid-nineteenth century, when canals had been overshadowed by the even more effective railways, there were over four thousand miles of inland waterways. This in itself was enough to break the stranglehold on both urban development and on industry. It has been calculated that whereas a packhorse could carry one eighth of a ton, and a barge pulled by men or horses along a river bank thirty tons, one hauled along from the towpath of a canal could deal with a load of fifty tons. It was not only goods that the canals carried in their heyday. Passengers who did not mind the slow pace of the long boats, or who could afford no other form of transport, also patronized them. On many canals regular packet boat services were run. In 1817 travellers from Manchester or Liverpool who wished to visit 'that place of fashionable resort' Southport, could take the packet as far as Scarisbrick Bridge, where carriages were waiting to take them on the last stages of their journey.

By then the roads too had been much improved. The wealthy travelled in style and comfort in their own conveyances, changing horses at regular posting inns and accompanied by a postillion and, if ladies were travelling alone, by a man servant, or at least a maid. Travellers who did not possess their own carriage had a choice of public transport. They could take a stage-coach or the royal mail. Even genteel females from what were coming to be described as the middle classes had the freedom of travelling thrown open to them because it was now possible, though often uncomfortable, to use a public conveyance. Miss Weeton, a governess who, fortunately for posterity, kept a very full journal and letter book, enables us to see this kind of travel through contemporary eyes (Ellen Weeton, *Miss Weeton: The Journal of a Governess*, ed. E. Hall (1939) 314–17). In 1824 she made the journey from Wigan to London and back by coach. Partly for economy and partly from preference she occupied an outside seat, which was cheaper. Stops were short. Having left Prescott at two in the afternoon they stopped for tea at nine p.m., by which time it had grown very cold. The next stop was at midnight at Lichfield where for ten minutes the shivering passengers were allowed to warm themselves by the kitchen fire. At Lutterworth she took 'a hearty breakfast of coffee'. There was another stop at Northampton for lunch. The return journey was more eventful. The first part was enjoyable. She left the Spread Eagle in Piccadilly at 5.45 on a lovely morning and when the coach stopped for a full half hour in the evening she got 'a good warming at the kitchen fire'. But from Birmingham, where she had to change coaches, things went wrong. They had taken up 'six Irishmen of the lowest description', one of whom appropriated her seat so that she was forced to ride 'the rest of the night on a very dangerous outside seat behind, backwards'. As if this were not enough, she wrote, 'The man on my left kept a constant motion with his head upon my shoulder, up and down the night through, being heavy to sleep, the brim of his hat endangering my eyes.' Next morning another woman on the coach confided to her that she too had 'passed a dreadful night, an Irish pig driver on each side of her, and another in front, snoring and resting their heads against her, to prevent themselves falling'. This journey had lasted from 5.45 on the morning of 29 July until 11 a.m. on 30 July when she reached Liverpool. In spite of her discomfort she was full of praise for the new roads, writing 'Mr McAdam's name was on many a board as we approached [London], thanks, ten thousand thanks to him I say for the easy ride. I should have been more shook if I had journeyed from Wigan to Southport'. Nevertheless there were shortcomings. On another occasion, when there had been no rain for three weeks she found the dust intolerable, writing 'The roads laid on McAdam's plan are better for carriages and easier for draught horses, but for humans they are one continued cloud of dust, blinding to the eyes, filling the nostrils, going down the mouth and throat by quantities to suffocation and completely ruinous to all decent clothing. Houses by the road are inundated with dust, and all cleanliness destroyed and useless. The fields are so covered on each side, according as the wind blows, that they are much less value an acre than those more distant from it. If Mr McAdam could lay the dust as well as the roads he would be a clever fellow' (ibid., 343).

Nevertheless despite its discomfort the era of travel had arrived. This in itself was a social revolution. McAdam and Telford between them had constructed roads that made both speed and punctuality possible. Coaches travelled at ten miles an hour, the changing of teams was reduced to split minute timing, meal stops, as Miss Weeton found, were brief. Only three of about twenty-five minutes each were allowed on the journey from London to Edinburgh, which took only forty to forty-three hours. The modern 'comfort stop' was apparently non-existent. The rapid spread of the urge to travel is attested by the amount of capital that went into the new equipment needed to satisfy it. Though the royal mail was a government monopoly the stage-coach services were financed by private enterprise. This meant a considerable investment in horses and coaches as well as the payment of drivers, guards and ostlers. This life of the road for the twenties and thirties captured the imagination of the age. Men of wealth and breeding attempted to emulate the expertise of the professional coachman, 'tooling' their own elegant equipages and wearing the many-caped coats that were their protection against the weather. Sir Vincent Cotton even drove the famous *Brighton Age*. Later Dickens, already overtaken by the less glamorous railways, looked back and wrote nostalgically of the coaching days. Their convenience and delights were, however, confined by pecuniary considerations to the middle class. On the fast day coaches the fares for inside passengers, where four people could sit in comfort, were from 4d to 5d a mile. Passengers travelling outside, where they were exposed to any kind of weather paid from 2d to 3d. Fares on the mail were almost double. When agricultural workers often earned less than 12s a week and an artisan thought himself well off with 30s coaches were not for them. But for their betters well-made roads had brought a new mobility. Jane Austen's heroines go to Bath, pay visits, explore Derbyshire and even contemplate a tour of the Lakes.

Important though the influence of the coaching era was on the pattern of social behaviour, making new pleasures and new experiences more easily available to the middle class, even to its womenfolk, and helpful though the canals had been in the economic sphere, large-scale industry, large towns and the mobility of the working class as a whole were only made possible by the coming of the railways. With industry speeding up its output every year, and with the population increasing at an alarming rate, there was every incentive to push ahead with new forms of transport. Moving coal, now more essential than ever both as domestic fuel and for industry, had long been a problem. It was from this necessity that the idea of a railroad was born. Rails, first of wood, then of iron, were laid down along which to pull the coal trucks from the pit head to the nearest river or canal. The next stage was to employ a stationary engine to pull them up a slope. If the engine could move with the trucks then still more advantage would accrue, and men set about this problem also. The details of this achievement belong to the technical history of the Industrial Revolution, but with the opening of the Stockport to Darlington railway for freight in 1825 and the Liverpool to Manchester for goods and passengers in 1830 a new epoch had begun.

It is impossible in a short space to assess or analyse the social effect of the new railways because of their wide repercussions. Briefly, they made large-scale industry possible, partly because bulky raw materials could now be first concentrated, then processed and finally sold on a national market, and partly because railways stimulated the demand for iron to construct them and for coal with which to fuel them. They also made urban development on a large scale practicable now that the railways could transport the materials with which to build them, the food with which to feed them and the coal with which to warm them. Mass production meant that more workers could be concentrated in larger factories. More workers and their families meant more shopkeepers, more managerial staff, more professional men: as a result the urban population snowballed and towns sprouted everywhere. Where a town of some importance already existed, then the coming of the railway both stimulated such of its economic activities as could be adapted to a national market and affected the urban layout and social zoning of the town. To the working man the railways gave a new mobility that eventually was to transform his way of life. True, third class travel was uncomfortable, the early carriages were little better than open cattle trucks, but compared with the coach it was both fast and cheap. The fare on the latter between London and Edinburgh had been £10, including the tip, for inside passengers, and £7 for those riding outside. The train carried passengers for £2 at not ten miles an hour but, by the mid-century, at least fifty. If in these decades the population was doubling, the speed at which men could be transported from one place to another had increased fivefold. Speed, like mobility, had become a new factor in the pattern of society. It was to be the solvent of the traditional way of life. A hundred and thirty years later the *Rocket*'s thirty miles an hour was to seem like the slow speed of the tortoise when compared with the planes which first broke the sound barrier, and to have no speed at all in comparison with the moon flights of the *Apollos*.

By the opening of the Great Exhibition Britain had more than a mere skeleton railway network. Like so many of her industrial achievements, the process was piecemeal and unplanned. Every businessman wanted to take advantage of this new and efficient way of getting the raw materials to his factory and of dispatching his finished goods. The money was available locally for such enterprises and as a result many small lines were built. Had it not been for the dominating part played by the Stephensons this might have been disastrous, because until 1846 there was no legal standard gauge, and this must have delayed the integration of the country's railway network. Not every engineer considered the narrow gauge of 4ft 8½in. desirable and in the west country the broad gauge of 7ft advocated by Isambard Brunel was adopted. No engine could have run on both, and time and money would have been lost while trucks were emptied and reloaded. As things were, the advantages of through traffic were soon realized and running rights over other companies' permanent way arranged. Gradually mergers took place between the smaller lines. In 1846 there were some 200 of these but by 1851 they had been reduced to some 22 important lines, though a few small ones did still retain their independence. In these formative years in addition to such amalgamations new track was laid down with the result that the mileage in the United Kingdom, which had been 2,036 miles in 1843, was 8,280 by 1855. Both the dates and the mileage are important from the angle of social development because they provide a measure of the impact of this new form of transport over twenty years. By 1840 a traveller from London could take the Great Northern line as far as Doncaster, where he would have a choice of routes to Scotland via either the East or West coast. The railways had not yet made England an economic and social whole but they were well on the way to doing so. So normal had it become for all classes to travel by train that the Railway Act of 1844 decreed that one train in each direction per day should carry third class passengers and stop at every station. This was the famous, or notorious, 'parliamentary train'. On it third class passengers were to be carried for 1d a mile at a speed of not less than twelve miles an hour, though in practice third class coaches were generally attached to ordinary trains.

Interesting social consequences came from the general acceptance and use of railway travel. The provision that they made for first class, second class and third class passengers emphasized the class distinctions of the new society. Workmen travelled third, the middle class second and the gentry first. Any deviation from this was felt to be unacceptable. A middle class traveller, who for motives of economy, travelled third, was frowned upon as one who was evading the responsibilities of his station in life. He was disliked by the railway companies as diminishing their revenues in a shabby way and by the workmen as intruding into company where he did not belong. One argument for not increasing the amount of third class accommodation was that except at Easter or Whitsuntide few of the working class could afford to travel, except on workmen's early trains in some areas. Nor was it thought advisable to provide more than the parliamentary minimum of comfort, because to do so might be only to encourage more people who could afford the second class fare to travel third. Nevertheless working class people did take the train as a matter of course in increasing numbers, though for many their first journey was 'a matter of wonder' as Mary Barton found it, even though, as

Mrs Gaskell observed, railways were common 'in all places as a means of transit, and especially in Manchester'. For superior artisans and the lower middle classes the speed and cheapness of the railways was making travel for pleasure, and not merely for work, a growing possibility. Railways began to run excursion trains, and those that ran from London to Margate on Sundays were crowded. England had traditionally been a nation of seafarers, though in fact the majority of the labouring poor had never seen the sea. Now, first within a limited radius and then, as the decades went by, within a larger one, they were able to visit the seaside.

To the middle class railways gave a greater range to their activities, whether for business or pleasure. It was easier for women to travel alone, and to that extent it favoured their social emancipation. Visits to friends and relations no longer needed to be a matter of weeks or months, now that journeys were less expensive and hazardous. Whole families, complete with governess and servants, could take an annual holiday by the sea. The benefits brought by the railways were not confined to the working and middle classes. First class travel was comfortable, quick, and, compared with that magnificence demanded when the aristocracy, or even the gentry, travelled by road, much cheaper. This enabled the aristocracy to indulge in increased mobility with economy. Where for instance, in the past a great landowner who had possessed estates in various parts of the country had found it necessary to keep an adequate staff of servants in each because of the expense of transporting any but the personal servants to and fro, now only a skeleton staff need be permanently employed, local help being engaged for additional labour and the key domestics transferred from one great house to another by train. Not only was the domestic economy of the aristocracy altered in this way, the pattern of their hospitality was also affected. Now that travel was less of an under-taking, visits of one or two months began to give way to shorter house parties. The weekend visitor was already on the horizon. For the aristocracy even death became cheaper because of the railways on those occasions when the head of the family died far from his ancestral vault. Instead of the impressive cavalcade of hearse and mourning coaches making its solemn journey the coffin could now be placed with quiet decorum on the train, and from thence with dignity, but much less expense, to the place of interment. Funerals were still an occasion for sombre black, for magnificent horse-drawn hearse, for ostentatious grief, but class distinctions were beginning to disappear. A wealthy banker might be given a funeral as magnificent as that accorded to a noble lord. In other ways also the railways helped to destroy class distinction. In their eyes there was no difference between the wealthy parvenu and the gentleman; they were both 'first class'.

A similar revolution in transport was taking place at sea, though in the first part of the nineteenth century this had less impact on the pattern of society than the railways. This was partly because the daily lives of the majority of people were unaffected by it. The need for better facilities for seaborne traffic was due to the increased demand for imported raw materials and the increased outflow of finished goods which meant that serious attention had to be given to the provision of more adequate docking arrangements. At the end of the eighteenth century those of London were lamentable. In 1799 the building of docks was started to replace the older method of unloading from lighters onto the quays, and during the first three decades of the nineteenth century their area was enlarged tenfold. In the north Liverpool was similarly improving her dock area, as were Hull and Grimsby and Bristol. Nevertheless the steam engine took longer to conquer sail on the sea than it had taken to conquer the horse on land. Even by the mid-century ships were paddle-steamers. Miss Weeton, when she saw them on the Mersey in 1817 described them as making 'rather a laughable appearance; they go puffing and blowing, and beating their sides and labouring along with all their might'. She made a trip to Runcorn herself in one of them which she said 'had a rough tide to work upon', adding 'it is very unusual for passengers in a Steam-boat to be sick; but few escaped it that day' (Weeton, op. cit., 155–6). It is not always remembered that these tiny paddle-steamers were carrying passengers on rivers, and even between England and Ireland, before locomotives were carrying them on land. Nevertheless even by the mid-century the battle of the steamship had not been won. The wool crop from Australia and the tea from China still came in the fast and beautiful clippers that were the pride of the British and American shipyards. In the first half of the nineteenth century therefore the main social impact, apart from the impact of the increased immigration of Irish labourers, on the social pattern made by the developments in sea transport was due to the enlarging of the dock areas to meet the increased volume of overseas trade rather than the type of ship employed in it. Great numbers of casual labourers were needed to build the docks and later to load and unload the ships that used them. The parishes that had abutted onto the Pool of London had always been rough places, abounding in taverns, bawdy-houses and low-grade housing. With an extension of these areas the great docklands of the East End became a permanent part of the London scene. The same thing was happening in Liverpool and Hull. It was to leave to posterity a legacy of slum houses and underemployment, of casual labour and of drink, that was to provide a headache for the social reformers of the late nineteenth and twentieth centuries and which lies behind many of the labour troubles of the nineteensixties.

Important though the transport revolution was in creating the conditions which made a common social and cultural unity possible, it was only one factor in the general movement that historians have christened the 'Industrial Revolution'. This process was less rapid than the word 'revolution' might suggest. Yet though the seed-time stretched much further back into the seventeenth and even sixteenth centuries, the changes that technological invention brought in its train fully deserve, in their effects, if not in their time sequence, to be described as revolutionary. On the industrial side there was a tremendous increase in the productivity of basic commodities, such as textiles and iron goods, for which there was an enormous potential demand, both at home and overseas. The milestones in this story are well marked and well known, and need no elaboration here. The spinning jenny invented by Hargreaves, the waterframe introduced by Arkwright, and finally Crompton's mule, which incorporated the virtues of both, meant that by the seventeen-seventies spinning was slipping out of the hands of a multitude of women, scattered over the length and breadth of the land, and was being concentrated in factories. This in itself produced a social revolution of no mean order. The married working women of Britain lost what had been the traditional way of supplementing the family income, while the unmarried woman, the spinster, had taken from her even the poor living that she had. Now both would have to go into the factories or find alternative employment in the home. Obviously this change did not happen overnight. Factories had to be built, or older mills adapted to use the water power necessary to drive the new machines, though the early jennies could still be worked by hand, so that the entire family might be set to work spinning in some shed. This, however, afforded only a brief respite. Even by the seventies, particularly in the cotton districts of Lancashire and Cheshire, the dilemma had to be faced. Wool, which was less amenable to the new processes, took longer to go over. It should be noticed, too, that the results of technical change did not hit every part of the community, nor even similar social groups, at the same time. Industrialization was always a patchwork and piece-meal affair.

Had technical advances only affected the spinners, the consequences would have been disastrous for them yet the disruption of the existing social pattern would hardly have followed. But technical advances, like sorrows or swallows in spring, rarely come singly. Except for the odd accidental discovery, such inventions are the product of a pur-poseful search. The entrepreneurs who had organized the manu-facture of cotton and woollen goods had been painfully aware of the inconvenience of working with so scattered a labour force. Mechanical spinning and weaving had been a goal long before it had become a reality. The breakthrough in weaving did not come until the nine-teenth century, though the theory had been mastered by Cartwright, who had produced and patented a prototype of the power loom by 1787. The first power looms which could be regarded as commercial propositions were installed in a Manchester mill in the early nine-teenth century, but it was not until the twenties and thirties that the use of them became widespread. Until the forties there were still more hand-loom weavers than those working on the power loom, even in the cotton manufactory. It was this long struggle between the old and the new that was responsible for much of the misery of these years. Here again was the stuff of a new social revolution as the machine bit into the pattern of the traditional domestic industry. Inexorably textiles, first cotton and then wool, were moving into the factories. It was no longer a question of the wife losing her by-employ-ment; the whole family was affected. In clinging to the old methods in spite of falling wages the weaver was defending a way of life and refusing to accept the pattern of the future.

Technical advance in the manufacture of iron led to less change in the traditional organization of the industry and brought less hardship to the men who worked in it. By its very nature it had never been a domestic industry, nor had it employed a large labour force. Never-theless its social impact, both directly and indirectly, was great and, like the movement of textiles into the factories, it put its stamp on the new age. To understand this impact it must be remembered that until 1709, when Abraham Darby used his new process, iron ore could only be smelted by using charcoal. This meant that because British forests had been exhausted, and what timber was available was needed for other things from the making of furniture to the building of ships, the production of iron was limited to those areas where not only deposits of ore existed but where there was room to grow the coppice wood from which the charcoal was made. In turn this meant that the industry was forced to be migratory, charcoal-burners and furnace-men moving to where iron deposits and coppices were in close proximity and then, when the local fuel supplies were exhausted, moving on again. Until the seventeen-sixties the new process made little impact on the traditional methods, partly through secrecy, partly because it was of limited application. It could produce cast iron but not iron suitable for the smith to use. By 1760 there were still only seventeen blast furnaces using coke in Britain. With the growing demand for iron for industrial purposes, combined with the invention of a steam-driven blast furnace powered by Watt's engine, the number increased rapidly. By 1790 only twenty-five furnaces still using charcoal remained in operation. Meanwhile two men, Henry Cort and Peter Onions, working independently, by 1784 had dis-covered how to remove the impurities that spoilt the quality of cast iron by the use of a process of puddling in a reverberatory furnace. Together these two inventions revolutionized the making of iron. Coal, which was abundant, replaced charcoal and, instead of small units, mass production was possible. From these facts flowed two important social consequences. The industry was no longer migratory: it could be developed wherever coal and iron were to be found to-gether. Secondly, because the demand for iron mounted every year, its manufacture provided employment for a growing labour force at a time when the population was also growing. Nor was this employ-ment confined to the making of the iron. To the old crafts of the nailer, the chain-maker and the domestic manufacturer of small-scale iron goods were now added the necessities of the modern age, steam pumps, engines, rails and cast iron bridges, all of which afforded work on an extended scale. The iron age had begun and with it the smoky towns of the Black Country.

The demand for iron had other consequences. Iron needed coal and coal meant the expansion of mining and the absorbing of more men, women and children into that harsh occupation. From the end of the seventeenth century an early version of the steam engine, invented by Newcomen, had been used to work the pumps in Cornish tin mines. When, improving on this, James Watt patented his new and more efficient design, and later went into partnership with the businesslike Matthew Boulton, together producing the new engine at the famous Soho works outside Birmingham, the age of steam, like the age of iron, had begun. Initially its social and even economic impact was small. This was partly because Boulton and Watt defended their patent with tenacity, partly because the new engines needed skill to maintain, and partly because many of the early factories had adopted water power and were slow to change. In the first decades of the nineteenth century, however, increasing numbers of manufacturers went over to steam. This also was to have momentous consequences for the siting of industry. The early factories, which had depended on water power, had perforce been built wherever this had been available. Because only a limited number of mills could use the same stream industry was necessarily spread out and many small manufacturing villages were created without much prospect of future growth. Now the three aspects of the Industrial Revolution, improved transport, power driven machinery and mass produced iron, came together to foster and promote what was to be the hallmark of the nineteenth century—urbanization.

The growth of large towns, more than any other single factor, transformed the Britain of the past into the Britain of the future. The effect on every aspect of social development was immense. With so much to encourage it, urban growth is not difficult to explain. Nevertheless it is staggering. Though not primarily an industrial city, London led the way. With its outlying areas, London in 1801 contained some 957,000 people; in 1851 it contained 2,362,000. A cluster of Lancashire towns showed tremendous increases. In 1801 Blackburn had a population of 12,000, Preston's was similar. Salford had 14,000, Bolton 18,000, Oldham 22,000 and Manchester already 70,000. Liverpool, one of the most populous cities in Britain, had achieved 82,000. Fifty years later the figures for these towns were: Blackburn 47,000, Preston 70,000, Salford 63,000, Bolton 61,000, Oldham 72,000, Manchester 303,000, and Liverpool 376,000. (These figures are to the nearest thousand.) Yorkshire can show some even more dramatic increases. There were only 13,000 people in Bradford in 1801; by 1851 there were 104,000. Sheffield, which even in the eighteenth century had been a considerable town, had increased its population from 46,000 to 135,000 in the same period. The same spectacular urban growth was taking place in South Wales, where the iron and coal town of Merthyr Tydfil had shot up from a mere 10,000 to 63,000. To summarize the situation, in 1801 there had been only fifteen towns in England and Wales, and five in Scotland, with a population of over 20,000. By 1851 there were sixty-three in the former and nine in the latter. Nor was this urban growth taking place only in centres of industry. Though many of the smaller ports were showing a tendency to decline when the coasting trade found itself in competition first with the canals and then with the railways, many small fishing villages found themselves blossoming as watering-places. As more and more people were forced by economic necessity to spend most of their lives in the dirt and noise of the industrial towns so the demand grew, first among the middle classes, and then among the working classes, for places to which they could make a brief escape. Blackpool was as much the creation of the Industrial Revolution as Bolton or Rochdale. In contrast to all this urban growth some of the older towns, which had once been centres of trade and industry but which had failed to attract the newer manufactures, though they had shared in the general increase, had done so less spectacularly. Norwich had not even succeeded in doubling its population, while Bristol, once one of England's leading ports, had grown only from 61,000 to 137,000 in the first fifty years of the nineteenth century.

As towns expanded and factories multiplied, the fortunes of more and more people came to depend on the state of trade. When that was good, manufacturers made profits, employment was steady, opportunities for the enterprising and the skilled were more plentiful, and even wages might swing upwards a little under pressure from the newly emerging trade unions. When mill owners and operatives alike had more money to spend, shopkeepers did well and so did the craftsmen who supplied them. When trade was depressed the reverse was true. Profits fell, spending declined as factory workers suffered from cuts in wages, short time and even unemployment. Social historians, therefore, though they are not directly concerned with the causes of the recurrent booms and slumps of the first half of the nineteenth century, are very much concerned with their consequences. Overseas trade was now vital to Britain's existence. Except when the harvest was especially good it was now necessary to import corn to feed the ever-growing population. This could be paid for only by the export of iron and cotton and the more traditional woollen goods. Luckily the world was greedy for these commodities and, as other countries began to industrialize after the end of the war, Britain sent them not only consumer goods, but also the capital equipment which they needed for their railways and their factories. Both public opinion and public men alike were concerned to promote overseas trade, and this concern was reflected in the discussion both in Parliament and in the Press. The result was the gradual reversal of the mercantilist policies of the past. Export duties went. Import duties, once protectionist in aim, were first made more reasonable and uniform then whittled away until those that were retained were retained only for revenue purposes, the financial gap being closed by what it was hoped would be a temporary measure, the re-imposition of a wartime expedient, an income tax. The old Navigation Laws also went; after 1849, and then only for a further four years, only the coasting trade was reserved for British ships. This free trade policy had been very largely sponsored by the new entrepreneurial classes, who wanted the maximum freedom in which to expand, and while it bears witness to their importance as an influential section of the population it was not a threat to the landowning gentry and aristocracy. This was not the case when the last bastion of protection, the Corn Laws, came to be debated. The manufacturers pressed for their abolition, arguing that this would both enable countries which sent us grain to buy our manufactures in return and would make food cheaper in Britain, an argument which the workers viewed with considerable reservations, believing that abolition would merely end in a lowering of wages. The long-drawn-out campaign, with the manufacturers attacking and the landed interest defending the traditional protection that agriculture had always received, did much to high-light the growing class differences that marked the first half of the century as both social groups mobilized to fight for what they believed to be their material welfare.

Certain aspects of the financial system also affected social development. Opportunities to borrow on reasonable terms can turn the small yeoman or the enterprising craftsman into a mill owner or capitalist. Opportunities for profitable investment can create a rentier class. Security for savings and encouragement to save can keep the independent working man from a degrading dependence on the Poor Law. In the financial world, as in the world of agriculture and industry, change was taking place. Even as late as 1776 credit and investment had been mainly the concern of the business world. The landed classes as a whole had used their profits to buy more land, or had ploughed them back into improving their estates. When they had invested it had been in government securities, 'the Funds', as the consolidated funds on the National Debt were called. If they wanted money to finance mines or quarries or foundries, they borrowed on the security of their estates. The middling sort for the most part had put their savings into their own businesses, or, like their betters, into the Funds. The Industrial Revolution both provided better opportunities for investment and new institutions for obtaining credit. To finance a canal, a turnpike or a railway needed more capital than an individual, or even a small group, could raise, so application was made to Parliament for the right to form a joint stock company. For the first time since the bursting of the South Sea Bubble a speculative mania seized the country. When the canal boom broke in 1793 and the railway boom in 1847 many were ruined but Britain had got her canals and her railways. She also had a new investing public.

Banking facilities were also becoming more available for ordinary people. By law the Bank of England was the only joint stock bank with the right to issue notes, and until the second half of the eighteenth century most private banks, which had grown out of individual money-lending and commercial enterprises, were in London. But by the second half of that century private banks with note issue were to be found in increasing numbers in the provinces also. These were at once a source of strength and of weakness. Because they were owned by local men they were good judges of local conditions and local characters. This made them ready to advance loans to finance new enterprises on what was often inadequate security. When they miscalculated the market, or had insufficient reserves of cash to back their notes, they broke. Readers of Mrs Gaskell's novel *Cranford* (1853) will remember the distress that the breaking of a bank could cause, when modest savings were wiped out by such a failure. Because private banks with note issue were limited to six partners by law, in bad years they could go down like ninepins, spreading havoc in the business world and among the retired gentlefolk in many a small town.

The population explosion, the improved means of communication, which was mental as well as physical with the declining cost of paper and printing, the mechanization of basic industries and the growth of the industrial town all combined to produce a new rhythm in Britain's economic life that was reflected in her social development. Hitherto this, as in the rest of Europe, had been dominated by the harvest. When this had been bad, or failed. the mass of the people had been pushed down to subsistence level. Some had starved; none had money to spend on any but bare necessities. In consequence industry slumped, craftsmen were on short time, their purchasing power was affected and the whole economy, except for those farmers who could sell their grain at high prices, faced stagnation. In contrast, if the harvest was good and food cheap, then ordinary people had a margin over for clothes, household goods and minor luxuries. Towns flourished; industry picked up; the economy was buoyant. War, too, affected the rhythm of the national economy. Some men were withdrawn from the labour force. Resources were diverted to non-productive activities and inflation followed. Industries that catered for the army, whether in the provision of munitions or military clothing, received a boost. Agriculture boomed. Up to 1815 these two factors, the harvest and war, dominated the economic life of Britain. After the end of the Napoleonic Wars this was no longer so. Britain was at peace and her population so large that, except in years of abundant harvest, her own resources were too small to feed it. Increasingly Britain had to depend on imported food. There was also a change in the eating habits of working people, who were beginning to consume articles like tea and sugar which could not be produced at home. Britain therefore had to depend more and more on exporting manufactures in order to buy the food, the timber and the raw materials, such as cotton, without which her industries would have collapsed. Moreover as a great proportion of her people were living in towns they could no longer supplement their diet by even as much as a tiny garden or a potato patch, though it is surprising how many people contrived to keep a pig, even in a town like Manchester, where the nuisance, dirt and smell that they caused were being complained of as late as the eighteen-forties. In both town and country the number of persons who depended on wages for their livelihood was growing steadily. As the manufacturers' ability to pay these depended to a large extent on overseas markets these assumed an ever major importance. While Britain carries the population that she does, she must export to live. This was one of the greatest changes brought about by the Industrial Revolution. Men could still starve but the reasons why they did were no longer the reasons of the past.

Society adjusted itself to these new conditions with difficulty. The rich preached resignation and blamed a too-generous scale of poor relief. The workers preached revolution and with bitter resentment blamed the government for their misery. At such times the social historian must expect social stress; in the first decades of the century it seemed to many men as if revolution could not be far away. From 1793 to 1814 harvests were poor. Indeed in 1810 they were so disastrous that had Napoleon decided to cut off continental grain supplies, Britain might have been starved into submission. Instead he argued that to let us buy vital grain for gold would be a more mortal blow to the economy. Even so there was rioting and bitter distress, particularly among urban workers. Luckily during the war years Britain managed to find markets for her goods. Economic warfare and blockade was as yet an imperfectly understood weapon, and trading with the enemy hardly recognized as a treasonable activity. French soldiers marched to battle in greatcoats of British cloth. Only in the latter stages of the war did Napoleon's decrees and British Orders in Council create a situation that threatened to become desperate for British industry. After a short post-war boom came depression. Army contracts fell off. Men returned from the forces looking for employment. Manufacturers had optimistically stockpiled goods which the rest of the world was too poor to buy. As a result 1816 and 1817 were years of great distress, particularly in the Black Country. For some years trade continued to fluctuate; 1818 and part of 1819 were bad, then business picked up, only to run into another depression in the early twenties. The reason for this was at least partly financial. Speculators had invested heavily in the newly emerging countries of South America, but the expected profits did not materialize. If Britain was now the workshop of the world she depended on the world for customers and, like the manufacturers, had to learn when to expand credit and when to withhold it. The lives of her inhabitants were now dependent on forces that were only half realized and which men in charge of the country's finances and trade had not yet learnt to control. Industrial Britain was creating great wealth but also new social problems and patterns that were to affect her people profoundly. It is because the cycles of boom and depression in these formative years explain so much that the social historian cannot afford to ignore them.

Yet one must not exaggerate the impact of the new England on the England of the past in the first decades of the nineteenth century. It is easy to concentrate on what was new, cotton mills, railways, gas lighting in the streets and factories, and the blaze of the great ironworks, that lit the night sky like a violent smoky pall from hell in the Black Country, and to forget how much of the past remained. Even by 1851 only half the population lived in what could be described as genuinely urban conditions. The rest were still to be found in villages, in scattered hamlets and in small market towns. The open country was still at almost every man's back door. There were 1,904,680 persons employed in agriculture as opposed to 144,998 in cotton, which was the greatest employer of labour among the new mechanized industries. There were only 193,111 men and boys employed underground in coal mines. Iron and steel, the latter still a small-scale industry, employed only 95,350 persons. Far more people still worked in the traditionally organized industries. Sheffield cutlery was still made in small workshops. Silk was still woven in Spitalfields by weavers working in their own homes for capitalist employers. Handloom weavers, though reduced to almost a living death, hardly able to exist without some assistance from the parish, were still

struggling to survive in the forties. Wool combing had not yet succumbed to mechanization. Steel, though now made with coal, could
be produced only in small quantities by the Huntsman process.
Building, perhaps surprisingly when it is remembered that within
fifty years an additional nine to ten million people had to be housed,
remained basically unchanged in organization and technique. In the
countryside, once the shock of the loss of commons and the open
fields had been absorbed, and in small market towns, life went on
much as it had always done. Tailors, milliners, cobblers, still worked
on individual orders, though inventions like the sewing machine had
helped to speed up their labours. If the candlestick-maker was finding
fewer customers in towns large enough to have a gas works, in most
localities his market remained untouched. Butchers still bought and
killed locally and towns were full of slaughterhouses; the baker
baked and the poor, when they could afford one, still took their
Sunday joint to be roasted in his oven. The rural crafts were as necessary as ever. Farmers still used horses and iron ploughs and so kept
the blacksmiths busy. The thatcher had not gone out of business
where thatch was the customary roofing. Nevertheless even the
tempo of rural life had been speeded up. Letters and newspapers came
by train, though their swift delivery depended on how far away the
nearest station was; it is easy to forget that many villages lay away
from the path of the new railroads and remained remote until the
coming of the internal combustion engine and the local bus. Improvements in the wholesale production of pottery enabled the countryman to discard his wooden trencher and his pewter pot and to adorn
his mantelshelf with gay Staffordshire figures. Newer cottages were
equipped with iron ranges, so that cooking had no longer to be done
over an open fire. Life in the country, therefore, was more convenient
for many people. Nevertheless its essentials changed very little with
regard to employment. Some by-employments had disappeared, such
as spinning, but it is astonishing how many remained to give work in
the long winter evenings, thus adding a little to the cottager's or
smallholder's income. There were still more women employed in
domestic service than in cotton mills; even men had not yet come
to despise it, and everywhere the life of the 'big house' went on.

   But though by 1851 English society was only half-way to its modern
pattern, the economic changes that historians are pleased to call the
Industrial Revolution laid the foundations for a society that was to
be both a class society and an urban society. The traditional mould,
if not yet completely shattered, had been severely chipped and cracked.

Though it was not yet clear what the future would bring it was increasingly plain that there could be no going back, and that further economic changes were likely to emphasize the country's urban, industrial character.

Chapter 2   Urban England

Few things have affected the pattern of English social development as profoundly as the increasing industrialization of the nineteenth century. Before the technical changes of the Industrial Revolution English society had been geared to the needs of agriculture and the seasons. Even the meeting of Parliament had been dictated by the determination of country gentlemen not to sacrifice their rural pleasures to their obligations as M.P.s. By 1851 this situation had changed radically. The census of that year marked the watershed between an England that was rural and one that was urban, because by that date the two were more or less in balance. In the second half of the century the process of urbanization gathered pace; today it is 'the man in the street', not the countryman, who is its representative figure, the trade unionist and not John Bull. This was a social revolution comparable to that which was reshaping industry and transport. It constitutes one of the great milestones in English social development. Because more and more it was the town dweller who was shaping the future, though he was not yet dominating the present, some knowledge of urban England is an essential prerequisite to the understanding of much that was happening to English society during the Industrial Revolution.

The old and the new were co-existent but had little in common. Apart from London, which was in a class by itself, English towns can be divided into those that looked forward to the future and those that looked back to the past. Foremost in the first category were the great industrial towns and the growing industrial villages of the midlands and the north. It was there that the new patterns of urban living were being worked out. They were both creating and being created by the new class society. It was no accident that Engels's *The Condition of the Working Class in England in 1844* had Manchester as its background. Representative of the past were such cities as Bristol and Norwich, which had once been provincial capitals, and the host of small market towns, which were little more than part of the surrounding countryside. Halfway between the two, with one foot in the future and the other in the past, were the towns whose business was recreation. Bath was redolent of the eighteenth-century gentry, when travellers arrived by carriage or coach, took elegant lodgings and stayed for several weeks. Southend was the product of working and lower middle class needs, whose patrons came down by excursion train for a day by the sea. Yet though to the cursory observer nineteenth-century towns may seem to fall into distinguishable groups the historian must never forget that in fact almost endless variations existed within these definable groups. Liverpool and Birmingham, Sheffield and Manchester, on closer examination prove to be very different in both their industries and their class structure. What is true of one industrial new town is not necessarily true of another. Only the local historian can hope to draw a reasonably accurate picture of his chosen town, giving due weight to the stresses and strains within it.

London's place in the development of English society is not easy to define, partly because it is both many-sided and subtle. Many of the problems that arose out of urban living, problems such as housing, sanitation and water supplies, it shared with other big towns. These, to save repetition will be discussed later. But in many ways London was unique; it was everything. It was a great metropolitan market, drawing not on one district but on every county and half the world for the food it ate and the goods it sold. It was the political centre, the administrative centre, the social centre of the nation. Within its confines were to be found not one society but many, ranging from the beggars and thieves who congregated in the rookeries of St Giles, the dockers and stevedores of Rotherhithe and Wapping, to the merchants and financiers of the City and the country gentlemen and nobility of Westminster. In it the pull of urbanization had long been effective. Its growth since the Great Fire had staggered contemporaries. Until 1801, when it was credited with a population of 850,000, there are no official figures. In 1776 a reasonable guess in round figures might be 700,000. With the conclusion of peace in 1815 expansion was rapid. The shape this took is in some senses a commentary on the changes that were transforming society, in matters both of taste and of convenience. Throughout the eighteenth century fashionable people had been moving west. Now prosperous business and professional men were following their example, so that every year saw a further demand for good urban houses. The result was the creation of the dignified area of linked squares known as Bloomsbury. To wander through Beford Square, Russell Square, Mecklenburg Square and some of the surrounding streets of civilized and restrained Georgian houses is to step back a hundred and fifty years in urban architectural history. This kind of demand was being transformed into bricks and mortar all over London. The fashionable world still tended to go west, particularly after 1821, when Buckingham House was enlarged and converted to become Buckingham Palace, but aristocratic London was now being flanked on all sides by middle class London. Sussex Gardens was built during the thirties and by 1843 Paddington was described as 'an elegant and recherché' part of the town, at least 20 per cent of the males who lived there being described as 'capitalists, merchants and professional men'. The upper middle class were moving into Kensington, those of more moderate incomes into Bayswater. Gradually the outlying villages were absorbed, so that Knightsbridge, Kensington, Hampstead and Highgate became parts of London. As the circumference of London grew ever wider and Georgian England began to give place to Victorian England, the style and layout of middle class houses altered. The formal squares with their homogeneity of design gave place to the detached or semi-detached villa standing in its own garden, which abounds in districts such as St John's Wood. Suburbia was coming into being and with it a new style of middle class life. Professional and business activities were more and more divorced from the home. Many prosperous business-men still went to their offices in the City on horseback or in their own carriage, but by the forties the omnibus was making it easier for the less opulent to live further from the centre of business.

The defeat of France had given a great boost to British pride. Though the twenties and thirties were hard for working people, and though recurring depressions plunged the midlands and the north into periodic misery, London, under the influence of the Regent, afterwards George IV, and his architect Nash, began to assume some of the conscious splendour of a great capital. Regent Street, designed by Nash and called after his patron, provided a broad and imposing thoroughfare from the new residential areas in the north to Whitehall and Westminster, separating the now slightly disreputable district of Soho from the fashionable west. In 1830 Trafalgar Square replaced the old royal mews and New Oxford Street penetrated the notorious slum of St Giles, though Charing Cross Road and Shaftesbury Avenue had to wait until the eighties to carve a way through the labyrinth of mean streets that had grown up round Leicester Fields. Money was also spent in the service of learning and the arts. When George IV presented the Royal Library to the nation, the British Museum designed to house it replaced an older building of the same name. The modern structure, begun in 1823, took thirty years to build. In 1832 work was started on the National Gallery. Clubland also dates from the Regency, and is itself an indication of the growing exclusiveness of upper middle class London society. Though the eighteenth century had seen some exclusive establishments, for instance Almack's and White's, the centre of masculine sociability had been the coffee house. Though most attracted a particular kind of patron, whether these were men of literature, wits, East Indian merchants or shipping men, socially they were not exclusive. Indeed foreign visitors were amazed to see the lack of embarrassment that a mere artisan displayed in calling for refreshment and in reading the papers provided in coffee houses frequented by his betters. By the nineteenth century this mingling of different social groups was disappearing. Perhaps because people no longer accepted their traditional place in the social hierarchy, class distinctions had to be more formally enforced. The new clubs were specialized and expensive. The first to be housed in a new and splendid building was the United Services, which was intended to provide a meeting-place for army and militia officers after the peace in 1815. Clustering round Pall Mall and Suffolk Place, these handsome establishments soon became an essential part of male aristocratic and upper class life and to 'go to the club' was as much an occupation of the well-to-do as 'to go to the pub' was of the working class Londoner.

If Regency London was providing a pleasant and even splendid environment for the upper and middle classes, the situation was very different in what had once been known as 'the East End of the Town'. Here the vast expansion of commerce and the needs of a maritime war had made it imperative that adequate docks should replace the old 'legal quays'. In 1799 the City, in conjunction with a joint stock company, procured an Act enabling them to build an up-to-date dock on the Isle of Dogs, which became known as the West India Dock. A period of almost frenzied dock construction followed. The London Dock was started at Wapping in 1802, two years later work was begun on the Surrey Dock. In 1805 the East India Dock was sited at Blackwall. Much thought went into the planning of these docks and good architects were employed to design their warehouses. But for the men who lived and worked in dockland nothing was controlled. In the eighteenth century Rotherhithe and Wapping had always catered for a rough waterfront population, though Dr Johnson refused to hear anything against the latter, rather to Boswell's surprise when later he visited it. With the new dock area extending over some ninety acres the population of Shadwell and Wapping grew rapidly. Unlike the West End, there was no attempt at planned development. Small speculative builders bought such plots as their funds or their credit allowed, and built to their pleasure. The result was a mass of mean streets of terraced houses, which engulfed the older, more dignified, residences where merchants and sea captains had once lived. Though the East End had never attracted men of fashion, many substantial citizens, men connected with the sea and its commerce, had lived there earlier. Behind the streets full of shops selling everything that a seagoing population might require, and the public houses with names like 'The Jolly Tar', clustered innumerable courts and alleys full of cheap lodging houses. Mayhew, whose description of dockland makes a vivid reading, tells how he and a companion 'dived down a narrow court, at the entrance of which lolled Irish labourers smoking short pipes. Across the court hung lines, from which dangled dirty white clothes to dry; and as we walked on, ragged, unwashed, shoeless children scampered past us, chasing one another' (*Mayhew's London* (1854), ed. P. Quennell (1969), 550). In these places a motley collection of London's poor, who picked up a living from the waterfront, dockers, ballast heavers, lumpers (who handled timber cargoes), coalheavers, mudlarks, men who combed the filthy sewers that emptied into the Thames to glean what they could, were all crammed together.

In this misery there was nothing new, though more people were caught in its meshes as London's population grew. London's poor had always lived in appalling squalor. What was new was the creation of large districts in which they alone congregated. The comparatively small space originally occupied by the City and Westminster, combined with lack of transport, had meant less social segregation. Substantial houses and mean courts had been jumbled together, particularly in the City. Later in the West End, which had been developed piecemeal by such families as the Russells, the Cavendishes and the Southamptons, because each great square represented a separate promotion, between them lay land on which the small builder erected more modest houses, which were occupied by the people who provided the goods and services for their wealthier neighbours. Some of these were little better than slums. For instance very poor property lay behind Hanover Square. The construction of the London docks created a new situation. They were built on low-lying and unattractive land; nobody wanted to live there unless forced by necessity.

London had always been more a commercial than an industrial city, but what industry there had been, particularly as the small craftsman declined, while the workshops and factories grew, tended to be concentrated in the East End in order to be near the docks. As a result men who had only their strength on which to rely, or the street seller of hot pea soup, or hot eels or doubtful pies, and all the hangers-on to the fringe of society, scrounging, thieving, running brothels for sailors, or picking up a living in other dubious ways, congregated there. This created a vast new urban sprawl, peopled by the poor and the lower middle classes who catered for them, small shopkeepers, publicans and the like. This increasing social division of London into aristocratic, middle class and working class districts is one of the most interesting developments that took place during the first half of the nineteenth century. By 1851 one cannot speak of London in any but a geographical sense. The West End, the East End and suburbia all represented ways of life, conventions and patterns of behaviour so different that they might have come from different continents instead of all being found within the limits of the metropolis. One corollary that sprang from this social segregation was that the City became almost neutral ground to which men flocked during the hours of business and which they deserted at the day's end.

Though the form that the expansion of London took was creating new social norms, the headlong growth of the industrial towns of the midlands and the north was doing so even more obviously. Between 1776 and 1851 in parts of Lancashire, Yorkshire, Cheshire, Derbyshire and Warwickshire the prevailing way of life had become urban rather than rural, industrial rather than agricultural. It was not a uniform development. Each town, or group of towns, had come into being to serve the needs of a particular industry in a special way, cotton in Lancashire and Cheshire, woollens in Yorkshire, heavy industry and metal working in the Black Country. The layout and character of these towns was largely dictated by their history. Liverpool had grown in response to the demand of industrial Lancashire for a port to handle both the imports of raw cotton and the export of its finished goods. It grew with cotton and remained a commercial rather than an industrial town. Manchester, on the other hand, had originally been the organizing rather than the manufacturing centre of that manufactory. Leeds had performed a similar function for Yorkshire. This remained the case while mechanical spinning was dependent on water power; new manufacturing towns grew up round the perimeter wherever this was available. In 1792 Byng described 'the village of Accrington, where they are building rows of houses, as every vale swarms with cotton mills; some not bigger than cottages—for any little stream, by means of a reservoir will supply them' (J. Byng, *The Torrington Diaries*, ed. C. Bruvyn Andrews, 1936, vol. 3, 113–14). Not until the steam engine had freed spinning from its reliance on water power could manufacture invade towns like Manchester and Leeds in a major way. Then mills were built, a great pall of smoke hung over them and their streets were filled with factory hands. The influx of industry made the centre of the city a less attractive place in which to live. By 1830 the leading citizens were moving out to the suburbs and converting their erstwhile residences into warehouses. In Manchester, therefore, as in London, social segregation became a feature of urban growth. In the new manufacturing towns there never had been much social variety: the reason for their existence had been their mills and most of their inhabitants had been either directly or indirectly dependent on them economically. They were in consequence largely working class urban enclaves in the countryside, apart from such professional or middle class men as were needed to supply them with lawyers, doctors, teachers and managers. In such places the mill-owners constituted the ruling oligarchy and there was often a well-recognized antagonism between them and the mass of the inhabitants.

The general state of the towns, combined with the gruelling work in the factories, makes it easy to understand this working class resentment, though in reality many of the evils from which they suffered were due to the new circumstances and not to the inhumanity of the capitalists. Towns had always been unhealthy, dirty places, which had grown rather than been planned, except in a few instances when one landowner had been able to impose some order and regularity of design, as had happened in Ashton-under-Lyne. Omnibuses, even where they existed, were too expensive to be used by working people. Working men and women had to walk, and after a twelve hour day nobody wanted that walk to be a long one. So it was desirable to live near the mill and that meant accepting any available accommodation. To provide houses at all was something of a feat; several factors combined to make it unlikely that they would be either well sited or well built. In the first place it was nobody's business to see that they were or indeed to see that they were built at all, unless a progressive mill owner decided that it would be to his advantage to have a steady, well-housed labour force attached to his factory, or, if the mill was isolated, because he would need houses to get a labour force at all.

Whether such houses were good, bad or indifferent depended solely on the manufacturer who built them. Even if the urban authorities had considered the supervising of housing to come within their province, which they did not, they had no legal authority to act without first obtaining a local act for that purpose. Even after the remodelling of the corporations in 1835 their powers were very limited; moreover many manufacturing towns were over-grown villages, without any authority more potent than the vestry, and not corporate towns. The second reason for building low-grade houses was the economic pressure on national financial resources. In the early stages of urban expansion the major effort was being put into the war with France, which, by withdrawing resources from domestic capital expenditure, had an inflationary tendency. Later, in the post-war period, years of depression alternated with booms and whatever capital was available was wanted to equip the factories and foundries and ironworks, and to build the railways needed to feed them. It is true that good-class houses continued to be put up, witness the development of Bloomsbury, or the new suburbs on the outskirts of the manufacturing towns. But working class property did not appear to offer enough profit to attract the big contractor. Rents were often difficult to collect from low wage earners, who also might be faced with long spells of unemployment when trade was slack. There was always the risk when so many families lived on or near the poverty line, and when their furniture was so scanty, that if rent arrears became too great, such families would abscond. As a result cottage property was usually put up by small builders

without regard to either the personal comfort of the inhabitants or the necessities which congregation requires. To build the largest number of cottages on the smallest allowable space seems to have been the original view of speculators and the having the houses up and tenanted the *ne plus ultra* of their desires . . . The land has been disposed of in so many small lots, to petty proprietors, who have subsequently built at pleasure, both as to outward form and inward ideas, that the streets present all sorts of incongruities in the architecture; causeways dangerous on account of steps, cellar windows without protection, here and there posts and rails, and everywhere clothes lines intercepting them, by which repeated accidents have been occasioned. (Edwin Chadwick, *Report on an inquiry into the Sanitary Condition of the Labouring Population of Great Britain*, 1842, 40).

The resulting picture seems more like a Neapolitan slum than a description of Leeds in the early forties.

Whole areas, often undrained and quite unsuitable for building on, were rapidly covered in this way in the closing decades of the eighteenth and the first decades of the nineteenth centuries. The favourite layouts followed by such small speculators were narrow back-to-back houses in rows or grouped round courts. Sometimes the two methods were combined to give the worst of both worlds. When the houses were built in terraced rows the streets themselves were usually narrow. At Preston, in the working class districts, some were only nine feet wide. The better type of houses faced these principal streets. Some had just one room up and one room down; the larger ones rarely had more than two bedrooms, a living room and a slip of a scullery. Behind them, and backing onto them, so that neither house could have windows except at the front, which made through ventilation impossible for both, was another row of houses. These looked on to a much narrower street or back lane, which also had to serve as a dumping ground for all the filth and rubbish of the neighbourhood, as well as acting as a thoroughfare to the houses in it. Shepherd's Buildings, in the Stockport Union, was typical. It consisted of

> two rows of houses, with a street seven yards wide between them; each row consists of what are styled back and front houses—that is two houses placed back to back. There are no yards or out conveniences; the privies are in the centre of each row, about a yard wide; over them is a part of a sleeping room; there is no ventilation in the bedrooms; each house contains two rooms, viz, a house place and a sleeping room above; each room is about three yards wide and four long (ibid., 17).

Altogether there were forty-four such houses in the two rows. When these small houses were arranged in courts the evils were, if possible, worse. Such courts were usually entered by a narrow passage running through the houses that fronted the street. The courts themselves were very small. Local attempts were made to mitigate this evil. For instance Liverpool procured a Health of Towns and Building Act in 1842 which prohibited the erection in future of courts that were closed at one end unless the entrance to them was at least fifteen feet wide. Manchester in 1830 had obtained a local Act which forbade any street, lane, way, court or square to be built that was less than twenty feet in width. Before this there had been no minimum; many of the older streets were narrower. In Birmingham the minimum was a more generous forty-eight feet. Houses situated in the old, small courts inevitably were badly ventilated, an evil that was often increased by the presence of the privy or privies for the use of its inhabitants, which occupied part of this already restricted space. In addition there was often an ash pit or midden, which acted as a general receptacle for all the refuse from the houses. Sometimes the common privy was placed at the entrance to the court, poisoning the air that entered it. The atmosphere in such places can hardly be imagined by the modern reader. Even the inhabitants, accustomed as they were to smells, found some courts quite intolerable and complained that they were forced to keep their windows shut and in some cases even to stuff up the keyhole with rags. In Liverpool it was reported that only 478 courts out of 1,982 were open at both back and front, so admitting a through current of air. No less than 55,534 persons were housed in such courts, 'some of which are of the most objectionable construction' (*Second Report of the Commissioners for inquiring into the State of Large Towns and Populous Districts*, 1845, vol. 1, 379).

The cellar dwellings to be found in so many Lancashire and Yorkshire towns were, if possible, even worse. In the early stages of the Industrial Revolution, when the handloom weavers, not yet a poverty-stricken breed, had flocked into the expanding towns in order to be near the mills on whose yarn they depended, houses had been built with cellars in which to place their looms. The family lived in the house place and slept in the bedroom above it. It was in the older houses, therefore, in the narrower streets and courts, that the majority of these were to be found. When the handloom weavers could no longer afford a whole house, or had begun to decline in numbers, at a time when the increasing population was putting an ever-growing pressure on housing, the cellars were used as separate dwellings. Most of them were ill-drained, badly ventilated and poorly lit. In the back-to-back houses previously described in the Stockport Union there were twenty-two cellars let off as separate dwellings. These were described as 'close, damp and very low, not more than six feet between the ceiling and the floor'. Liverpool was notorious for the number of its cellar dwellings, though it had never been predominantly a textile town. One doctor reported:

I visited a poor woman in distress, the wife of a labouring man: she had been confined only a few days, and herself and infant were lying on straw in a vault, through the outer cellar, with a clay floor impervious to water. There was no light or ventilation

in it and the air was dreadful. I had to walk on bricks across
the floor to reach her bedside, as the floor itself was flooded with
stagnant water. This is by no means an extraordinary case, for
I have witnessed scenes equally wretched (ibid., 382).

By 1844 Liverpool was struggling to deal with the worst of these,
forbidding any cellar without a fireplace and window and the height
of which was less than seven feet to be used for 'human habita-
tion'. In better cellars such as these their tenants were described as
living in 'comparative comfort', but to attempt to raise the standard
without providing additional accommodation only too often meant
that the poor wretches who could afford or find nothing better
would be, and were, left homeless. One witness estimated their
number at 23,000. Not all industrial towns were honeycombed with
cellars. Birmingham had few. Nor were they common in the north-
east, where geology did not lend itself to their construction. But
where they abounded too often their unfortunate inmates existed
'in a state revolting to humanity'.

Though railways eventually helped to relieve urban congestion,
during the period of construction they tended to intensify the pressure
on working class housing and to create new class zones. Where, as
frequently happened, the original terminus of a local line was some
large town, such as Manchester or Birmingham, some demolition
was unavoidable. Cottage property was particularly vulnerable. If
the owner were a considerable landowner the sale of the land might
be financially rewarding so that he had every inducement to sell. If
it were divided among many small proprietors they were likely to
be voteless and unable to make their protests effective. Railway lines,
like rivers, took the way of least resistance and a good deal of small
and low grade property was destroyed in the process. The people
evicted, like those driven from the Liverpool cellars, had to crowd
into whatever accommodation still remained. Moreover, the existence of a railway attracted additional labour to its vicinity, much of
it casual manual labour, all of which had to be housed near the depôt.
At the same time better class people disliked living near the railway
with its dirt and noise. In Manchester, for instance, no rebuilding took
place in what had previously been a residential district once the line
had been cut through it. New better class suburbs grew up elsewhere.
Railway arches soon became the haunt of vagrants, adding to the
squalor, so that such areas grew more and more disreputable. This
was as true of the environs of Waterloo as of those surrounding the

terminus and goods yards of any northern industrial town. For working people the benefit of the railways lay in the future.

Because the gentry eschewed the grimy growing manufacturing towns which were inhabited for the most part only by people who worked there, and because the majority were artisans, mill hands and casual labourers, there is a danger of slanting any analysis of the problems of urban mass living from the angle of the working class. Indeed it is true that as the more prosperous of their inhabitants moved out to the healthier suburbs it was wage-earners and the poor, who could not afford to do so, who bore the brunt of the evils thought to be inseparable from urban life. Nevertheless to some extent they were shared by everyone who lived in any sizeable town or city, not excluding London. Before towns could be anything but 'devourers of men' they had to be well drained, clean and supplied with plentiful and pure water. It was the heavy death rate in the towns, and particularly in the working class districts of the industrial towns, that first forced these problems on men's attention. Chadwick included an investigation into the comparative expectation of life in various parts of Britain in his Inquiry into the Sanitary Condition of the Labouring Population. The figures are startling. In a predominantly rural county, Rutland, professional people and gentry might look forward to a span of 52 years, tradesmen, farmers and shopkeepers to 41 years, mechanics and labourers 38. In Liverpool in 1840 the figures were 35, 22 and 15 years. Manchester was a little better. Here the expectation of life of the three groups was 38, 20 and 17 years (*Report on the Sanitary Condition . . .*, 157). Even Whitechapel was an improvement on these northern figures, though housing conditions for the poor were, and always had been, appalling. One Whitechapel doctor declared: 'When they attend my surgery I am always obliged to have the door open', adding 'When I am coming down stairs from the parlour, I know at the distance of a flight of stairs whether there are any poor persons in the surgery' (ibid., 64). Yet even in Whitechapel the average expectation of life for labourers and their families was 22 years. For tradesmen it was 27 and for gentle and professional families 45.

Towns of the standing of Manchester and Liverpool had already begun to tackle problems of sanitation when Chadwick made this report, but it was its impact on public opinion that first made people aware of both the size of the problem and the fact that its evils were not confined to any one section of the population. Consequently it was followed by the appointment of a Royal Commission on the State of Large Towns and Populous Districts, which reported in 1845.

This, combined with Chadwick's earlier report, provided a careful analysis of the fundamental evils and outlined a set of constructive proposals for overcoming them. The picture that emerged from their investigations is grim, particularly when it is remembered that every year more and more people were getting their livelihood in towns and that urban living was becoming the pattern of the social development of the future.

The problem of drainage was fundamental but, though it affected all parts of a town, lack of drainage, like so much else, hit the poorest areas worst. Because there was no authority to ensure that land was drained before building operations were commenced, the small operator, who was cutting his costs to a minimum, frequently bought low-lying, waterlogged land because it was cheap. As the houses he built had no damp courses, inevitably they were damp inside, while outside stagnant water accumulated. Sometimes poor-grade houses were built along the banks of a stream that was liable to overflow. As most streams and rivers were also used as main sewers the consequences can be imagined.

In the past drainage systems had been exceedingly simple, depending largely on the use of natural declivities to carry off rainwater and other liquids. The favourite method was to slope the street slightly towards the centre, down which ran an open gutter, the contents of which, sooner or later, found its way to the nearest stream, river, lake or sea. As towns increased in size such a procedure was plainly inadequate. One witness describing Wigan stated: 'There are no regulations for draining the town. The general declivity of the streets is favourable for the discharge of surface water. There are some streets, which, being unpaved and undrained, retain wet and refuse thrown from the houses . . . There are many stagnant pools and open ditches in the town' (*Report on the State of Large Towns . . .*, 361). Fiction bears out the official reports. Mrs Gaskell in *Mary Barton* (1848) describes one such street. 'It was unpaved; and down the middle a gutter forced its way, every now and then forming pools in the holes with which the street abounded. Never was the Old Edinburgh cry of "Gardez l'eau" more necessary than in this street. As they passed women from their doors tossed household slops of *every* description into the gutter.' This, it is true, was in a poor part of the town, but even the Bartons, who were a respectable operative family, lived in 'a little paved court, having the backs of houses at the end opposite to the opening, and a gutter running through the middle to carry off household slops, washing suds, etc. The women who lived in the court were busy taking in strings of caps, frocks, and various articles of linen, which hung from side to side.'

Even when there were sewers, as in London, the situation was not much better, except for the elimination of stagnant water, because they had originally only been constructed to deal with rainwater. It is sometimes forgotten that this, and not the removal of human excreta, was their original purpose, and that the invention of the water closet put on them a burden for which they had never been intended. As a result sewers became choked with what was euphemistically described as 'offensive matter'. This an inadequate flow of water was quite incapable of removing. At intervals therefore the sewers had to be opened up and the filth removed manually and carted away! There were other hazards. Sanitary engineering was in its infancy and house drains, even where they existed, were often inadequately connected to the main sewers. As a result sewer gas often seeped back into the basements of the well-to-do who had adopted the new-fangled water closet. Where these were not connected to a sewer but emptied into a cesspool this frequently drained into the subsoil and contaminated the nearby springs and wells, on which many houses depended for their water supply. Drainage, therefore, as towns grew, became less and less a mere matter of disposing of surface water and more and more one of fundamental sanitation.

The majority of people, however, in the first part of the century still used the traditional 'privy', or 'necessary house', or 'bogs'; all three names were common. This faced urban communities with a double problem, the provision of an adequate number of such conveniences and the organization of a satisfactory method of cleansing and removing the nightsoil. Today it is taken for granted that every house will have access to some sort of sanitation, however unsatisfactory and inadequate, but in the first part of the nineteenth century this was not so. It is difficult now to realize the appalling conditions with which people in the poorest parts of a town were faced. In Manchester it was possible to find whole streets, inhabited mainly by the Irish, where there were no conveniences at all. In other parts for all practical purposes the situation was as bad. In Oldham Road and St George's Road 645 houses, with an estimated population of 7,095 people, had only 33 necessaries between them! In Liverpool the Health Committee of the Town Council stated that in some courts there were no privies at all, and that of 26 streets, containing 1,200 front houses, two-thirds had neither yard, ash pit nor privy. These were extreme instances, dug out by reformers anxious to shock public opinion into taking action, but the generality of cases was bad enough. A court consisting of sixteen houses which, in the over-crowded conditions that prevailed, might shelter some 80 persons, usually only possessed two privies. Their condition can be imagined. Moreover in many Lancashire towns these privies had attached to them large open cesspools, into which all the nightsoil, ashes, and general refuse went. In a court some fifteen to twenty feet wide, entered by a narrow passage, and with no through current of air, the stench must have been appalling, even to contemporary noses. As, in addition, the privies were often badly constructed the filth from them, and from the adjoining ashpit or cesspool, often soaked into the nearest house. Where there was no drainage in the court, other than a surface drain, which soon got blocked up, there was little chance of even the liquid filth getting away. Conditions were quite as bad in parts of London. Behind one house in St Giles's High Street a surveyor, called in to inspect the property, found the yard 'so covered with nightsoil from the overflowing of the privy, to a depth of nearly six inches, and bricks were placed to enable the inmates to get across dry shod; in addition to this there was an accumulation of filth piled up against the walls, of a most objectionable nature.' Such incidents were typical only of the poorer quarters. The more respectable working class streets were better supplied. In Hulme, which was one of the later areas of Manchester to be built on and which had the advantage of an open, airy situation, things were better. Here out of the 80 houses examined 64 had individual privies, in 14 two families only shared one while in the remaining couple there was no information available. On such conditions at least some decency could be observed.

Nevertheless until adequate main drainage could be constructed and earth closets be replaced by water closets the problems of emptying them was bound to grow more formidable with the building of more and more houses. This was something that better class houses in more attractive parts of the town had to share with their poorer neighbours. In much of London the work was done by contractors. In the provinces the practice varied from town to town. Sometimes there were no public arrangements; each household made its own, carting the nightsoil to a dump or tipping place in the nearest river, or into a private cesspool. In some houses a cellar was used for this purpose. In London it cost a shilling to have a cesspool cleaned out, which meant that the poorer families incurred this expense as infrequently as possible when a shilling could represent a day's wages. Many towns had a regulation forbidding the nightsoil men, who collected it for sale as manure to take their filthy loads through the streets during the hours of daylight. Only the most wretched types undertook this kind of work and householders complained bitterly that to collect the maximum amount in the shortest possible time the nightsoil men pulled apart, and tore down, the privies which they were supposed to be emptying, often leaving behind any residue difficult to remove in the process. As the usual pay was around 3s for two loads, which was as much as the men and their families could hope to collect in the course of a night, it is not surprising that they were not over-particular in discharging this disgusting assignment. In some towns the responsibility for the physical emptying of the privies remained with the householder, but its removal was organized by the town authority. In Birmingham this type of refuse was supposed to be placed outside the houses at night. As, however, the work was often carelessly done the streets were frequently littered with fragments of a very disagreeable kind. The problem of dealing with the sanitary needs of any large community was becoming so crucial that one commentator declared that man was in danger of being buried in his own excreta.

Overflowing privies were not the only sanitary nuisances from which the urban population suffered. There were many other types of refuse to be dealt with, both domestic and industrial. As these were also very inefficiently handled the streets remained littered and filthy, a condition augmented by deplorable drainage in many towns. Even in the most aristocratic parts of London the crossing sweeper was a regular figure, most of them working on the same pitch day after day, making a path with their brooms through the debris and dirt. Some towns employed paupers to sweep the main streets. Courts and alleys were regarded as private property and little, if any, attention was paid to the unpaved streets in the poorer parts of the town. The superintendent of the Manchester scavengers informed the commissioners that all the paved streets were swept once a week. The commissioners remained unconvinced. In their opinion the task could not have been effectively done in under a fortnight. Imagination shrinks from the state of the centre of any large modern town so neglected. In Liverpool the situation was apparently even worse. One witness said that at certain times of the year the streets near the docks were nearly impassable. Some smaller towns, like Frome, had no scavengers at all. Bath, on the other hand, where there was a steady flow of well-to-do visitors, was kept reasonably clean. Manchester, too, was just investing in a new street-cleaning machine and was hoping, the commissioners were told, to reach a better standard by this means.

Even when streets were cleaned there was still the problem of what to do with the sweepings. In Leeds the contractor concerned leased two plots of land on which he dumped all the refuse from the streets and the market, both general and vegetable. There they were left to rot until they could be sold as manure. Both these plots were in the centre of crowded working class districts whose inhabitants complained that the terrible stench afflicted them night and day, making it quite impossible for them to open their windows. The practice of letting nightsoil and rubbish accumulate until it had rotted and could be sold as manure seems to have been general. What could not be sold in this way was frequently tipped into the nearest stream or river, which then became little better than an open drain, particularly offensive in hot weather. In Bristol, for instance, when in summer or autumn the Frome was low the stench was so great that 'the inhabitants of the houses adjoining it, mostly of the poorer class, as scarcely any others will live in them, describe it at times as making them turn sick' (ibid., 249). The Irwell and its tributaries were as bad as, if not worse than any. Having collected all the sewage of Bolton, Bury and Rochdale, it was then further contaminated by that of Manchester. Among other unpleasant matter one geologist stated that 'an abundance of dead dogs and cats are to be seen in various stages of decomposition'. Indeed so bad was it that in the cholera epidemic some of the courts fringing its banks were all but depopulated and had to be pulled down.

Slaughterhouses added their own quota of deleterious matter to the normal domestic and industrial waste. Many of these were situated in densely populated districts. Cattle had always been driven on the hoof to the towns where they were to be consumed as beef, and, unless urban families were to live on salt beef, before the days of refrigeration there was little alternative, though slaughterhouses would have been less of a hazard to health if they had been situated on the outskirts. But because, in the eyes of the law, courts were private property, there was little that the authorities could do to mitigate the evil without fresh legislation. A respectable shopkeeper in Bristol, whose accommodation overlooked a yard where pigs imported from Ireland were slaughtered, declared:

Often the pigs, in coming over in the packet, die, and I have seen as many as 30 dead pigs at a time brought into the yard. They

are thrown under that shed there, until there is time to cut
them up, and by that time, I have seen the maggots fairly drop-
ping out of them. Then they are cut up and I believe made into
salt bacon or sold for sausages. The entrails of such pigs . . .
are thrown into the dunghill. When the dunghill is stirred up
to be taken away, Oh, Sir, the smell is awful.

Apparently no redress was possible. Moreover he did not like to
complain for, as he explained, 'the owner of the yard is a very good
neighbour and tries to keep things as clean as he can, but his occupation beats him at that' (ibid., 274). A secondary evil caused by the presence of these slaughterhouses was the amount of dung that the cattle,
sheep and pigs deposited on the streets leading to them. Sometimes,
too, the terrified animals ran amok, to the danger of the passers by.

Such evils were largely confined to the poorer parts of a town but
nobody, unless they took refuge in an outlying suburb, could avoid
the heavy canopy of smoke that the factory chimneys poured out.
In Manchester it turned the water collected in rain butts into an inky
liquid. Clothes required constant washing, houses constant painting.
In the Black Country the smoke came from the ironworks and from
all the small forges of the domestic nailers. In Newcastle the steamers,
plying up and down the Tyne, belched it from their funnels. All this
was in addition to the smoke from domestic fires which so often
obscured the sun even in non-industrial cities like London. Many
people considered it inseparable from the use of coal and it was little
use for experts to point out that industrial smoke was not only harmful but also uneconomic, and that by careful stoking fuel costs could
be cut by 5–20 per cent. Progressive manufacturers might agree, but
no northern mill-owner was going to be dictated to by 'know-alls'
from London. So to the dirt under foot was added the dirt in the air,
and there is little wonder that persons of sensibility shunned the
unlovely industrial towns where the nuisance was at its most obvious,
though Londoners accepted the pollution of the air by the innumerable domestic fires very much as a matter of course.

¶ The filth of the towns was closely linked with the lack of an adequate
and convenient water supply. The early siting of towns had usually
been connected with the availability of water, either drawn from a
stream or river or from wells and springs. As population grew these
local sources became more and more inadequate. Water was needed
for industry as well as for domestic use. Because rivers had become
the main means of getting rid of garbage and nightsoil their water

had become increasingly unpleasant and unsafe for drinking, for cooking and even for personal and domestic washing. In spite of this London's supplies for a horrifyingly long time were pumped by the water companies from near Westminster, though somewhat cleaner supplies were also taken from above Chelsea. After 1829 the Chelsea Water Company did at least use a sand filter but the East London Water Company contented itself with using settling reservoirs before the water, untreated in any other way, was piped to consumers. It was not until 1852 that the London water companies were legally obliged to take their supplies from above Teddington Lock, and even this puny measure was held up for some time. In the provinces, as local supplies became inadequate, joint stock companies were floated to bring more distant supplies to the bigger towns, where the venture promised to be profitable. Many of these dated from the eighteenth century and their technical expertise was rather of the *ad hoc* variety, the original pipes being made of hollow elm trunks. This method of supplying the growing towns suffered from two major defects. The piping was technically inefficient largely because when the revolution in the manufacture of iron, in pumping engines and in the general field of engineering could have been used to give a much better service the companies had already sunk their capital in the older equipment and set their face against the need to replace this by more modern types. The second defect was that water was regarded as an article of trade and not a necessity of urban life. Therefore water companies were formed only where there seemed a good hope of profit, and smaller towns had to struggle along without even the dubious supplies that the companies could provide. Even in the larger towns the same profit motive operated. The company often only laid pipes in the middle class districts where a return on their capital seemed most likely. Even that service was by modern standards pathetically inadequate. Pressure was low and supply intermittent, the excuse being that the pipes could not stand a constant flow of water at high pressure. In Liverpool water was only turned on for 1–2$\frac{1}{2}$ hours on alternate days. By 1845 Manchester was doing rather better; water was available every day for 1–4 hours. Even London suffered from the curse of intermittent supplies at low pressure. By the eighteen-thirties such inefficiency was quite unnecessary, as the experience of the Trent Water Works demonstrated. This enterprise had employed a first-rate engineer, Thomas Hawksley, and had no difficulty in providing Nottingham with an unlimited supply, even to working class houses, for a penny a week.

Normally water piped into individual houses was a luxury confined to 'the more affluent classes' as at Clifton, where only 404 enjoyed this amenity. In Birmingham out of around 40,000 houses some 8,000 were provided with this convenience, in Newcastle perhaps a twelfth, in Coventry between 300 and 400 out of some 7,000. Not many working class families were among this fortunate minority, though occasionally a progressive landlord equipped his cottage property with piped water. Even when working families were lucky enough to live in a house which had piped water their troubles were not over. Because it was turned on just for a few hours, sometimes only every other day, either the house had to be equipped with expensive cisterns or some one had to be at home to collect it in tubs and pails. In overcrowded houses this storage was an additional problem.

For most households, therefore, water for domestic use came from springs or wells or from public conduits and fountains, often the legacy of ancient benefactors. It was calculated that in Bristol 73,443 persons were wholly dependent on water obtained from public or private wells. Better class houses often had a pump attached to their own well; landlords of courts often supplied one for their tenants, though some leased it to a particular individual who charged for the water taken from it. In Bath the corporation provided six conduits in the poorer districts. Some water companies by the terms of their charter were obliged to provide public standpipes. For those middle class families who depended on such sources the hardship was lessened by the fact that they had servants to draw and carry the water. For working people once again the problem was one of timing. Where the system of intermittent supply prevailed angry crowds at the standpipes, all struggling to be first, caused constant friction between neighbours. If supplies had to be brought from an itinerant water cart the cost might amount to 1d a day, which was a considerable expense to the poorer families. If water had to be fetched from a distant well or pump, even though it might be free and available at all times, yet the labour of fetching it after a hard day's work was a genuine obstacle to its lavish use. A man in Bath, who had to carry his water about a quarter of a mile, declared 'It is as valuable as strong beer. We can't use it for cooking or anything of that sort, but only for drinking and tea.' When asked where they got their water for cooking and washing he replied, 'Why, from the river. But it is muddy and often stinks bad because all the filth is carried there' (*Report on the Sanitary Condition* . . ., 70). Yet, knowing this, he preferred to use it rather than face the fatigue and inconvenience of carrying better water. As a doctor emphasized, in such circumstances 'cleanliness does not and cannot exist'. Historians enumerating the advantages of cheap cotton clothing stress the fact that it was more easily washed and dried than the old heavy woollen garments. What they do not explain is where the water in which it is to be washed is to be got, or how in smoky industrial towns with huddled houses and few backyards, so that washing lines had to be stretched across the courts or street, the clothes once washed were to be dried in the polluted atmosphere. One White-chapel doctor, speaking of the local poor, declared: 'I find they have only a very scanty supply of water in their tubs. When they are wash-ing, the smell of the dirt mixed with soap is the most offensive of all the smells I have to encounter. They merely pass dirty linen through very dirty water' (ibid., 64).

It is incontestable that many English towns in the early nineteenth century were in a deplorable state through lack of water (which even when sufficient in quantity was seriously deficient in quality, scaveng-ing and sewering) quite apart from the badly built houses, the narrow streets and the confined courts where the workers lived. It should be remembered nevertheless that these evils were not new; nor were they the peculiarity of the growing industrial towns. Even the royal borough of Windsor, where 'a double line of open, deep, black and stagnant ditches' ran between the gas works in George Street and Clewer Lane and gave forth 'an intolerable stench' (ibid., 13) could show sights and produce smells quite as offensive as any in the newer towns of the north. Old market towns, such as Tiverton, were equally insalubrious. There it was reported that 'the open drains in some cases ran immediately before the doors of the houses', some of which were almost surrounded by them and into which went all the animal and vegetable refuse of 'not only the houses in that part, but those in other parts of Tiverton' (ibid., 5). All towns were traditionally regarded as unhealthy. In the summer anyone who could fled from London with its dirt and smells, but obviously the bigger the town the greater the hazard to health.

Nevertheless too great a reliance on the reports of reformers and on fact-finding commissions tends to produce a distorted picture of urban life. Edwin Chadwick and his colleagues were out to shock and shame people first into facing the situation and then into taking action, or at least into allowing action to be taken. Therefore they concen-trated on the worst parts of any town they visited. Such reformers spoke the truth and nothing but the truth, but they rarely spoke the whole truth. The districts in which the upper and middle classes lived were not squalid and outwardly filthy, though they were frequently unhealthy not because of stagnant pools and unpaved streets but because the rich as well as the poor were threatened by contaminated water supplies and deficient drainage. Most members of the royal family contracted typhoid at one time or another. As a girl Queen Victoria nearly died of it, and it proved fatal to her husband, the Prince Consort. Nor, even in working class districts, did filthy streets necessarily mean squalid and wretched homes. G. R. Porter in his *Progress of the Nation* noted that in Sheffield many of its working class population had comfortably furnished homes, with carpets on the floors and substantial mahogany furniture. Mrs Gaskell gives the same impression in her novel of Manchester life, *Mary Barton*. Unlike Dickens, who enjoyed hunting out social exploitation as a terrier enjoys smelling out and hunting rats, and who in *Hard Times* painted what was essentially a southerner's picture of the industrial north, Mrs Gaskell wrote out of a long knowledge and deep sympathy with its people. The hatred of social exploitation is there and she did not shut her eyes to it. Her description in *Mary Barton* (1848) of the cellar in which the destitute and unemployed operative died, a man whom his mate described as 'always a steady, civil spoken fellow though somewhat of a Methodee', is as grim as anything quoted by Chadwick. At the same time she knew, and showed by her description of old Alice's cellar in the same novel, that they were not all equally horrifying.

> It was the perfection of cleanliness: in one corner stood the modest-looking bed, with a check curtain at its head, the white washed wall filling up the place where the corresponding one should have been. The floor was bricked, and scrupulously clean, although so damp it seemed as if the last washing would never dry up. As the cellar window looked into an area in the street, down which boys might throw stones, it was protected by an outside shelter. In one corner was a sort of broad hanging shelf, made of old planks, where some old hoards of Alice's were kept. Her bit of crockery ware was ranged on the mantelpiece where also stood her candlestick and box of matches. A small cupboard contained at the bottom coals, and at the top her bread and basin of oatmeal, her frying pan, teapot and a small tin saucepan.

Her furniture consisted of two rush-bottomed chairs and a small round table. In describing John Barton's home at a time when he was in work the picture that she paints is one of modest comfort, though that which she depicted later when he was out of work and everything pawnable had been pawned, was very different.

> The room was tolerably large and possessed many conveniences. On the right of the door, as you entered, was a longish window, with a broad ledge. On each side of this, hung blue and white check curtains . . . Two geraniums, unpruned and leafy, which stood on the sill formed a further defence from out-door pryers. In the corner, between the window and the fireside was a cupboard, apparently full of plates and dishes, cups and saucers. . . . On the opposite side of the door and near to the window was the staircase, and two doors; one of which led into a sort of little back kitchen where dirty work, such as washing up dishes, might be done, and whose shelves served as larder and pantry, and storeroom and all. The other door, which was considerably lower, opened into the coal hole—the slanting closet under the stairs.

This was probably typical of the home of the respectable mill hand of the north when trade was brisk. Though water had to be brought from a nearby pump, and there is no mention of what the sanitary conveniences of John Barton's dwelling may have been, there is nothing degrading in the circumstances of his home. When friends come into tea Mary runs round to the shop to buy eggs and a pound of ham. For the mill workers, who in good times could afford comfortably furnished rooms and nourishing food, the major concern was with wages, full employment and shorter hours. The Ten Hour Bill was a burning issue. Cuts in wages drove them to organize strikes and to half murder blackleg labour. Few of them showed much interest in Southwood Smith's Health of Towns Association. Today it is difficult to realize how little people were shocked by sanitary deficiencies that were traditional. Yet this is understandable. Until the turn of the century earth closets had been the only sanitary convenience for rich and poor alike. Not only were they taken for granted but in better class houses, and where there was no difficulty in arranging for them to be kept clean, they were not even a hazard to health. In some of the best suburbs of Johannesburg as late as 1927, to my own knowledge, the majority of houses still had outside privies, and the long lines of the bullock carts, with their red lanterns swinging, were a common sight as the nightsoil men came on their rounds to empty them. Even Girton College in 1917 relied on inside sawdust closets and oil lamps. In the same way the danger from polluted water was unguessed. It was only slowly realized that the terrible cholera epidemics of 1831–2 and 1848–9 were the result of infected water supplies. Bad as conditions were becoming in the great industrial towns, the inhabitants of the smaller ones were still largely oblivious of their hidden dangers. Bad spots, narrow and overcrowded courts and lanes, hovels of houses, there most certainly were, particularly in the poorer parts of the town, where long familiarity with dirt and squalor had made it normal. But it was only where more and more of the labouring population congregated and were crammed together, and where industrial waste was added to household garbage and human excreta, that disposal by the old methods became impossible and rivers hopelessly polluted. In parts of London, and in ports such as Bristol, the situation had long been grim. It was only when they were reproduced on a grand scale in the new towns that enlightened opinion began to realize the sacrifice of human life that was involved.

There were many reasons why this realization came slowly. Historians are often tempted to concentrate on what was new and to forget how little for most people urban life changed in those peaceful backwaters, the cathedral and market towns of England. In the former the Industrial Revolution had the effect of making them still more conservative, at least until after the Municipal Act of 1835, by drawing away from them the industries that had once played so important a part in their lives. Cities like Exeter and Norwich had been the organizing pivots for the woollen manufacturers of Devon and East Anglia, as well as the centres of county administration and the seats of bishops. Now, from the industrial angle, year by year they were declining in face of the competition from the north. What remained were socially the most conservative elements. A recent study of society and politics in Exeter considered that its history provided an illustration of a society which continued to be linked to the habits and standards of a pre-industrial age. Because there were few opportunities to make rapid fortunes, money remained of less importance than status, and both the administration of the city and the leadership of its society were in the hands of the gentry, the clergy and professional families. It was not quite acceptable to be a Nonconformist or to vote Liberal. When after 1835 tradespeople began to take a more active part in local government, the gentry gradually dissociated themselves from any active participation. In that year the first mayor under the new Act was a Unitarian ironmonger; by 1848 no less than eleven of the councillors were members of the licensed trade (R. E. Newton,

'Society and Politics in Exeter 1837–1914', in *The Study of Urban History*, ed. H. J. Dyos (1968), 302). This made local government no longer attractive to the leaders of the old society. This was the England of Trollope and of *Barchester Towers*, where the gentry and the clergy still dominated, looking with patronizing condescension on such of the middle class who knew their place and with smouldering dislike on those who presumed. In every way these cities were a complete contrast to the smoky, bustling, thrusting new manufacturing towns, and the societies that they nurtured could not have been more different.

In market towns there was even less visible alteration. When they lost their industries the old provincial capitals had had to accept change, if only that of decay. But the market towns, at least for the first half of the century, followed very much the even tenor of their ways. Many small towns had a fair sprinkling of maiden ladies, widows and retired gentlefolk of limited means. Such a society is enshrined for ever in the pages of *Cranford*, whose ladies practised 'an elegant economy' and where a new carpet was so precious that careful housewives provided a newspaper path from door to chair so that it could not be muddied by the feet of careless callers. Gentility was cherished as the hallmark of their status and their major concern was to keep up appearances on the most minute of incomes. In such circles money was considered vulgar; gossip, gently spiced with social nuances, an enduring interest. When the widow of a Scottish baron, a Lady Granville, came to Cranford on a visit the one topic of serious debate was the correct mode of addressing her. Modern readers may smile at these preoccupations, so redolent of the past: nevertheless they were typical of small-town England. Here the deferential society lingered on. Tradesmen were respectful, maid servants were not allowed 'followers' without their mistress's permission, the lower orders still accepted their station as ordained of God. But it must be remembered also that the gentry accepted the obligations that went with their status. When the local bank broke Miss Matty chose to suffer financial disaster herself rather than allow an honest working man to lose his money. Life in such places lacked the excitement of bigger towns. They could offer little to the ambitious, who tended to leave them, but the shopkeepers and craftsmen, tailors, shoemakers, milliners and their helpers, seem to have been contented. On market days the local farmers and their wives came with their produce to sell and bought whatever they required for their regular needs or for special occasions. Then the inns would be full of farmers and the

alehouses of their men. Such towns had their poverty, their corners
of squalor, their haunts of fever, but these things merged into a back‡
ground of acceptance. Even vice was still personalized. It was Elizabeth
Walker who was suspected of being 'no better than she should be' or
Tom Smith who got drunk and beat his wife. Outwardly there were
some changes. The china that adorned the tea table might be the
latest design by Mr Wedgwood. The occasional visitor came and went
by train, but in essence life went on untouched by the problems which
the Industrial Revolution was bringing to the larger towns. When one
speaks of urban England one must therefore remember the old that
remained as well as the new patterns that were emerging.

If London belongs to all time, the industrial towns to the future
and the cathedral cities and market towns to the past, those resorts
where pleasure, sometimes thinly disguised as a concern for health,
was the main attraction, link the eighteenth and nineteenth centuries
to modern England. Such towns *par excellence* are Bath, Cheltenham
and Brighton in the south, with Scarborough, Harrogate, Southport,
and later Blackpool, in the north; these, though they had many
imitators, had few rivals. Bath had been noted for its medicinal
springs since Roman times, as the ancient baths, rediscovered in 1755,
bear witness. In the eighteenth century it became a place of high
fashion, to which everybody of note went at some time to take the
waters. The result of its popularity among the nobility and gentry
was the creation of a very fine town, full of elegantly designed cres-
cents and squares and broad pavements, on which the 'ton' could
parade safe from traffic at a time when most towns were content with
a few posts and chains. Like all cities Bath had its poorer squalid parts,
though even its working population had a better expectation of life,
namely twenty-five years, than most of their urban counterparts. It
was perhaps the first town in England to be created for gracious living.
The Assembly Rooms, built in 1771, and the Pump Room, which
dated from 1797, were the centres of its social life, and their patrons
were expected to conform to a rigorous code of behaviour and dress.
So well were its amenities, its codes and its geography known that
though the town figures prominently in many of Jane Austen's
novels she takes it for granted that her readers are as familiar with
them as she is herself. If the northern towns were created by the new
industrialism and dominated by the new capitalists, Bath was equally
the creation of the aristocracy and gentry and equally mirrored the
society of 'order and degree'. The same is true of Cheltenham. It also
owed its rise to the discovery of medicinal springs and its social fortune

was made when George III went to drink the waters there in 1788. Like Bath it was designed to attract the world of fashion and wealth by the creation of a suitable environment. Much of this building took place in the early nineteenth century, which left its stamp on the town and its architecture. From a mere 3,076 inhabitants in 1804, by 1841 the population had swollen to 31,411. Throughout the century Cheltenham remained a place to which the gentry, and in particular ex-army officers and their families, retired. Though it never attained the magnificence or reputation of Bath at its peak, it was a town of considerable charm.

Brighton was another creation of the fashionable world. Up to the middle of the eighteenth century Brighthelmstone, as it was then called, was little more than a fishing village, often ravaged by severe storms. However, when Richard Russell, a fashionable physician, began to recommend sea water for a variety of complaints he suggested Brighton as a suitable place for the new treatment. The idea proved popular and in 1754 he built himself a house on the Steine from which he could supervise his patients. To modern readers the treatment sounds both unpleasant and spartan. As a preliminary preparation of the body for sea bathing, because few people were used to total immersion, the patient had first to drink considerable quantities of sea water. When the body had been sufficiently conditioned Dr Russell permitted the bathing to begin, but only in chilly weather when the pores of the skin were adequately closed. The spectacle of delicately bred females like Mrs Thrale and Fanny Burney complaisantly taking a dip before dawn on a November morning should remind us that our ancestors were tougher creatures than some of their descendants! Later other medical men made the convenient discovery that it was better to bathe in warm water so that the poisons could be more easily dispelled through the open pores. A new building was then erected on the now fashionable Steine to provide both hot and cold sea water baths.

Medical whims come and go. What placed Brighton securely on the map of fashion was the visit of the Prince of Wales in 1782. Brighton was near enough to London for visitors to drive down in a day. The air was invigorating, sea bathing an amusing pastime, and though costumes were decorous to the point of absurdity and no mixed bathing was allowed, much masculine amusement could be derived from the use of spyglasses. The Prince enjoyed the atmosphere of social relaxation, which he helped to create. Two years later he began to build himself a summer residence there, the fantastic Royal Pavilion, which took its final shape in 1827. The younger set flocked to Brighton, with the result that here too a spacious town of elegant streets, squares and terraces grew up to accommodate them. This was Brighton's heyday of fashion. With the death of George IV it lost its royal patron and with the coming of the railway in 1841 it began to attract a very different section of the public. The railway was a great leveller. It brought the coast within the reach of ordinary people and even, as the century progressed, of working class families. In response to this demand watering-places began to grow, some catering for middle class patrons and some frankly for the working classes. South-end became the lungs of London. In the north Southport and Black-pool did the same for the Lancashire towns. This in itself was a proof of a changing society. In the past travel for pleasure had been the prerogative of the well-to-do. The middling sort had looked for entertainment nearer home; in London, for instance, flocking to the tea gardens that had ringed the metropolis. The labouring poor and craftsmen had found their relaxation in rough games, in low taverns and in the traditional fairs where sideshows and stalls had catered for amusement and appetite alike or, more reputably, in glee clubs. The new watering-places were a response to a new public demand, though until the second half of the century this was neither steady nor sustained.

The industrial town and its inhabitants represent the active, creative influence of the Industrial Revolution on the development of English society. The situation in rural England was different. It, too, was subject to pressures, but these were in general alien and unwelcome. In the social changes which they brought rural England was a passive rather than an active participant. As far as it could it resisted them, was bewildered by them and morally perplexed by their results. The attitude of the countryside was traditional; men clung to their rights and status in society as something that pertained to them as Englishmen. This was as true of the labourer as of the squire and was something that the townsman and the radical thinker found difficult to comprehend. The values of town and country increasingly clashed. It would be too sweeping a generalization to say that in 1776 the gap was between London and the rest of England, whereas by 1851 it was between urban and rural England. Nevertheless, as is the case with most generalizations, there is more than a grain of truth in it.

Though no section of rural society was immune to the new pressures, outwardly the first half of the nineteenth century brought less change to the gentry and aristocracy than it did to the farmers and to the labouring poor. The former still dominated the life of the countryside. As late as 1867 Bagehot could still describe English society as 'deferential'. Until at least the end of the Napoleonic Wars there were very solid economic reasons for this deference. Agriculture was still the greatest single source of wealth, and between them the aristocracy and gentry owned most of the land on which it was dependent. In discussing the leaders of rural society these two are difficult to separate. The relationship between them may be likened to that between the senior and junior officers in the services; the one conscious of their right to lead, the other of their obligation to follow. But both recognize the same traditions, accept the same responsibilities, observe the same code of behaviour and, as far as their differences of income allow, enjoy the same pleasures. The colonel or the captain entertains his young officers and their wives; he does not expect the same scale of entertainment in return. In the same way the peers made their country seats the centre of hospitality and, though this was less obtrusive, of authority, in their own locality. Before the ministry of the younger Pitt, the peerage was an exclusive body, numbering less than 200. Even after his fairly extensive use of the royal power to create new peers in return for political services, the peerage was socially less diluted than might at first sight have been supposed. Scottish and Irish peers were promoted to the English peerage, thus securing a hereditary seat in the Lords, old country families secured baronies. But there were no direct promotions from the ranks of commerce and industry. Fortunes made in that way still involved climbing the social ladder in the old accustomed way by buying land and being accepted by the local gentry before new men were trusted with so much as a baronetcy. As a result county society was tightly knit; if everybody did not know everybody else they knew about them, knew their ancestry and their connections.

Many of the peers were very rich. The Dukes of Bedford and Northumberland had incomes of around £50,000 a year, though £10,000 was a more usual figure. But their expenses were correspondingly heavy. An income of this size was more a family than a personal asset. Estates swallowed up money, particularly when capital investment was needed for new farm buildings, new cottages, new fences or hedges. Moreover the head of the family was rarely able to use his nominal income. Much of it was tied up in settlements. A widowed mother's jointure, which usually consisted of 10 per cent of her original dowry, was a charge on her son's estate. Younger sons and brothers had to be helped in their careers. Sisters and daughters had to be given dowries, though the bluer their blood in comparison with that of their spouse the less this was expected to be: a wealthy financier was resigned to paying heavily for the honour of marrying an earl's daughter, or even a baron's. Peers were expected to spend lavishly, to live magnificently and to maintain a splendid house as well as at least one country seat. Many peers had more than one for, unlike the gentry whose estates were normally confined to a single county, their estates, the fruit of successful marriage alliances, were scattered nationwide. Places like Chatsworth and Woburn required hundreds of servants to run them. Large house parties were the order of the day, but apart from formal entertaining the term 'family' was so widely interpreted, and family obligations so punctiliously honoured, that there were nearly always dependants, from young married couples to spinster aunts, paying a protracted and money-saving visit to their wealthy kinsman. Large house parties were more than an opportunity for pleasure and display. They were almost one of the organs of government. While this was largely confined to men of birth, policy was as often hammered out on the race course or at the dinner table as in the Cabinet room. Such parties were also a marriage market. In many spheres the peers and their relations were allowed by convention to lead singularly uninhibited lives. Socially they were so secure that, if so inclined, they could dispense with the outward trappings of their rank. They could consort familiarly with grooms and bruisers, if athletically inclined, or with artists and men of letters. But in their choice of a marriage partner they were not free. Wealth and the land on which it rested needed constant replenishment; if young men hunted the fox by day they were equally bound by the necessities of their situation to hunt for a well dowered wife when the day's sport was ended. Both during the pleasures of the country house party and the London season alike this was one of the serious businesses of life.

Within their own part of the country peers were little kings. Public rejoicing marked the birth of an heir, the coming of age of an eldest son, the birthday of the peer himself, public mourning his death. On such occasions hospitality was of an almost royal magnificence, and could be a crippling burden. Death could be equally expensive if this took place in London far from the family vault. Until the railway provided a less ostentatious and less costly form of transport for the noble corpse the funeral cortège with its hatchments and its mourners made a dignified progress to the tomb of his ancestors. The villages *en route* tolled their bells and people stood bareheaded when the procession passed. It was this involvement of the whole of the countryside that made these activities, whether gay or sad, socially significant. The tenants and the villagers were an integral part of them and the interest that they took was a personal one. Rural society might be 'deferential' and its detractors might use the word 'feudal' as one of condemnation, but at least it was not a society where human values were ignored. George Grenville, whose world it was, described the celebration of the birthday of the Duke of Rutland in 1838. A grand dinner was given in the servants hall for 145 retainers and servants about which Grenville observed:

I should like to bring the surly Radical here who scowls and snarls at 'the selfish aristocracy who have no sympathy with the people' and when he has seen hundreds feasting in the Castle,

and heard their loud shouts of joy and congratulation, and then
visited the villages round, and listened to the bells chiming all
about the vale, say whether 'the greatest happiness of the
greatest number' would be promoted by the destruction of all
the feudality which belongs inseparably to this scene, and by the
substitution of some abstract political rights for all the beef and
ale and music and dancing with which they are made merry and
glad even for so brief a space. (P. W. Wilson (ed.), *Grenville's Diary*
(1927), vol. 1, 29.)

Grenville then goes on to discuss the Duke's attitude towards his
social obligations:

The Duke of Rutland is as selfish a man as any in his class—that
is, he never does what he does not like, and spends his whole
life in a round of such pleasure as suits his taste, but he is neither
a foolish nor a bad man, and partly from a sense of duty, and
partly from inclination, he devotes time and labour on his estate.
He is guardian of a very large Union, and he not only attends
regularly the meetings of the Poor Law Guardians every week
or fortnight, and takes an active part in their proceedings, but
he visits the paupers who receive outdoor relief, sits and con-
verses with them, invites them to complain to him, if they have
anything to complain of, and tells them that he is not only their
friend but their representative at the assembly of Guardians, and
that it is his duty to see that they are nourished and protected.

Grenville then went on to express the opinion that 'To my mind
there is much more "sympathy" in this than in railing at the rich and
rendering the poor discontented, and weaning them from their
habitual attachments and respects and teaching them that the political
quacks and adventurers who flatter and cajole them are their only
true friends' (ibid., 305). He was no doubt prejudiced in favour of the
old order but, as other extracts show, he was very far from being
complaisant when faced with 'the vast extent of misery and distress
which prevails, and the evidence of the rotten foundations on which
the whole fabric of gorgeous society rests', asking 'Can such a state of
things permanently go on?' (ibid., 305). It must be admitted that the
conditions which produced this outburst were those prevailing in
Bethnal Green and not in rural England. Nevertheless in writing of
both he was describing something with which he was well acquainted,
even if he viewed them from an aristocratic angle.

For the majority of country people the squire rather than the peer was the most important local figure. The noble owners of vast estates normally left their management to agents, spending only a limited time at each of their country mansions. The squire, using that term loosely to describe the most important non-noble landowner in the neighbourhood, was an ever-present reality. The word 'squire' so inevitably calls up the picture of those two eighteenth-century characters, Squire Weston and Squire Alworthy in Fielding's *Tom Jones*, that it is difficult to banish them from the mind and to picture the Victorian squire as a gentleman with side-whiskers and a sense of propriety! In reality there was no archetype, though the squires of 1776 differed in many respects from those of 1851. In the cause of simplification and generalization one can distinguish between the squire who was mainly interested in country pursuits, hunting, fishing, shooting and all manner of bodily activity, and the squire who in addition had cultural and political interests beyond those of the rural community of which he was so important a part. In both the eighteenth and nineteenth centuries such men had collected libraries, had spent some time at one of the universities and had enjoyed the advantage of foreign travel. Some of them, more particularly in the latter century, were deeply religious men, often of an evangelical turn of mind. Two men who could be said to typify this contrast are Squire Osbaldestone and Sir John Boileau of Ketteringham in Norfolk. The former was an outstanding sportsman and rider to hounds, the kind of squire that earlier Lord Chesterfield had categorized as English Bumpkin Country Gentlemen. At Eton he was perpetually being flogged for some high-spirited prank, a retribution which he seemed to take very much as a matter of course. On attaining his majority his mother's ambition, combined with his possession of extensive estates, led him to taking the conventional step of standing for Parliament, to which he was duly elected. He found politics 'a great bore'. He confessed 'I had, however no taste whatsoever for public life; I was so entirely engrossed with hunting, shooting and athletic feats, that I could not turn my thoughts to politics' (E. D. Cummings (ed.), *Squire Osbaldestone: his autobiography* (1926), 35).

Sir John Boileau was a complete contrast. He too was a rich man, his father having made a fortune in India, but the family was an old one and when Sir John bought Ketteringham Hall in 1841 he immediately took his rightful place among the leading Norfolk gentry. In addition he had aristocratic connections; his wife was one of Lord Minto's daughters. A man of literary and scientific interests, he spent several months each year at his London house in Brook Street. When in Norfolk he prided himself on being 'the father of his parish', ruling his tenants with a firm, though benevolent, paternalism. He provided his labourers with decent cottages at moderate rents, paid wages to men who could not find work through no fault of their own to prevent them from having to go into the hated workhouse. He and his wife visited the sick, distributed coals at Christmas and provided a dinner of roast beef, plum pudding and ale to the poor men of the parish every January. In the grim year of 1847 he voluntarily raised the wages of his own employees and persuaded his friends to do the same. He was solicitous for the eternal welfare of his household, taking family prayers and even preparing his footman for confirmation, and of his tenants. In return he expected deference and gratitude. Once, when engaged in an acrimonious dispute with his vicar, with whom he differed on matters of religious observance, he told him 'I will turn every family out of the parish who dares disobey me' (Owen Chadwick, *Victorian Miniature* (1960), p. 99), and he meant it. In many ways he represented Victorian paternalism at its worst and its best.

Where the squire possessed this autocratic power much depended on his character and outlook. To the hard-riding Osbaldestone drunkenness and sexual laxity may well have seemed more venial offences than they did to the Victorian Sir John. He was quite unperturbed by the drunkenness that marked the celebrations of his twenty-first birthday. The tenants and any of the local poor who chose to come were entertained to dinner, with the result that the guests

> partook so copiously of the ale provided, that more than half of them were beastly drunk. This had been anticipated and arrangements made for those who should be incapable of reaching their homes; our stables and coach houses were extensive, and we removed the horses into a farmyard leaving the premises free for the temporary accommodation of helpless guests, who were made as comfortable as possible until they recovered. (Cummings, op. cit., 16.)

This tolerance was more characteristic of the eighteenth century than of the nineteenth, of which Sir John's moralistic standards were more representative. In some ways fiction is a better guide to the norm than fact, for whereas the historian is faced by the endless variety of the individual the novelist tends to reflect the contemporary image. The squire in nineteenth-century fiction, unless he is cast for the role of 'the bold, bad baronet' is more usually portrayed as a very humdrum gentleman, proud of his ancestry like Sir Walter Elliot in Jane Austen's *Persuasion*.

Few people questioned their authority over their dependants but what the private reactions of the villagers were is more difficult to gauge. Trained to submission and living in a community where tradition was all powerful, it seems likely that they accepted the squire for good or evil in much the same way as country folk accept the weather. He was important in their lives but outside their control and must be accepted as part of the nature of things, cursed when he was harsh and blessed when he dispensed the loaves and fishes. There was, however, one exception. Shooting was one of the major pursuits of both the aristocracy and the gentry, who protected their monopoly rights over bird and beast by savage game laws. The number of keepers was increased and shoots were more elaborately organized. No tenant, however extensive his farm, might shoot so much as a rabbit on it. Until 1831 even small landowners, that is persons possessing land worth less than £100 a year, might not shoot over their own property. Moreover until that year even the eating of game was reserved for the greater landowners and their friends because, in an effort to stop poaching, it was illegal to sell game by retail, though in practice much of it found its way to the tables of wealthy citizens. In 1831 certain dealers were licensed to sell game in the hope that the provision of recognized channels through which it could be purchased would make it easier to block up those available to the poachers. The grievances of the farmers and their labourers were not the same. The former were chiefly concerned with the damage that game, including rabbits, could do to their crops, and to blunt their resentment many landowners made *ex gratia* payments to their tenant farmers in compensation. Often after a shoot it was customary to make a present of some of the game to the farmers over whose land it had taken place.

For the rural poor there was no such sweetener; no single factor caused such bad blood and bitter resentment in the countryside as the determination of the landowners to enforce the game laws in all their savagery. Until 1827, when the most inhuman of these devices were prohibited by law, keepers protected their coverts against marauders by the use of spring guns and mantraps. Daylight poaching was regarded a trifle more leniently but night poaching carried with it the penalty of transportation, and in years to come many a prosperous Australian could trace his ancestry to some sturdy but unlucky poacher. Though in the eyes of the law poaching was a criminal offence, and though a squire as benevolent as Sir John Boileau harangued his labourers on the importance of preserving game, country folk viewed the subject very differently. To them pheasants, hares and rabbits were wild animals which it was sport to hunt and which, when caught, provided either food for the pot or a means of supplementing a meagre income if sold. At a time when wages were low, and employment often hard to find, the labourer felt the bitter injustice of not being able to take the occasional bird or rabbit to feed his hungry family. If he were caught red-handed he could expect little mercy from a bench of landowners, but, unless he were so caught, it was difficult for the magistrates to get evidence from a local population whose sympathies were with the poacher. Not all poachers were driven to law-breaking by the twin forces of hunger and resentment. There was an uglier side to the business which perhaps to some extent explains, though it does not excuse, the savage penalties which a Parliament of landowners imposed. Poaching was profitable and gangs of violent men, greedy for profit and holding life cheap, fought an endless battle with the keepers and there were casualties on both sides. Professional poachers, like the smugglers, were out to defeat the law by violent means in pursuit of illicit gains.

Hunting, the other absorbing pastime of the country gentleman, unlike the game laws, caused less social bitterness in spite of the risk to growing crops. By the eighteenth century the fox had replaced the hare and the stag as the favourite quarry and men with sporting interests expected to ride to hounds at least a couple of days a week, often more. When Osbaldestone was not hunting he was shooting, and when not shooting hunting; there were many like him. It became a status symbol to own a pack of hounds but it was an expensive hobby. A good pack might be worth £3,000 and in addition hunt servants had to be paid, so gradually the private pack was replaced by subscription hunts financed by their members. Good hunting country was parcelled out between them. By 1835 there were ninety-one in existence and some of them, such as the Pytchley and the Quorn, gained a nation-wide reputation. The hunt was more than a sport. It was a social institution, binding the whole countryside together. Unlike shooting it was not exclusive. The nobility, gentry and substantial farmers made up the field while country lads followed on foot. The popularity of this national sport provided a new subject for literature and fostered the growing appeal of the sporting journalist. Of these two men stand out: Charles Apperley, the son of a country gentleman, who, under the pen name of Nimrod contributed to the *Sporting Magazine*, and Robert Smith Surtees, himself the son, grandson and great-grandson of a master of hounds. It was he who created the character of John Jorrocks, the City grocer who rode to hounds in the sporting novels that are still to be found on some public library shelves. The popularity of the hunt was not, however, without its disadvantages. 'One of the greatest difficulties to be contended with in the Quorn country', wrote Osbaldestone, 'was the behaviour of the stocking-makers and weavers, who used to assemble and crowd at the covert side. It seemed impossible to keep them together at the right place in order to let the fox go away. At first we could not manage them at all' (Cummings, op. cit., 123). Having tried 'kind words and persuasion without success' the hunt resorted to force. This also failed and finally resort was had to bribery, and the goodwill of the villages where the weavers and stockingers lived was purchased by an annual gift of £2 drink money. Such episodes throw a rather unexpected light on the so-called 'deferential' society. Admittedly the offenders were not agricultural labourers and the rural craftsman was a very different breed, but their lack of respect for their betters is interesting.

Not all villages were squire-dominated. In those counties where the large estates predominated and the landowner was a peer seldom in residence for long periods, his place was taken by his estate agent or manager, who was more interested in the farmers and their rents than in the morals and behaviour of the cottagers. Where the land of the parish was owned by several proprietors, none of whom, either through the superiority of his birth or the size of his estate, predominated, there was much less dictation from above. In the north also where the farming population lived in isolated and scattered hamlets rather than in large villages the power of the squirearchy was much slighter and in parish matters it was the more substantial farmers who took the lead.

No description of the social structure of rural England would be complete without some discussion of the position of the clergy. This varied according to the wealth and connections of the incumbent. Much depended on who had the right to present to the living. When this was in the gift of the squire then, like Sir William Bertram of Jane Austen's *Mansfield Park*, he often installed a friend or younger son. When this happened the connection between the vicarage or rectory and the hall was close; social parity made intercourse easy. If the squire had no close friend or relative for whom he wished to provide, the living frequently went to his son's tutor, a common doorway to clerical promotion, or to some cleric lucky enough to attract his attention, as Jane Austen's Mr Collins was to attract that of Lady Catherine de Burgh in *Pride and Prejudice*. In such cases the vicar became a rather superior dependent. Though Mr Collins certainly did not regard himself in that light, equally certainly his noble patroness did. It is difficult to imagine him standing up to her on matters of either doctrine or parish management. On the other hand, if the living were in the gift of a bishop, a college or the crown the incumbent was more or less independent and, where there was no resident squire, likely to be the most influential person in the parish, unless he also was non-resident—in which case some of his power filtered down to his curate-in-charge.

Where, as could easily happen, there was both a resident squire and a resident parson who was under no obligation to him, clashes could and did occur. In the eighteenth century these were more likely to be the result of clashes in personality than to be caused by doctrinal differences. Religion was normally regarded by the upper ranks of society as an instrument for ensuring right conduct than as a matter of theological debate. Even the Deists, though they might question the divinity of Christ, were content that humble folk should still be taught from the pulpit their duty to their neighbours and respect for their betters. By the end of the eighteenth century this situation was changing. The evangelical movement was producing a new breed of clergy who, in their campaign for righteousness, were prepared to challenge the authority of a more latitudinarian squire. This happened at Ketteringham. Sir John Boileau was no lax or indifferent Christian but he found parson Andrew's strict evangelical outlook, his disapproval of dancing and his insistence on the strictest observance of Sunday a sore trial. There were continuous quarrels over the school, the school house, and the fabric of the church. The villagers, as villagers always are, were well aware of the tension between the two men, and on occasion found themselves facing the awkward dilemma of offending the squire, whose tenants they were, or the vicar who was responsible for their spiritual welfare. Usually bread and butter won! The situation at Ketteringham was in no sense unique, and after 1833 such possibilities were increased by the doctrinal and ritualist convictions of the Tractarian movement.

If such clashes could create friction between the parson and the squire, the former could equally easily find himself at loggerheads with the farmers over the payment of tithe. Indeed much of the smouldering dislike of the clergy was caused by this obligation. The great tithe, consisting of a tenth of the corn, grain, hay and wood, was the property of the rector. The small tithe payable on livestock and such produce as was not covered by the great tithe, went to the vicar. How substantial these tithes could be is illustrated by the large, and often beautifully built, tithe barns still to be found in many agricultural English villages. By the eighteenth century the tithe was deeply resented, particularly by dissenting parishioners and in parishes where the parson was non-resident and the church was represented only by an underpaid curate. As well as being a financial burden its collection could be the cause of considerable inconvenience when crops could not be carried until a tenth part had been earmarked for the Church. By the thirties the Church was under attack from many sides. This resulted in the tithe's most objectionable features being removed by an Act in 1836 which converted it into a rent charge on the land, based on its value and the average price of grain over the previous seven years. This measure at least removed the physical irritant of seeing the grain or hay gathered into the tithe barn, or of having to hand over the tenth piglet to the vicar, but that the tithe had to be paid at all remained a grievance, particularly when the farmer was a Methodist or Quaker who had no love for the established church. Even strict orthodoxy rarely reconciled the farmers to its payment and it remained a constant source of friction between them and the rural clergy. It was not only the tithe that involved the latter in the fortunes of agriculture. Part of the incumbent's income came from the glebe, which was that portion of the parish land that had originally been assigned for his support. Richer rectors might rent it out but many farmed it themselves, drawing a considerable amount of their income from it. Here again the interests of the parson seemed to conflict with those of some of his parishioners. When a parish was enclosed the parson got compensation for his glebe in the form of a section of the newly enclosed land. When the commons were enclosed he was compensated for the loss of his grazing and other rights attached to his glebe. In the eyes of the villagers their spiritual pastor therefore benefited along with the other landowners of the parish and was disliked accordingly. When it is remembered that many of the clergy were also magistrates and that poaching was one of the crimes with which the Bench dealt most severely, it is easy to understand the gulf that separated some of the rural clergy from their flock. There were, however, many exceptions. Unpopular though many of the clergy were, there were always some who ruled their flock with benevolence and devotion and more who, being kindly men, did what they could to ameliorate the condition of the poor, running schools and dispensing charity. In this respect the evangelical clergy had a good record; they at least cared that their parishioners should find salvation.

Though the aristocracy and landowning gentry dominated the countryside and though many of them took an active interest in modern farming methods and in the management of their estates, they were essentially a rentier class. The actual cultivation of the soil was the task of the farmers and of the labourers whom they employed. Far more than the upper strata of society they were dependent on geographical factors. Though townsmen, then as now, often suppose it possible to dismiss everything that is not urban as 'the countryside', there was in fact as much difference in the way of life and in the pattern of society between Westmorland, with its hill farms, and East Anglia with its wide fields of grain, as between the elegancies of Bath and the murk of Manchester. The economics of farming had always been dictated by the natural features of the land, its elevation, its drainage, the richness or poverty of the soil, and nineteenth-century improvements in transport accentuated this dependence. In the past farmers had been forced to be partly self-sufficient. The hill farmer, though his main wealth lay in sheep, had found it necessary to culti-vate a few in-fields of oats or barley, crops which could be produced on his poorer soil. The arable farmers of East Anglia needed cattle or sheep to eat the turnips that were part of the rotation of crops, and to supply the meat, butter and cheese which supplied the local market towns. The cattle-breeders of Leicestershire, where the soil favoured pasture rather than arable, still required to grow some grain. With better transport for farm produce it became more profitable to con-centrate on what could be grown most economically. Hilly and mountainous country such as the Cotswolds, the Downs, much of Wales and the north of England concentrated largely on sheep, mainly for their wool and only secondarily for their mutton. In flatter areas the soil was the deciding factor. In Norfolk, Essex and Suffolk this was light and well-drained, which made it particularly suitable for arable farming. In the equally flat counties of the midlands the heavy soil produced good pasture for cattle and sheep; it is a mistake to suppose that only the less fertile areas were given up to them, as witness the famous flocks of Romney Marsh.

At first sight such factors may seem to have little connection with the social structure of rural England, but a moment's consideration will show that they are fundamental to it. There is a world of difference between the way of life in an isolated farm house, or in the scattered and tiny hamlets of the north, and that of the large villages to be

found in the arable regions. The demand for labour was different, the
type of labour was different, the type of farmer was different, even his
legal status was often also different. The greater part of the land was
farmed by tenants rather than by occupying owners, who by the end
of the eighteenth century had become a smallish minority. Legal
status, however, was no guide to their relative prosperity. The 'states-
man' of Westmorland, with his meagre freehold, lived little better
than a labourer, while the prosperous tenant farmer could live as
comfortably as many a small squire. It is true that the occupying
owner had some advantages in that he was secure in his holding, but
he had to face expenses which the tenant farmer had not to face. If
enclosure took place he had to pay his share; if new building were
required he could not look to his landlord to provide them. If times
were hard he had to cope with low prices or poor crops as best he
might while the tenant could press for an abatement of rent. It is
more satisfactory, therefore, to speak of small farmers, medium-sized
farmers and large farmers than to speak of occupying owners and
tenants. A small farmer was generally reckoned as working from 20
to 100 acres, a medium farmer something between 100 and 300, and
a large farmer upwards of this acreage. Large farms tended to concentrate on arable, small farmers on dairying, producing butter, eggs,
milk and cheese for a nearby town, but regional variations were very
great. If improved methods favoured the growth of large farms,
urbanization and better transport increased the opportunities of the
small farmer. Landlords, it is true, preferred to amalgamate farms
when leases fell in, or, when the waste was enclosed, to carve larger
farms out of it, because the fewer the farms the easier the problems of
management; also, larger farms producing for a wide commercial
market could pay more rent. But the number of potential large
tenant farmers was limited; most fell into the small or medium
categories.

It is difficult to know to what extent the farming community was
changing during the period under review. This difficulty is increased
by the fact that an earlier generation of agrarian historians talked about
'an agrarian revolution' to parallel what was taking place in industry,
and this assumed a much greater change in farming practices than
subsequent examination of the evidence has warranted. From the
late seventeenth century more efficient methods had been spreading
gradually even among the traditional farmers of the open fields, but
their progress was patchy. Nor did the spate of parliamentary enclosures at the end of the eighteenth and during the early decades of the

nineteenth century necessarily produce a spread of the new techniques. During the French wars farmers enjoyed a seller's market. The majority of farmers, especially the smaller ones, tended to be conservative, and with high war-time prices they had little inducement to experiment. The post-war years were more difficult. Though some were good, in general prices in the twenties and thirties only averaged some two-thirds of what the war-time boom had led farmers to expect; moreover averages give little idea of the actual fluctuations which make forward planning so difficult. Some marginal land went out of cultivation. Better and cheaper systems of drainage made wet and waterlogged land more profitable. Larger farmers began to look to more efficient methods to keep up their profits. Landlords were faced with demands for lower rents. The worst hit were the small occupying owners. But though the depression may have lessened their ranks it seems to have had little effect in reducing the proportion of small farms. Until the mid-nineteenth century, in spite of the occasional introduction of threshing machines and the use of better ploughs, English farming remained more traditional in its methods and outlook than is always realized.

It was the prosperity of farming rather than its innovations which brought with it a rising standard of living in the late eighteenth and early nineteenth centuries. Improving landlords enlarged or rebuilt farmhouses. When several small estates were amalgamated, either by purchase or by marriage, their small manor houses often became redundant and were demoted to become farmhouses. In the past the great farm kitchen had been the centre of the household, 'the houseplace' in northern parlance. Here the family and hired hands lived together, though they usually ate different food at separate tables. With prosperity a separate sitting-room, or even a best parlour for entertaining, began to appear. Furnishings varied but in addition to substantial chairs, tables, benches and stools in oak, ash or elm, many had elaborate linen chests and cupboards. Better-off farmers had feather beds; the less fortunate slept on mattresses filled with flock or straw. Most were well supplied with sheets woven on the loom and blankets. By the end of the century Wedgwood's enterprise in producing pottery that was cheap and attractive led to its use rather than that of the traditional wooden trenchers and pewter tankards. Socially perhaps the most interesting development within the farming community was the appearance of the gentleman farmer or, because these men were rarely of gentle birth, it might be more accurate to describe them as farmers who were beginning to ape the way of life of the gentry. They were emerging from the ranks of the large farmers and were frequently pioneers in trying out new farming practices, which attracted the attention of both contemporaries and historians. For their improved and experimental methods both have praised them, but when increasing prosperity tempted some of them to abandon the farmers' traditional way of life, their contemporaries condemned them. The reasons for this were social. Prosperous farmers made desirable tenants who were approved by the landowning gentry, but when they began to copy the manners and ways of life of their betters such presumption was frowned upon. It was a topic on which Arthur Young expended much eloquence, declaring that though a farmer was entitled to everything that 'yields comfort; those who chuse to give up that enjoyment for liveries or show of any kind, arrange themselves with another order of mortals' (Arthur Young, *Annals of Agriculture*, vol. xviii, 152). In other words they were transgressing against the canons of due order and degree.

This social revolution seems to have originated among the wives. In the past their lives had been hard. In addition to being responsible for the dairy when the farm servants were hired by the year and lived in the farmhouse, the farmer's wife had to cater for, organize, and often cook for a considerable household. This continued to be the practice on smaller farms, particularly those in isolated districts, even into the twentieth century, but on the bigger ones by the late eighteenth century the farm servant was being replaced by the farm labourer who lived out with his family in a cottage, which was often the property of the farmer who employed him. This lightened the burden on the farmer's wife. Moreover, as her husband's prosperity increased she began to employ more domestic help in the house, which in turn left her and her daughters with more leisure. Her contemporary critics declared that the consequence was that she was tempted to indulge in a way of life above her station. She was no longer content to go to market wrapped in a cloak and riding pillion behind her husband. Instead she demanded a smart chaise. Traditional clothes no longer satisfied her and her daughters. They studied avidly such London fashions as penetrated to their market town, employed local milliners and mantua makers to copy them and flaunted their new finery at church or when they received company. Daughters had to be educated to fit them for a more genteel social role and were sent to one of the new boarding schools, now springing up, to learn the manners and accomplishments of the gentry. When they returned to the farm the parlour was equipped with one of the new-fangled pianofortes, on which they performed when receiving company or entertaining their neighbours. How widespread such aspirations were cannot be known, but by the end of the eighteenth century those who cherished them had become the butt of satirical writers and cartoonists. In Trollope's *Barchester Towers*, written in the mid-nineteenth century, there is a delightful vignette of a social climber. When Miss Thorne gave her annual party for her neighbours and tenants it was her custom to receive the former in her drawing room and entertain them on her lawn, while the latter were feasted in the park beyond the ha-ha, which acted as a social barrier. As a hostess she was in something of a quandary about the Lookalofts. Mrs Lookaloft, as Trollope indicated by her name, was a social climber. She had changed the name of her house from Barleystubb Farm to Rosebank, had installed a pianoforte in her drawing room and sent her daughters to a fashionable seminary in Barchester. 'Mrs Lookaloft', lamented Miss Thorne, 'won't squeeze her fine clothes on a bench and talk familiarly about cream and ducklings to good Mrs Greenacre. Yet Mrs Lookaloft is no fit companion and never has been the associate of the Thornes and Grantleys. And if Mrs Lookaloft be admitted within the sanctum of fashionable life, if she be allowed with her three daughters to leap the ha-ha, why not the wives and daughters of other families also? Mrs Greenacre is at present well content, but she might cease to be so if she saw Mrs Lookaloft on the lawn'. In the end Miss Thorne contented herself with stressing in her invitation to that ambitious guest that all the tenants had been invited, hoping that if they did not want to be counted with the rest of the tenantry they would stay away. But she had not reckoned with Mrs Lookaloft's resolution. On the fateful day mother and daughters, all outrageously overdressed, presented themselves at the house, where a perplexed footman found himself admitting them. Though they were most coldly greeted by their unwilling hostess and ignored by the other guests, Miss Thorne was correct in supposing that Mrs Greenacre would be seriously put out, though she found some comfort when she heard that they had been gate-crashers and not invited guests when they invaded the drawing room, and that their reception there had been frigid. Mr Lookaloft, who knew his place, torn between his wife's ambition and his own sense of propriety, had a diplomatic bilious attack and stayed away. Most farming families had no such pretensions to gentility, even though sporting farmers rode with the hunt. The furthest that Mr Lookaloft was prepared to go was to wear a red coat on such occasions. Social revolutions, like other revolutions, are pioneered by the few. The Lookalofts and their kind found the going hard. The significant thing is that they entered the race, even if they usually brought up the field. By the mid-nineteenth century the ranks of the gentry were being successfully assailed by rich farmers as well as by wealthy merchants.

The mass of the rural population, however, were ordinary villagers, rural craftsmen, cottagers and labourers. For them the French wars and their aftermath brought more kicks than halfpence. Although with the coming of peace every section of the rural community had to face difficulties and make adjustments, a combination of circumstances prevented the agricultural labourer from sharing in the prosperity of the wartime years. Historians have argued over the effects of the wave of parliamentary enclosures on the villagers when the open fields were enclosed. For many the shock of seeing the old landmarks and the old practices disappear was psychological rather than material, but it did mean that the frugal had lost the chance of buying land in very small parcels and of thereby gradually accumulating a tiny holding. The village poor were more likely to be adversely affected by the enclosure of wastes and commons, which, under pressure to produce more food, began to disappear rapidly after the General Enclosure Act of 1801. How valuable an adjunct to village life and village economy the waste had been has been hotly disputed by both contemporaries and historians. Originally the waste had been part of open field farming, and even for non-open-field villages it had supplied additional rough pastures for cows, sheep and, above all, for pigs. It had also been a source of fuel, wood, or in some regions, peat. Timber, with the permission of the lord of the manor, could be used for building. Some northern parishes, my own for instance, once possessed small quarries, a valuable material in a countryside of stone houses and stone walls. Originally only certain villagers, in open field villages only those who also held land in the open fields, were allowed to use these rights, which were carefully apportioned. But by the eighteenth century, though not all the inhabitants enjoyed a legal right, in practice all who wished to use them did so. Indeed squatters had often built flimsy hovels on what were the fringes of the waste. Arthur Young frequently declared that the poor who used the commons derived little benefit from them because overcropping and neglect had destroyed much of their fertility. According to him they were more a breeding-ground for idleness than a help to the frugal. He argued that families who could keep a half-starved cow and a few sheep on them, who could collect fuel and live in a miserable or low-rented hovel, would never exert themselves to do an honest day's work and would bring up their children to be as idle as themselves. Probably commons did encourage scroungers and the work-shy, but many families must have lived more comfortably because of them. To be able to keep a pig, or even a few hens, or to collect sticks for a fire, were important additions to a poor man's budget. Certainly whether they were valuable, or whether the poor only thought them to be so, their disappearance caused bitter resentment because only those with legal rights received compensation. This was often so small and so burdened with the expenses of enclosure as to be of little use, even if the temptation to sell for immediate cash were resisted. There is some scattered evidence to suggest that enclosure could lead at times to an increased reliance on the poor rates.

It has been argued, probably correctly, that the new work created by enclosure gave so much more employment that the cottager would live more comfortably working for wages than he had done when tempted to rely for part of his livelihood on the fringe benefits of the waste. This, however, depended on the adequacy of his wage. Unfortunately the same forces which were encouraging landowners to enclose the open fields and the waste were also working to push up the price of everything that the labourer wanted to buy, while the wages, on which he was increasingly dependent, did not rise in the same proportion. No one who has studied the earlier situation of the labouring poor can have much faith in the Golden Age of which Peter Gaskell and, following in his footsteps, Engels, drew so idealistic a picture. Life for them had always been hard. The dictum that before enclosure they had been labourers with land and after enclosure without land can only have been true of the few. It has not stood up to historical criticism. Even medieval villages were not devoid of landless labourers; nor were those of eighteenth-century England. Nevertheless there is a sense in which it is true to say that the agricultural labourer, as the nineteenth century was to know him, was as much the creation of the new economic and demographic pressures as the factory worker of the towns. In the eighteenth century when a farm had been large enough to employ a full-time farm worker, in line with the practice of the past, he had been hired by the year and had lived in the farm house, or at least, like the Northumberland hind, in a cottage whose occupancy formed part of his wages. When extra help was needed for haytime or harvest, or for scouring ditches, or hoeing turnips, it was hired by the week or even by the day, from the nearest village. If local labour was not enough it was supplemented by itinerants from as far away as Wales or Ireland for seasonal tasks. In the villages this reserve of labour was made up of men who reckoned to make good money during hay and harvest and, in the arable districts, by winter threshing. Between bouts of agricultural employment many of them worked at some cottage industry. The women spun. In Bedfordshire the children, when little more than infants, were sent to lace-making schools, as in Madeira today they are sent to learn embroidery. In Hertfordshire they plaited straw. In osier country baskets were made. In Northamptonshire, where cattle-breeding supplied the leather, shoe-making was widespread. Small local cottage industries abounded, and there were few villages where an industrious family could not find some such employment.

But to secure even a very modest degree of comfort required from such families good health, steady application and good harvests. Their main item of food was cereals. In the early eighteenth century in the south bread was made with a mixture of grains; wheat and rye was common. In the north the normal cereal was oats, which was made into oat cakes or porridge, or barley, though barley dumplings were so tough that one man declared he could hardly get his teeth into them. Another said that rye bread made of grain harvested in a wet season was so heavy that it sank to the bottom of a basin of milk! It is not surprising that with good harvests the poor began to eat bread made of pure wheaten flour, which today would be described as wholemeal. Good harvests, which prevailed in the first half of the century, meant a larger crop to get in and therefore the opportunity to earn more wages. Also there was more grain in better condition to be got by gleaning. When the corn was cut by sickle it was not possible to cut it close to the ground and some of the ears were shed in the process. Most farmers allowed poor women to glean in the fields once the crop had been carried. It was a custom as old as the story of Naomi and Ruth. Abundant harvests also meant lower prices, at least until later in the century, when, with the pressure of a growing population, demand increased. When harvests were good and prices low the cottager was able to improve his standard of living by having something over for luxuries, such as butcher's meat and tea, as well as eating a better bread. It is almost impossible to know to what extent the rural population bought these articles. The poor keep no accounts which the historian can check and the statements of contemporaries are unreliable. The eighteenth-century pamphleteers were appalled that the poor should drink tea at all, or indulge in habits which they considered extravagant. In consequence they tended to blow up such examples as they had come across merely for propaganda purposes.

It does look, however, as if, except for a few years when the harvest was deficient, the diet of the cottagers was improving. The increased use of potatoes also helped, and in some parts there appears to have been more consumption of other vegetables, such as onions and cabbages. In the north the more traditional diet seems to have continued as far as the consumption of oats and barley went, but potatoes were better liked than in the south. Could this have been due to the influx of Irish labourers into Lancashire, one wonders? Also more milk was available there. In some southern villages, particularly in those near towns, this was becoming a scarce commodity because farmers were finding it more profitable to make it into butter or cheese, or to dispose of it in bulk to a dairyman rather than to retail it in pints and half pints to the cottagers. Even today the presence of cows does not necessarily ensure local supplies of milk. In one Highland village where I used to stay in the thirties, the milk went into Inverness, and only later in the day was it brought back and retailed by the dairy that had bought it. But before the coming of the automobile milk once taken to the town did not come back, and unless there were small farmers prepared to supply their poorer neighbours, these had to go without. In the north where the stress was on cattle and sheep, and where there were many small farms remote from the industrial belt, the countryman could still enjoy milk on his porridge.

In addition to having a monotonous diet, the rural poor were badly housed. To some extent this was the fault of the Poor Law. By the Act of Settlement and Removals (1662) each parish had to bear the responsibility for its own poor. In consequence when a parish was in the hands of one or two landowners they were careful to restrict the number of cottages. Such parishes were known as closed parishes. Where, on the other hand, the land of the parish was divided between many small owners, cottages, often of the flimsiest description, were run up for rent. But the economic situation was as much to blame as the Poor Law. The rent which a labourer could pay, even with the assistance of the earnings of his wife and children, when his wages varied between 7s and 9s a week, hardly encouraged the building of decent cottages. Moreover at least some proportion of the rural poor owned the hovels in which they lived. The better ones were the relics of the open field villages and had once had a few strips attached to them, but more had been run up on the waste, sometimes with the permission of the lord of the manor, sometimes by squatters. Judging by contemporary prints, for their fabric was too slight for any of them to have survived, they were for the most part low thatched structures, made of whatever local material was available. Many agricultural labourers lived in cottages owned by the farmer or the local land-owner. These varied from the wholly deplorable to the neat dwelling on some large estate. Chadwick produced some horrifying examples of the former in his *Report on the Sanitary Condition of the Labouring Population* (1842). It is unlikely that sixty years before they had been any better. According to one report of a Poor Law doctor in Dorset, most of the cottages there were 'of the worst description, some were mere mud hovels, and situated in low and damp places with cesspools or accu-mulations of filth close to the doors. The mud floors of many are much below the level of the road, and in wet seasons are little better than so much clay' (op. cit., 9). 'Persons living in such cottages', he continued, 'are generally very poor, very dirty and usually in rags, living wholly on bread and potatoes, scarcely ever tasting animal food.'

Instances of appalling housing can easily be multiplied. At Todding-ton in Bedfordshire it was reported that 'Very few of the cottages were furnished with privies that could be used, and contiguous to almost every door a dung heap was raised upon which every species of filth was accumulated ... Scarcely any cottage was provided with a pantry, and I found the provisions generally kept in the bedrooms. In several instances I found whole families, comprising adult and infant children with their parents sleeping in one room' (ibid., 12).

In the Epping Union the medical officer stated that 'many of their cottages are neither wind nor weather tight. It has often been my lot to attend a labour where the wet has been running down the walls, and the light to be distinguished through the roof, and this in the winter season, with no fireplace in the room' (ibid., 14). Not all rural families were so miserably housed. Even in Dorset many cottages were reported as 'consisting of a day room and two bed-rooms, constructed with due regard to ventilation and warmth, pantry, and fuel house, with a small garden and pigsty adjoining' (ibid., 9). Generally the best cottages were to be found on the estates of improving landowners who took as great a pride in their 'good cottages and farms as others in fine hunters and race horses'. Some of the cottages which the Earl of Leicester had built at Holkham in 1819 were described as 'perhaps the most substantial and comfortable which are to be seen in any part of England; and if all the English peasantry could be lodged in similar ones, it would be the realization of an Utopia'. His example was unlikely to be followed; the Earl let them for £3 a year and this rent included a spacious garden, a wash house, a dirt bin, a privy and a pig cot, whereas the minimum economic rent for such a three-bedroomed house would have been £6. This rent, it was stated, very few labourers would be prepared to pay, 'for reckoning the rate of wages at 12s a week (which would be high for some parts of the country), very few would be willing, out of that sum to expend 2s 3¾d a week, or nearly a fifth of their earnings, for the rent of their cottage' (ibid., 264–5).

To make even the roughest approximate assessment of the position of the poorest section of the rural population at the outbreak of the French wars is all but impossible. Yet the attempt must be made because what had been was the measuring rod of what was to come. In matters of housing, by-employment, wages, diet, availability of waste and commons each region had its own norm: any attempt to strike a national average would be more misleading than illuminating. There was not even a uniform rate of change common to all regions. When the historian turns from material satisfactions to the even more elusive psychological ones then the problem has to be faced of trying to see life with the eyes of an eighteenth-century villager. His diet was monotonous in the extreme, and often deficient in much that the modern dietician would consider necessary, but was this a cause of discontent to people who had known no other? The Indian or Chinese peasant, if his rice bowl is full, does not complain bitterly that it only contains rice. Traditionally the English poor had lived mainly on cereals. Bread was the accepted staple food in the south, oat cakes and porridge were eaten in the north. If this were of good quality and could be supplemented by cheese, by butter, or lard and bacon from the pig then, provided he could eat his fill, the rural cottager was content. Moreover the rhythm of this limited fare was broken by moments of equally traditional feasting. Harvest Home, when the grain had been carried and the barns were full, was celebrated with beef and mutton pasties, puddings and beer and ale in profusion. Births, marriages and even deaths at the Big House were again occasions on which the villagers could eat and drink their fill. Christmas and Easter, as well as lesser festivals such as May Day, brought their own pleasures when the local gentry supplied food and drink for the mummers, or distributed largesse to the young folk who came collecting. Such events were the highlights of rural existence and were savoured to the full. Sometimes a fair was held within walking distance. Legs were tough in those days; they had to be. Then all the neighbourhood flocked there from miles around. Briefly the yokels made contact with the outside world, gazing at the mountebanks and spending a few precious pennies at the stalls, entertained by the bustle and storing up enough memories to see them through many a winter's evening. Occasionally too a pedlar came to the village with his chapbooks and store of simple luxuries or necessities. Even to go to the nearby town on market day to sell a bit of produce, or to drive the farmer's sheep or cow made a welcome break. When nothing better offered there was always the local beerhouse where a man who had the modest price of a pint could meet his cronies. The younger men had their traditional sports often crude and brutal but bringing into their lives an element of excitement. Like their betters they would go miles to see a cockfight. which was no exclusive sport, or to watch a wrestling.

To a more sophisticated age these may seem simple pleasures to balance against monotonous food, that was sometimes scanty in addition, deplorable housing and the ill health and rheumatism that came from working hours in all weathers before the age of waterproof clothing. A day that meant work from dawn to dusk in winter and a full twelve hours in summer, sometimes with a long walk at either end, was exhausting; damp and smoky cottages with little fuel for drying clothes were a hazard to health. It was almost impossible for such families to save anything for an emergency. Illness or even a lying-in often meant an application to the parish. Overseers were frequently asked for help when some major article of attire had to be replaced. Many people lived out their lives near to subsistence level with only the Poor Law, stretched like a safety net, to save them from starvation in old age or illness. Yet foreign visitors from countries that had not even this safety net were unfailingly impressed by the higher standards of the villagers in comparison with that of most European peasants. According to them they worked less hard, wore better clothes and could contrive to spend time at the ale house, though to some extent this rosy picture may be due to the fact that foreign tourists, then as now, rarely penetrated much beyond London and the home counties, one of the most prosperous regions of England. Yet, balancing the bad with the good, if the historian cannot believe in a Golden Age before the Industrial Revolution it can still be argued that perhaps since the fifteenth century the rural poor had never 'had it so good' as in the first half of the eighteenth century, in so far as the majority had enough to eat, adequate clothing and a life that was not without its alleviations and pleasures.

In the last decade of the eighteenth and during the first part of the nineteenth century this simple standard came under increasing pressure, though an American visitor as late as 1810 could still declare 'the poor do not look so poor here as in other countries'. He found 'that poverty does not intrude on your sight and it is necessary to seek it'. Of the people he said that they 'appear healthy, and not in rags but not remarkably stout' (Louis Simond, *An American in Regency England; the journal of a tour in 1810–11*, ed. Christopher Hibbert (1968), 18–19), and he was particularly impressed by the fact that even in poor houses the casements were in good repair and that in the north, near Kendal, honeysuckle and roses grew against the cottage walls, which to him seemed proof of 'a great degree of ease and comfort among the lower ranks' (ibid., 71). Nevertheless the pressures were there. More babies were being born and were living to bear children themselves for it to be possible for agriculture to absorb them. At the same time subsidiary industries, such as the wife's spinning, were either going into factories or moving nearer to the towns to use their facilities or feed their factories. In the countryside there was no longer enough work to go round. In the north the situation was more readily handled because in Lancashire, in Cheshire, in Yorkshire and in Nottinghamshire so many erstwhile villages were growing into industrial towns. Most immigration into them was from the neighbouring countryside rather than long-distance, as the more energetic or ambitious moved from the farm to the factory. But for the southern labourer, and for the family whose parish lay in a remote pastoral area, this was hardly possible in the days before cheap transport and labour exchanges. Moreover the Poor Law discouraged any such adventurous conduct. By the terms of the Act of Settlements and Removals people could only get relief, other than casual and *ex gratia*, in that parish where they were settled inhabitants. To leave one's own parish therefore was the equivalent of deliberately sacrificing all one's social benefits and social security today. If a family did not obtain a settlement in the new parish, and as many obstacles as possible were put in their way of doing so, then, if years later they asked for relief they were liable to be sent back to their original parish, with which they had long lost all links. As a result, from tradition, inertia and fear, people stayed where they had lived all their lives.

Too many hands chasing too little work encouraged employers, if not to lower wages, certainly not to raise them comparably with the rising cost of living. It was therefore a disaster for the agricultural labourer when a series of poor harvests drove up the price of grain. Between 1730 and 1760 prices had been remarkably stable, then they began to rise, somewhat irregularly, depending on the harvest, the growing pressure of population and some wartime inflation. By 1792 over thirty years there had been a rise of about 40 per cent. Worse was to follow when war broke out with France; between 1793 and 1813 prices doubled. For a few sections of the working population, the weavers, for example, before their trade was overstocked, wages rose even higher, but for the rural poor, whose numbers gave them no opportunity for bargaining, the position rapidly became desperate. It was realized that something would have to be done. The question was what? There was in fact legislation still on the statute book authorizing the magistrates to fix wages according to 'the plenty or scarcity of the times' but this relic of Elizabethan paternalism had long been a dead letter. In 1795 a group of day labourers in Norfolk tried to form an association to press for a sliding scale which should vary with the price of wheat, in other words to peg wages to the cost of living in a somewhat crude way. In the same year Whitbread tried to get a bill through the Commons to fix a minimum wage for labourers in husbandry. Neither effort succeeded but the idea was very much in the air and magistrates up and down the country started taking *ad hoc* action. The Poor Law, combined with a certain amount of semi-public charity, had always been used to help the poor in a sudden emergency when the harvest had failed and prices soared. Now, probably believing that the current crisis would be of short duration, a practice, not unknown before, of making up wages to an agreed minimum linked with the price of grain was adopted. This method of bridging the gap between wages and prices is usually known as the Speenhamland system because of the publicity given to the resolutions of the Buckinghamshire magistrates who met at the Pelican Inn at Speen, but it seems to have come back into being independently in other parts of the country as being a mere extension of traditional practices. [See A. E. Bland, P. A. Brown and R. H. Tawney, *English Economic History: Select Documents* (1914), 656 for text.]

That wages should be linked to the labourers' cost of living was made more necessary by the reluctance of the farmers' wives, already mentioned, to have farm servants living in. At a time when prices were rising steeply and when more and more farm workers were both marrying earlier and having to provide all the necessities for themselves and their families, including often the rent of a cottage, it was impossible to manage without either wages going up or assistance from some other source. The pitiful budgets collected by Sir Frederick Eden in *The State of the Poor* (1797) are evidence of this. One Huntingdon family, consisting of a man, his wife and four small children, could afford neither cheese, meat or milk but lived on coarse bread, largely composed of barley meal, some potatoes and tea. The man earned 7s 3d a week and his wife 1s 2d. Out of this meagre income he had to pay £2 7s a year for rent, somehow squeeze out £4 6s for shoes, clothes and domestic replacements and put £1 1s aside to pay for sickness, a lying-in, or a burial. A pathetic monument to the family's self-respect was a weekly expenditure of 3¾d for soap and blue and of 1½d for thread and worsted to mend their clothes. Again and again both Eden and Davies found a gap between earnings and expenditure that must have meant either a chronic burden of debt and hopelessness, or reliance on parish relief to fill it.

The result over forty years was the semi-pauperization of the rural poor. This was not universal. In the north the proximity of factory towns kept wages up. Agriculture was flourishing, farmers needed labour and could not let all but the most inefficient depart to the factories. The worst hit were the purely agricultural counties of the south and west when there was no other source of employment. Such employment need not be industrial; the new watering-places along the coast provided a good deal of work, though most of it unfortunately was seasonal. Even in purely agricultural counties not every farm labourer was driven to seek help from the parish. Men working on piece rates, particularly if they had a prudent wife and not too many children, were able to earn enough to preserve their independence. It was generally acknowledged that where a cottage had a small garden it was easier for its inmates to remain independent; at least potatoes could be grown and perhaps a pig kept. Nor would it be accurate to suppose that parish relief was given indiscriminately to all those who would have liked it, though the skilful propaganda of the Poor Law report of 1834 endeavours to give just this impression. What the parish did during the war years was to provide something in the nature of an unofficial cost of living bonus and a family allowance combined. This varied from county to county, both as to the number of children needed to qualify and the amount paid per child. Generally a man and his wife were expected to manage without relief if they had only one or two small children. Some parishes gave an allowance for the third child, some only for the fourth.

The situation deteriorated with the coming of peace. Harvests were better, with the result that prices fell and farmers' profits diminished. Also, after a brief post-war boom severe industrial depression in 1817, 1818, and in most of 1819 hit the towns, so that the demand for meat declined while armies, too, had no longer to be fed. The problem now was not just one of low wages but of massive unemployment as farming faced years of intermittent depression. The buoyancy of the war years was over. It is from these years when small and individual parishes were attempting to shoulder a burden too heavy for them and seeking to improvise some method of finding work for their unemployed settled inhabitants, a problem that has baffled even modern governments despite all their resources, that semi-pauperization seemed to be a creeping disease threatening all rural England. One common method was to send a man on the rounds, that is he was sent to a rota of farmers, who found work on which to set him if they could, but at such low rates that they had to be made up by the parish to bare subsistence level. In other parishes occupiers were forced to employ a quota of the unemployed labourers according to their rateable value, whether they had any work for them to do or not. These systems were doubly pernicious. Farmers were tempted to dismiss men, so throwing them on the parish, and by so doing get their wage bill subsidized from the rates. Life was made difficult for the man who wanted to remain independent. There was little point in doing an honest day's work when the cards, or so it seemed to many, were stacked against them, while to be hawked around the farmers lessened self-respect. Employing the workless in meaningless tasks, or in badly supervised gangs in gravel pits or on the roads, which was a third alternative, merely led to further demoralization.

How this attempt to use the Poor Law to deal with chronic unemployment in the rural areas worked it is difficult to know. The smoke-screen of propaganda is too dense. In investigation after investigation leading questions were asked and conflicting evidence ignored. This is as true of the Select Committee of 1817 as of the famous report of 1834. No doubt some work-shy and unsatisfactory persons did take advantage of the loopholes in an inefficient and amateur administration, but how great a proportion of the whole they were we have no means of knowing. Nor can we hope to be able to assess the social dependence on the Poor Law of a great many people who ought never to have been put in that position. But from what evidence we have it seems as if these decades took the heart out of the rural workers. As long as they could, they fought back. This misery of the countryside was acknowledged even by authority. The Agricultural State of the Kingdom, published by the Board of Agriculture in 1816, reported widespread distress, with one out of every three or four unemployed and the wages of the rest cut, sometimes from 15s to 9s a week. In the same year the price of grain sharply rose and ugly sporadic rioting began to appear. This was particularly marked in East Anglia, a corn-growing area where the labourers were congregated in villages rather than isolated in hilly terrain. Though the magistrates later tried to say that the riots were the work of outside agitators, who had seduced the ignorant labourers, there is no evidence that this was so. Resentment and distress were everywhere; the news that one village had taken to violence was enough to infect the next one. Often in this, as in subsequent outbreaks, the leading local organizer was a shoemaker or cobbler. There was apparently something in his solitary reflective work that turned him into a radical and a natural leader. The forms that rural violence took were arson, when the barns of unpopular farmers and landowners were fired, machine-breaking, mostly the new threshing machines and mole ploughs that did the work formerly done by spade digging for purposes of draining, and threatening crowd demonstrations demanding that prices be lowered and wages increased. In the latter many women took part. In most cases these crowds confined themselves to demanding contributions for 'refreshment' from the gentry, clergy and farmers, whose dwellings they mobbed, but sometimes they got out of hand; windows were broken and in the towns butchers' shops and millers' premises were ransacked. There were full-scale riots in Norwich, mostly by unemployed weavers, at Downham Market and Ely. Sometimes the magistrates panicked and made concessions which they took back afterwards, sometimes the military were called out to restore order, but once authority had had time to collect its resources the rioters, even though on occasion they seem to have been led by returning soldiers, who gave them some rudimentary ideas of attack, were dispersed, and leaders put on trial and sentenced. At the assizes at Norwich in August nine men and six women were sentenced to death, though in the end only two were hanged and the remainder transported. At Ely assizes twenty-four were similarly condemned but only five executed. (See A. J. Peacock, *Bread or Blood: The Agrarian Riots in East Anglia, 1816*, 1965.)

In 1830 the same pattern was repeated on an even wider scale. This time the point of ignition was Kent, where in August the first threshing machine was destroyed near Canterbury. By the thirties these machines were sufficiently widespread to seem a threat to winter work, though they do not yet appear to have been common. Machine-breaking was combined with the usual outbreaks of arson, and threatening letters began to appear promising further violence if wages were not increased. As the movement spread it began to be associated with the name of Captain Swing, who was supposed to be the leader, though the contagion of misery is enough to explain the movement's rapid spread. The most serious disturbances occurred where wages were lowest in the grain-growing areas, and the least in the pastoral districts of the west, but they spread from county to county like a heath fire, flaring into flame and destruction wherever smouldering heat met combustible material. In some regions arson was common, in others machine-breaking predominated. In places cattle were maimed. Everywhere threatening crowds assembled in the villages, once again organized by the cobbler or some rural crafts-man. Everyone was compelled to join in the march to the house of the nearest justice or parson, demanding a promise of better wages and an immediate contribution to their funds. Few substantial houses in the vicinity escaped such visits but the greatest destruction to property took the form of arson, which was more likely to be the work of a minority of the more desperate men. It never took long for authority to re-establish itself and retribution followed. Eventually nineteen rioters were executed, sixteen of them for arson, and 481 were transported. Nevertheless both the magistrates and the ministry were shaken, seeing political agitation and social revolution just round the corner. In so doing they were wide of the mark. All that the rioters wanted were wages on which a family could live decently, and an end to unemployment. Many of them still cherished the belief that if only the King and his ministers realized their distress they could take steps to end it. It has been suggested that some of the farmers themselves, reacting to the depression in agriculture, were not averse to the rioters putting pressure on the clergy to reduce or abandon the tithe, and on landowners to reduce rents, on the plea that then, and only then, could they raise wages. (See E. J. Hobsbawm and George Rudé, *Captain Swing*.)

Although in some areas wages were somewhat raised, any hope that the propertied classes might listen sympathetically to claims backed by violence were shattered by a new and harsher Poor Law. Its intentions were laudable. It aimed at arresting the danger of a creeping semi-pauperization and at restoring a free market in labour. The argument was that this would force the farmer to pay a living wage and the labourer to do an honest day's work in return. (See chapter 8, below.) Chadwick and his colleagues were soon congratu-lating themselves on the way in which the rural areas were depauper-ized, but the individual hardships that this involved cannot be assessed. Relief to the able-bodied was only to be given in 'a well-regulated workhouse' and these establishments were so hated that people went to any lengths of deprivation in order not to enter them. Women burnt crusts of bread and drank the brown liquid instead of tea. Children lived mostly on potatoes and salt. A turnip, if one could be stolen or fell off a cart, was a luxury. One man later in life declared that as a child he had been perpetually so hungry that time and again he had sat under a hedge crying and promising God how good he would be if only He would send him bread. Though after 1830 there were no more national labourers' revolts, local riots and disturbances against the Poor Law continued. So did arson and poaching.

Though it had to be smothered for fear of the consequences, resentment together with a sense of the hopelessness of endeavour added a new and dark ingredient to English village life. It would be inaccurate to paint the picture as one of unrelieved gloom. Provided the labourer 'knew his place' the gentry and the squire, for the most part, continued to accept their traditional responsibilities towards their poorer neighbours. Visiting the poor, the sick and the aged became one of the recognized social duties of their wives and daughters. Sir John Boileau, it will be remembered, voluntarily raised the wages of his workmen in the hungry forties to prevent their going to the workhouse. On many estates the tenants were provided with well-built cottages that had good gardens. In many areas the younger farm servants still lived in and though they worked hard and had little comfort they did not go short of food. As members of the household, though subordinate ones, the relationship between them and their masters was at least personal and human, if not always humane. It was in the regions where large farms grew commercial crops that conditions were at their worst and relations most depersonalized. In Norfolk, because there was little employment for the women and children, they too were forced to swell the numbers of those seeking work on the land. Even small children were forced to earn a few pence scaring birds. Out of this surplus pool of labour arose the notorious gang system. At certain times of the year large additional labour forces were required and gang-masters recruited unemployed men, women and children for this purpose, hiring them out and moving them from farm to farm. Because they were nobody's responsibility the gang-master could, and usually did, exploit them so that they worked, lived, ate and slept in deplorable conditions. What upset Victorian opinion was not so much their hardships as the fact that these conditions encouraged promiscuity and fostered immorality. Perhaps no group in nineteenth-century England, except the child workers in the earlier factories, were so much the victims of circumstances over which they had no control as the agricultural labourers of the south.

The years between 1776 and 1851 saw the transformation of rural England, both in its outward appearance and in the significance of the part it played in the economic and social structure of the nation. The outward signs of change were easy to observe. The open fields had gone. So had the wastes and commons that were suitable for cultivation. Agricultural England was the checkerboard of fields and hedgerows that we know today. In the pastoral districts of the north stone walls crested the fell tops and delineated grazing rights. It was a much tidier England, crisscrossed by white dusty roads, busy canals and accustomed to the shrill whistle of the locomotive, which the cows grazing in the fields through which the railroad ran, and the people who watched its snorting progress, took for granted. By 1851 the isolation of the countryside was also being broken down, though farm produce travelled much further than the farm workers who produced it. Having survived the difficult post-war years and the fluctuating fortunes of the thirties and forties, agriculture was entering a new period of prosperity, though as yet only a minority of farmers had fought the challenge of depression by the adoption of new methods. These included the use of earthenware pipes for draining waterlogged fields, and the new artificial manures and the recently imported guano for feeding them. Nevertheless agriculture had lost its old economic predominance. In 1846 the manufacturers' campaign for the repeal of the old corn laws had been triumphant. Their success was the measure of their own importance in the country.

Social change was much less apparent. Outwardly the old landed classes retained their ancient predominance. The smaller owner-occupiers seem to have diminished somewhat under the stress of the difficult post-war years, but the big estates were, if anything, bigger and the position of the aristocracy and squirearchy was apparently unthreatened, though the economic foundation on which it was based was being subjected to increasing pressure. The great houses, with their retinues of servants, still kept up their old magnificence. Their owners still dominated country society. The squires continued to rule their tenants and their villages. There was little outward sign of any substantial class blurring, indeed in some ways underlying tensions and changing economic conditions seemed, as often in similar circumstances, to intensify class distinctions. The gap between the larger farmer and his labourers widened as fewer and fewer lived in, and as the gangs moved from farm to farm when the need for labour exceeded the local supply. The Poor Law Amendment Act, by destroying the sole line of the defence of the able-bodied, had made the agricultural labourer completely dependent on the goodwill of the farmer who employed him. This in itself induced outward sub-servience. This was particularly true in the richer agricultural areas. In the hillier ones, where the farms were more isolated, the social gap between the farmer and his men was less. Often the labourer was himself the son of a small farmer. Later, when he had saved a little money for stock, he too hoped to rent a small place and set up as an independent farmer. Even in the pastoral north, social inequality between master and man remained, though it was humanized by a social understanding which was absent on the larger and more im-personal agrarian farms. Among the farmers themselves there was a tendency for the social gap to widen between the working farmer renting a medium-sized farm and the man who worked a thousand acres or more. Such men could afford to live like the gentry, and some of them did. The Lookalofts among the rural communities were on the increase.

Though traditional rural society set its face against social change, new forces were burrowing and undermining the old structure, though on the surface it would need an observant eye to notice the tiny cracks that were occurring. Outwardly the middle class and the gentry, when they mixed at all, did so on terms either of deference or of aggressive self-assertion on the one hand and condescension or scarcely veiled *hauteur* on the other. The possession of land and a title still went hand in hand. Nevertheless, at least outwardly, the represen-tatives of both forms of wealth or rather of birth and of newly created wealth were meeting in some circles, though not the most exclusive ones, on something like socially equal terms. The sons of industrialists mixed with gentlemen's sons at schools such as Rugby. Disraeli made his hero Coningsby and Milward, the wealthy mill-owner's son, meet first at Eton, though the latter was looked down on by his snobbish companions until he gained their admiration by saving Coningsby's life. Industrialists were now buying estates, as rich merchants had done in the past, while older families who, through extravagance, misfortune and incompetence were forced to sell, were disappearing from the lists of county families. But it was indirectly that the middle class were most effective in undermining the traditional attitudes of the gentry and aristocracy. Victorian values, both in morals and money, were essentially those of the middle class, even though they had royal approval, and it was these that were influencing and chang-ing the outlook of men and women, who would not have dreamed of entertaining their unguessed-at mentors socially. Lord Melbourne, with his relaxed attitude towards morals and religion, belongs to the earlier, not the later, nineteenth century.

A new England was threatening the old in other subtle ways, as the interests and problems of industry began to take precedence over those of agriculture. It was prophesied during the debates on the Reform Bill that the field of coal would take over from the field of corn and it is noticeable how much parliamentary time was taken up after 1832 with such questions as factory reform, health reform, etc. Previously the emphasis had been on the maintenance of law, order and social stability, and the need to protect agriculture from cheap foreign grain. After 1832 neither the aristocracy nor the gentry had lost control of Parliament but their leaders, at least, knew that this control could no longer be exercised without the tacit co-operation of the industrial interests. In 1846 came the landmark whose shadow was to fall over the coming years, the repeal of the Corn Laws. This was perhaps less of a victory than it seemed. Many serious students of agriculture believed that their abolition would not hurt the landed interest; in the short run, until the depression of the seventies, they proved to be right. Nevertheless the disappearance of the Corn Laws marked the fact that the Manchester men had outwardly triumphed over what once had been the strongest economic force in England. With its economic base eroded, rural England and the social structure that it had maintained was increasingly forced from the fifties to adapt itself to a new world.

Chapter 4   The Changing Social Structure

English society had never been static, though over long periods change had come so gradually that to the casual observer it may well seem to have been so. But between the closing decades of the eighteenth and the middle of the nineteenth centuries the Industrial Revolution had been accompanied by a social revolution of so striking a character that even the blindest of contemporaries could not remain unaware of the changes that were taking place in the society of which he was a member. Georgian England thought in terms of status when describing an individual's place in society, Victorian England in terms of class. In the eighteenth century men belonged to the labouring poor or the middling sort, in the nineteenth to the working classes or the middle classes. In the earlier period the stress is on birth and the relationship of the individual to those above and below him in the social hierarchy, in the later the stress is on the solidarity of the economic group to which he belongs.

In 1776 land was still the foundation of traditional society. At the apex of the social pyramid were the great titled landowning families. Though individually not all of them were wealthy, as an order they controlled what was still the main source of all wealth. Next came the lesser nobility, baronets and the like, and the great mass of the landed gentry. Beneath them were grouped all those who, quite literally, occupied the middle ground between the aristocracy and gentry, and the labouring poor. These were accurately described as the middling sort, or the middle ranks of society. They comprised those merchants who had not yet bought their way into the ranks of the gentry, middlemen, factors, shopkeepers, industrialists, professional men who were not gently born and, in the country prosperous farmers. At the bottom of this pyramid, forming the broad base on which the prosperity of the country was acknowledged to rest, came all those who depended on manual skill or manual strength for their daily bread. These were, as their name most truly implies, the labouring poor. Within each of these orders there were subtle gradations of importance, separate rungs in the social ladder. The baron gave precedence to the duke, the baronet to the baron, the country gentleman to the possessor of a title. The merchant condescended to the shopkeeper, the attorney to the tenant farmer, the skilled craftsmen looked down on the semi-skilled, he in his turn looked down on the manual worker, who, however humble, could still scorn the pauper and the beggar.

All this was visible for everyone to see. Each order had its rights and its responsibilities; each man knew what was expected of him in relation to his fellows. It was a society in which acceptance was almost universal. It was not, and never had been, completely rigid. Men had always been able to move from one order to another, though in practice this was a feat beyond the mental and material resources of the vast majority. In medieval England the serf, with the permission of his lord, could become a priest, the priest a civil servant; the craftsman could become a merchant, the merchant a gentleman, the gentleman a nobleman. But while a man remained a member of the order into which he had been born, whatever that order might be, his status in society was fixed by it. Though aping their betters is a normal social activity, in the eighteenth century it was still usually possible to place people by the clothes they wore. A nobleman wore his star. Courtiers and men-about-town dressed the part; so did the country squire. The merchant adopted a decent sobriety of garment, the carpenter wore his paper hat, the smith his leather apron, the countryman his smock.

That this was both desirable and beneficial was the opinion of two great Englishmen, speaking respectively for Tudor-Stuart and Georgian England, Shakespeare and Dr Johnson. In the much-quoted speech from *Troilus and Cressida* the former saw order and degree as the great stabilizing principle that held society together and warded off chaos. The learned Doctor, in less lofty language, stressed the utility of a social order in which everybody knew what was expected of him without going into the niceties of moral worth or social value. In a society so ordered deference was so entirely impersonal that it carried with it no feeling of personal humiliation. Between the orders, in theory at least, there was social harmony, not social strife.

This did not mean that there were no personal ambitions, no personal resentments, no clashing economic interests. Men did not always behave as expected or conform to the social norm. Material factors often led to clashes. If the eighteenth century were not 'class conscious' in the way that the nineteenth became, it was certainly aware of the clash of 'interests'. Indeed its society has often been described as being vertical rather than horizontal in its economic structure, because superimposed on the broad pattern of order and degree were the various 'interests' which ran vertically from the top to the bottom. The greatest of these was the Landed Interest, followed by the Commercial Interest. Between them they embraced the greater part of the population. Very powerful too, and so closely connected with the latter as to be almost a co-partner, was the Financial Interest. More numerous, but less effectively organized, was the Industrial Interest. This was made up of a host of small manufacturers, who dependent on the merchants for capital and markets, geographically scattered and divided by the variety of their products, were never able to combine to present a common front to opposing interests.

These groupings must not be taken to imply any wide national organization. For the most part they were based on an instinctive acceptance of reality and of community of advantage. Anything more would have been beyond the administrative capacity of the age. Of all the 'interests' the Landed Interest spread its tentacles furthest. Men were well aware that all those whose livelihood was derived from the land, whether as landlords, as farmers, as yeomen, as rural craftsmen or as labourers, had a common interest in the wellbeing of agriculture, whether that interest were expressed in the form of an extensive rent roll or the chance to earn a meagre daily wage. Nor was this interest confined to those who worked on the land. The artisan-shopkeeper in a small market town, the professional man employed as an attorney or man of business for the local landowners, the apothecary and even the innkeeper, all depended on the prosperity of agriculture for their own. The same homogeneity bound together the members of the Commercial and Financial Interests. Their primary concern was with the nation's trade, though they too benefited from a prosperous agriculture, which increased domestic spending power. When trade flourished capital was in demand, merchants' profits high and the middlemen, factors and all of the middling sort, whose activities depended on it, better off. Even its labour force, porters, dockers, carters and seamen were sure of employment. Such interests were no threat to the social order. The dockers, the lightermen, the seamen had more in common with the merchants, the captains and commercial prosperity than they had with the wellbeing of the labourer or small tenant farmer. This failure of working men to identify their common interests as working men was intensified by geography and poor communications. The Durham miner might well have inhabited a different planet from that of the London porter or the

East Anglian ploughman. In such conditions the concept of class solidarity had no relevance.

It was the Industrial Revolution that first challenged and then shattered the traditional framework and substituted a society based on class. In the eighteenth century political power and the possession of land went hand in hand. With the coming of the new industry this dominance began to crack. Men who were neither landowners nor gentlemen could nevertheless create wealth through the possession of factories and foundries. It was no longer only the landowner and the merchants who could call the political tune. By the end of the eighteenth century it was no longer true that the majority of manufacturers were small, financed by the merchant who sold their wares. A few important figures were emerging from the ruck; the wealthy manufacturer was no longer a unique figure. In London brewers such as the Thrales and the Whitbreads were working with large capitals and organizing in a big way. In the provinces, Matthew Boulton at Soho and Josiah Wedgwood at Etruria were showing how a small local industry could be transformed into one of international repute by the adoption of new techniques and new methods of organization. Their numbers were not yet great enough to have any appreciable effect on social structure. Though these men were industrialists rather than merchants, contemporaries saw no difficulty in equating them in status with the wealthy merchants and bankers whom they already recognized as part of the traditional pattern. Just as the latter had intermarried with the gentry, so did the Thrales and the Whitbreads. But men such as these were no challenge to the social order. They were not numerous. They were wealthy and could be absorbed as English society had always been able to absorb the wealthy and the successful.

The mill-owners of the north were a more difficult proposition, partly because they were more numerous, partly because they were a different breed of men. The majority had come up the hard way, scraping together a little capital and investing in a few jennies, which they installed in any sort of a building that was available. Joshua Fielden, the father of the future reforming mill-owner and M.P., had started in this way. Some like the Peels, came from respectable yeoman stock, families who had always combined farming with some branch of the textile industry. For ambitious men with this background the transition to mechanical spinning was easy. By the turn of the century Robert Peel was already a wealthy man. Men such as these, with the necessary drive and business acumen, who had got in on the ground floor in the early nineteenth century were becoming the magnates of the textile world. But the magnates were not really typical of the average Lancashire or Yorkshire mill-owner. Many of these, at least in the early stages of their careers as industrialist capitalists, were the proprietors of very small concerns. Their standard of living was little, if any, better than that of the hands they employed. Often they were the first to get to the mill in the morning and the last to leave at night. Many of them were perforce slave drivers, expecting the same effort from their work people but for less reward. Once mechanical spinning was firmly established their numbers were swelled with men who had no previous experience of the industry and were concerned only with getting the greatest possible return on their capital. In most cases they were indifferent to, or ignorant of, the social cost of their profits. In periods of depression many of the smaller mill-owners went bankrupt, others hung on, eventually becoming proprietors of medium-sized flourishing businesses. By this time most of those who had made the grade had had much of any of the compassion they might once have possessed rubbed off in the process.

Widely though they differed as individuals, such men could not easily be absorbed into the traditional hierarchy. Their values and ambitions either lay outside it, or were in active conflict with it. Wealthy merchants purchased estates and merged with the gentry, but the majority of first-generation mill-owners had no such ambitions. Their profits went into the purchase of bigger and better equipped mills. As a class they were intensely proud of their achievements; they had no intention of paying any deference to birth. This did not mean that they were oblivious to the sweets of social recognition. Miss Weeton's Yorkshire employer, Mr A., told her that 'he thought a reigning monarch ought to confer titles on those who had, for two or three successive generations, been wealthy' (Weeton, op. cit., 118). Eventually a minority of them succumbed to the lure of social prestige and bought estates, though not necessarily in those counties where their money had been made, and passed into the ranks of the landed gentry. These, however, were the élite; the majority were content to remain successful urban business men who found their social sphere in the formation of powerful oligarchies in the expanding industrial towns. Later, when, as over the repeal of the Corn Laws, they came to believe that the interests of the agriculturalists conflicted with their own, they challenged the political domination of the land owners and broke it. For such men the traditions of the past had little relevance and, because of the financial power they possessed, they were able to challenge them successfully.

But though England was proud of Manchester and its achievements the mill-owner was not a popular figure. Peter Gaskell in *The Manufacturing Population of England* (1833) described them and their wives in savage terms. The men, he declared, were aggressive, crude, hard living and debauchers of their mill girls, whose virtue was perpetually at risk, their wives were intent above all things on 'keeping up with the Jones'. Gaskell's sweeping judgments are often suspect but John Fielden, who as a child employed in his father's mill and later a successful manufacturer therefore knew from his own experience both sides of the case, spoke of the curse of the factory system and of 'the avarice of masters' that had prompted many of them 'to exact more labour from their hands than they were fitted by nature to perform'. (J. Fielden, *The Curse of the Factory System* (1836), 34.) The Hon. John Byng, who found nothing to like in Manchester, declared that 'in places where wealth is procured it is ignorantly spent; for the upstart man of riches knows no better'. (Byng, op. cit., 117.) Miss Weeton would have agreed: 'the people in this part of Yorkshire appear to be all a money getting, but not a money spending people. Taste and Science are words I never hear.'

The picture that emerges of tight-fistedness combined with outbursts of vulgar display was the hostile product of a challenged traditional society. It is true that the northern mill-owner had to be very money-conscious, or he would not have survived, and to that extent he used money as the measuring-rod of his achievements. He could afford to waste neither time nor money on idle pleasure, though when successful he might be glad to let his wife and daughters do so as a symbol of his success. The majority of them were not ogres. If the Carsons (*Mary Barton*) were heartless, Mrs Gaskell created a very different character in her mill-owner John Thorton, in the novel *North and South*. He was a hard man, but fair, proud of his success and independent to a fault. He would not be dictated to by his work people, he would not deign to explain to them why wages had to be reduced, though in fact his motive was mutual survival and not profit. He was 'the master'. In the same way he resented government interference. He was prepared to regulate the smoke from his factory chimneys, because excessive smoke meant wasted fuel, but he was not prepared to co-operate with legislators at Westminster who told him that he must do so. Nor was he an ignorant man. Like many of the new men, he was interested in literature, in philosophy, in religion; his world was not bounded by his business interests, though it was dominated by them. The hero of Charlotte Brontë's novel *Shirley* was also a mill-owner, who, though he came fom Belgian not north-country stock, shared many of Thorton's qualities. He too was prepared to defend his mill against riotous workmen, he too worked himself to the point of exhaustion, hanging on desperately in bad times, he too was a man of education and information. The type could be paralleled in real life; some of the keenest members of the Manchester Literary and Philosophical Society were mill-owners or connected with the textile industry. Even the censorious Miss Weeton had to admit that Mr A., however careful of his money, was 'a man of sense, talents, information and industry'.

Success often brought with it a sense of responsibility and a wider outlook. Sir Robert Peel and John Fielden were not the only manufacturers to become members of Parliament; cotton was well represented in the Commons after 1832. It was these men who campaigned against the worst conditions in the new textile factories. It was the elder Peel who sponsored the first bill to improve the treatment of pauper apprentices in cotton mills and who, later, in conjunction with Robert Owen, himself a manufacturer from New Lanark, steered the first Act to better the treatment of free children. It was Fielden, remembering the fatigue of his own early days when he worked in his father's mill, who strove tirelessly for a bill to limit the labour of the operatives to ten hours. Men of this type were not out 'to grind the faces of the poor' and were sufficiently intelligent to realize that a healthy and contented labour force was to their own advantage. Many of them were Methodists or Baptists. Doubtless some of them were hypocrites, and doubtless many of them were able to square a good deal of harshness in their business dealings with devout and regular attendance at church or chapel. Nevertheless there were many too who were concerned with the welfare of their workpeople, though they had very definite ideas as to the shape that this should take. Temperance, cleanliness and frugality were virtues to be fostered, and where possible enforced. Some manufacturers were men like Samuel Greg of Styal, a Presbyterian of Scottish descent, who built cottages for his people, opened a food shop which gave honest value, built a chapel, hired a minister, established an institute for lectures and social functions and opened a school where his daughter taught. One man, Titus Salt, a Bradford manufacturer of alpaca and mohair, even built an entire town, Saltaire, where everything necessary for the welfare of his workpeople was provided. In many cases the wives and daughters undertook such social duties as teaching in the Sunday school. Not all of them were would-be social butterflies. Though in the days of the early isolated mills some pauper apprentice houses were little hells, in others, such as those run by the Oldknows, the children were well fed and cleanly kept.

It is as impossible to generalize about the new manufacturers as about any other of the categories into which people fall. One can neither condemn nor praise without qualification. The time element is important. In the early days of mechanization, when men were innovating and experimenting, usually on the tightest of budgets, there was neither time nor money to devote to enterprises that would not show a profit in the balance sheet. To this extent their critics were justified in charging them with complete absorption in the making of money. Nevertheless gradually the more successful manufacturers came to create a new kind of urban society. They took a leading part in the life of their towns, serving on committees, acting as justices (by 1843 32 per cent of the Lancashire justices were bankers, merchants, executives of various kinds and manufacturers whom wealth, not birth or land, had raised to the Bench), and promoting legislation. When they could afford to do so they began to move from the smoky centre of the town into the pleasanter suburbs, instead of living, as had been the earlier custom, in a house adjoining the mill. Here they built those solid, ornate houses, plentifully adorned with gothic turrets and elaborate ornamentation, that still stand today, and from which they rode or were driven in their carriages to the mill each day. They were quick to adopt the comforts, and even the luxuries, that had once been reserved for gentlefolk. But for the most part they despised, or affected to despise, the artificialities of polite society. They prided themselves on their forthright manners, and were content to be what they were, prosperous businessmen who could afford solid comfort and had little use for idle show.

These men were the vanguard of the new middle classes behind whom a small number of modest urban property owners and professional men fell into line. As businesses multiplied and towns grew, the middle classes grew and multiplied with them. Small armies of clerks were needed. There were increasing openings for managerial staff, for commercial travellers, for building contractors, for hotel keepers and above all for shopkeepers. Some of these employments were lucrative, some poorly paid, but the men who engaged in them were united in the conviction that they were socially superior to the manual worker, however skilled. The struggling clerk, who earned less than the expert fine cotton spinner, underlined this superiority by his dress, his speech and his manners. These, and not his income, were what distinguished him from the working class. The rapid growth in the demand for professional services provided another breeding ground for the middle classes. The increased interest in education meant more schoolmasters, but the National and British schools were unlikely to tempt the gentry to staff them. Apothecaries were being metamorphosed into chemists or doctors. The embellishment of the new towns gave work to architects, the creation of the railways to surveyors and engineers, while legal business multiplied as the business community grew. With increased professionalism the men who followed what had once been considered humbler trades began to develop new standards and a new exclusiveness. The surgeons led the way by insisting that members of this company must take a qualifying examination. From 1832 students could read for medicine at the new University College in London and in the provinces the Medical and Surgical Association was founded to maintain the 'Honour and Respectability of the Profession generally in the Provinces'. Lydgate in George Eliot's *Middlemarch* (1871) was representative of this new professionalism in medicine, though he had the additional cachet in Middlemarch society of being well connected, which many provincial doctors were not. In legal circles the same change was taking place as the attorney struggled to improve his status *vis-à-vis* the members of the Inns of Court. His new professional society, later to be known as the Law Society, dates from 1825 and received a royal charter in 1831.

Therefore although the army, the navy, the upper ranks of the clergy and the bar were still largely the preserves of the gently born, other professions were providing increasing opportunities for middle class boys who did not want to go into business. As the middle class grew in numbers it began to split up into horizontal divisions. The poorly paid clerk, the small shopkeeper and what might be called the white-collared worker, men whose income ranged from £60 to £150, came to be regarded as the lower middle class; they were the families who had 'just made it'. Dickens's novels abound with them. The next layer was composed of moderately prosperous families living in well-furnished, often surburban houses. They kept a good table and could afford at least two respectable servants, where the lower middle class house could at most afford the little slatternly maid of all work, again so vividly portrayed by Dickens. The upper middle class lived in style. Yet despite the differences in income, with all that this entailed, it is possible to detect a certain uniformity in outlook and standards between the groups that it had become customary to count as middle class. Money was important but perhaps respectability even more so. Respectability meant sexual morality and the strict observance of Sunday, with regular attendance at some place of worship. Not all its members were in fact respectable but lapses were, as far as possible, swept under the carpet. Those qualities which later G. B. Shaw was to condemn through the mouth of Dolittle as 'middle class morality' were the product of Victorian England. The attitude of the aristocracy and gentry towards them was ambivalent, combining a mixture of amused contempt for their manners with a degree of patronizing approval for their virtues. They were 'a very good sort of people', though one did not necessarily want to entertain them in one's house. Dr Hall, Dr Gibson's predecessor in *Wives and Daughters* (Mrs Gaskell) 'had always been received with friendly condescension by my lady . . . but she never thought of interfering with his custom of taking his meals, if he needed refreshment, in the housekeeper's room, not *with* the housekeeper, *bien entendu*'.

Meanwhile in the smoky towns of the north a new pattern of industrial life was producing a new type of worker, the factory hand and the mill girl. The factories added a new and vigorous element to the shaping of the urban working class. The first generation were in a sense halfbreeds in that, because the towns had grown so rapidly, many of their inhabitants had their roots in the country. Psychologically most of them were still in tune with the rhythm of the semi-domestic industry of their youth. Even their children tended to retain much of the outlook of their parents. This made it hard for them to accept the discipline and confinement of the factory. In the early days of the Industrial Revolution this had been harsh. Twelve hours was the traditional length of the working day for wage-earners, with still longer hours at harvest, and from dawn to dusk for farm labourers in autumn and winter. Accordingly the twelve hour day was accepted as the norm for factories, but now there was no remission in winter because artificial light made it possible for the work to go on. Twelve hours therefore became the minimum. Because many of the early manufacturers had sunk every scrap of capital that they could save, beg or borrow, they wanted to work the machines to the maximum whenever the order books were full. On occasions thirteen, fourteen, even fifteen hours of toil might be demanded. It is true that in the past men working in their own homes had sometimes slaved for equally long hours, but the rhythm had been less regular. English craftsmen had been notorious for their worship of St Monday; sometimes Tuesday had also been kept holy. Then would follow days of furious application until the week's allotted work had been finished. Then, temporarily exhausted by this marathon effort, the worker once again relapsed into idleness, recruiting his energies in the rough games of the countryside or in the local beerhouse. Moreover he was the master of his time. However long the working day, he could always break off for a drink of ale, for a mouthful of bread and cheese, to stretch his legs and get a breath of fresh air, or to exchange a jest with a neighbour. He might be poor, even sometimes hungry, he might be tied by debt to one employer and have little option as to the work he would do or the pay he would be forced to accept. Nevertheless he had the illusion of independence, of being his own master; at least the petty details of his life were under his own control.

Once he went to the factory things were very different. It was not just that the long hours were a greater strain in the close, and often hot, steamy atmosphere, where a man had to adapt his motions to the remorseless monotony of the machine. The greatest hardship was the awful regularity of time-keeping. Hands had to be at the factory gates when they opened. If they came even a few minutes late they found them shut, knowing they would not be re-opened until the breakfast break, and that failure to be there on time would mean a loss of pay. If a man wanted a drink of water he could not leave his machine to get one and, unlike the chain gangs in America, factories had no water boy on call. Meals could only be taken at fixed times and the breaks were short, perhaps half an hour for breakfast and the same for the afternoon drinking with an hour for dinner when, if he lived near enough, he could go home. Practices varied from mill to mill. In some, apart from the main break, workers were supposed to eat when and how they could amidst the dust and whirring of the machinery. Even natural functions were a problem. In many factories workers could not go to the privy without permission from the over-looker. In one a tub was brought round for the male operatives to use three times a day! No wonder that the discipline of the factories was hated. It was a hard apprenticeship to modern industry and its product was a new breed of workpeople.

Factories did more than impose discipline on a hitherto undisciplined labour force; they upset the traditional balance of employment between men and women and between youth and maturity. They were greedy for both female and child labour, particularly for carding and spinning. The proportion between the sexes employed depended largely on the machines to be worked. Baines, the early historian of the cotton manufactory, estimated that spinning with the throstle was largely done by women but that men predominated where the mule was in use. In spinning mills it was normal to employ as many children of both sexes as adult operatives. Indeed the mills could hardly have functioned without the cheap labour of the women and children. There was no novelty in this massive employment of women and children. In the traditional cottage or domestic industry the family had always been an economic unit, with the wife and children working alongside the husband. It was he who had dictated the pace and he had not necessarily been a lenient taskmaster. Domestic tyranny could be brutal. It was not surprising that men resented a change which put them, as well as their wives and children, under the same iron discipline. This in itself did not necessarily break up the family as a production unit. Unless the indispensable little piecers were pauper apprentices they were not normally either recruited or paid directly by the mill owner. The usual practice was for the adult spinners to hire and pay them, and where possible they used their own children in this capacity. Also women were usually employed in the same factory where their husband or father worked. Nevertheless the new conditions soon began to undermine the old economic authority of the male. Propagandists such as Engels made great play with the argument that the demand for female and youthful labour was forcing unemployment on the men, but though it may be true that, in a town where throstle spinning prevailed, men found less demand for their labour, it was not the norm for a man to have to stay at home, turning himself into a domestic drudge while his wife and children were the bread-winners. Doubtless such cases could, and did, occur, though their likelihood was increased if the husband were a sick man, or an idle drunkard who preferred to live off his wife's earnings.

The challenge of the factory was more insidious. For the first time a working woman had the opportunity of becoming reasonably economically independent. Small though the wages of a mill girl were in comparison with those of the male operative, they were much greater than she could have earned by spinning on the wheel or by her needle. In the past rural families had been patriarchal. Until the sons and daughters married they had remained under the family roof, contributing to the family income and accepting the authority of their parents. Now a son could earn a full day's wage by his teens, and there was no family holding to induce him to wait for dead men's shoes, not even so much as a cottage on the waste, because the urban worker rented, not owned, his house. A daughter too could fend for herself and bring home as good wages as her mother if they worked in the same mill. Cheaper clothing tempted her to spend her wages on her back; contemporary accounts stress the smart appearance the young women of the working class assumed on Sundays. Often she too resented parental control, particularly when her parents tried to enforce old-fashioned standards of behaviour, to which they had had to conform in their own youth. The generation gap is not a modern invention. The result was that sons and daughters alike were tempted to leave home and go into lodgings. This was a blow to both family life and the family income. If the wife and mother herself worked in the factory there was probably little home comfort to anchor them there in any case. The wife who went out to work was another by-product of the factory. Many of them had worked in the mill from early childhood with the result, as critics were quick to point out, that 'they were totally ignorant of all those habits of domestic economy which tend to render a husband's home happy and comfortable; and this is very often the cause of the man being driven to the ale house to seek the comfort after his day of toil which he looks for in vain by his own fireside' (*Report on the Sanitary Condition* . . . , 139). That there was often little comfort to be found there is not surprising. When too often the houses were crammed into dirty courts where even the ordinary decencies of sanitation and water were lacking, the most houseproud women must have found it difficult to surmount such conditions. It is surprising how many Lancashire and Yorkshire women managed to make a comfortable home despite them, attaining a standard of almost fanatical cleanliness indoors to compensate for the squalor outside. However, when the wife went to the factory, and worked a twelve-hour day, except on Saturday when most factories stopped earlier, it is not surprising that the housework suffered. Those critics who thought she would have been wiser to stay at home also pointed out that the working wife was an extravagant wife. One Birmingham commentator stated that

> Tea, coffee, sugar, butter, cheese, bacon (of which a great deal is consumed in this town) and other articles the working people purchase in great quantities from the hucksters, who charge an enormous profit upon them, being as they state, compelled to do so to cover the losses which they frequently sustain by bad debts. . . Meat is purchased in the same improvident manner, the working man generally contrives to have a good joint of meat upon a Sunday, the dinner on the other days of the week is made

from steaks or chops, which is the most extravagant mode of purchasing or cooking meat (ibid., 138).

It is difficult to see what alternative a working class wife had, whether she stayed at home or went to the mill. Wages were not paid until Saturday, and until she had the money she could not do the weekend shopping. Among the various suggestions that Edwin Chadwick made to promote the general health of the labouring population was that wages should be paid on a Friday, or at least early on Saturday. When the housewife did not receive her money until late on Saturday evening she was forced to buy either from the inferior shops that kept open late enough on Saturday or who traded on Sunday or from the hucksters who 'sold an inferior commodity at a higher price'. The difficulty of buying untainted and unadulterated food in the first part of the nineteenth century is rarely realized by the modern shopper. Refrigeration was unknown. So was all but the most elementary hygiene. Meat and perishables were displayed all day on fly-infested stalls, and, after dark, exposed to the heat of flaring gas jets. Because there were no pure food Acts to protect the consumer, milk was watered down, sand mixed with sugar, and sweepings from the warehouse floor sold as tea. There was grit in the flour. Better-class shopkeepers dare not indulge too freely in such practices, but the small shopkeepers in the poorer parts of the town, who were often forced to give credit to keep custom, frequently protected themselves from loss by tricks of this type.

Nevertheless, in spite of the drawbacks of the crude industrial towns, the factories and the workshops did offer to women a new chance of independence. Not all married women availed themselves of such employment and many men, except under dire distress, refused to let their wives go back to the mill. But for the widow or deserted wife left with a family of young children, whose sole refuge formerly had been the parish, factory work was a boon. Instead of being regarded as a burden on the community, a woman with a large family was now welcomed as an asset in the rapidly expanding industrial towns. Indeed during the thirties, when the demand for child labour threatened to outrun the supply, one Lancashire manufacturer suggested to Chadwick that the Poor Law authorities in the rural and agricultural south might consider sending such families north. It was not only deserted wives or widows who gained a new independence. In 1840 it was estimated that a young woman who was prudent and saved between the ages of sixteen and twenty-five, if she remained unwed so long, could bring to her husband a marriage portion of as much as £100, which for a working woman was a very considerable portion. Probably few saved so rigorously, and probably too the estimate is over-optimistic, but that it could be made shows the possibility of a new economic independence for women who did not marry.

The most vulnerable section of the urban working class were the infants and young children. The death rate for those under five was appalling, though it must be remembered that a very high rate of infant mortality had been part of the traditional demographical pattern. In Liverpool 52 per cent of the recorded deaths were those of children under this age. In Lancashire as a whole in 1841 17 per cent of all the children born died before they had completed their first year of life. Several factors combined to produce this terrible record. Because young people reached their maximum earning quickly, they married early. Dr Strange of Ashton declared: 'It is no uncommon thing to meet married females at 15 and they are frequently mothers at 17, the fathers being but little older.' When marriage and child-bearing were postponed until the age of 20 or over he was of the opinion that 'the constitution of factory girls are not sufficiently consolidated, nor their frames firm enough at that age to bear strong and well constituted children'. (*Report on the State of Large Towns* . . . , 465.) This in itself is a commentary on the physical effects of the early and prolonged work under factory conditions. To make matters worse, he continued, 'comes the fact that in two, three or four weeks after delivery the young mother, if she hath but one, two or three children, returns to work in the mills, leaving the charge of her children either to some old woman or young girl or puts them out to nurse . . . the mother suckles it but at mealtimes and at night.' The horrifying con-sequence of this pattern of child rearing was the regular dosing of babies and young children with narcotics. One druggist stated that he sold about five gallons of 'quietness' and half a gallon of 'Godfrey' per week. As 'quietness' contained a hundred drops to the ounce and a teaspoonful was the prescribed dose this one druggist must have been supplying some 700 families, supposing each family to be buying an ounce a week. As he explained,

the mother goes out to her work in the morning, leaving her child either in charge of a woman who cannot be troubled with it, or with another child of perhaps 10 years old. A dose of quietness is therefore given to the child to prevent it being troublesome. The child thus drugged sleeps and may wake at dinner time; so, when the mother goes out again, the child receives another dose. Well, the mother and father come home at night quite fatigued, and as they must rise early to begin work for the next day, they must have sleep undisturbed by the child; so it is drugged, and in this manner young children are often drugged three times in each day (ibid., 454).

Describing the children subjected to this routine, another druggist said: 'You may know at once a child who is accustomed to the use of these drugs. It becomes so thin that you feel nothing but bone. Its eyes get sunken and fixed, its nose pinched; in fact such children look exactly like little old wizened men and women. They sink off into a decline and die' (ibid., 459). If the child survived infancy there was nowhere for it to play except in the filthy courts and streets. By the age of seven or eight, and in some cases as early as five or six before 1819, when officially the permitted age was nine, it was put to work in a mill or factory for twelve hours a day. For those children who were not employed in a textile mill there were no protective laws at all. These children were the urban workers of the next generation. There is little wonder that resort to opium was widespread among them, particularly when food and employment were short.

The textile operatives of the early nineteenth century clearly played an important part in shaping the development of the Victorian working class, but in the early decades they were not a predominant element in its composition. Their importance came from the fact that they were evolving a new social pattern based on new habits and new standards of value. It was because they were new, and alien to the society of the past, that they received so much attention both from their own contemporaries, who visited Manchester and recorded their impressions of the place, its way of life, and its people, as if they had been paying a visit to a strange and unknown country, and from historians subsequently. They are the prototype of the future working class. It was in these years that its folklore, with its bitter resentment against the capitalist and its passionate belief in the necessity for working class solidarity, originated.

Nevertheless to concentrate exclusively on the textile operatives during these formative years is to distort the picture. As Dogherty, who, as an organizer of the incipient trades union movement in the thirties, was familiar with the diversity of the manpower he was handling, exclaimed, 'we are not all cotton spinners'. Broadly speaking, occupations can be divided into those directly created by the Industrial

Revolution and those, though indirectly affected by the new economic atmosphere and often by the fact that the raw material on which they worked was the product of the new technology, themselves still worked in their own homes or in small workshops. Foremost among the new men, if the textile workers are omitted, were the engineers. They were needed to make the machines, and later to make the machine tools, with which to make still more elaborate machinery. They were needed to service the machines in operation. This in itself was a skilled job because, before the standardization of such simple components as screws and bolts, broken parts had to be made and fixed individually. Later, engineers were needed to make, to drive and to repair the railway engines. As year by year mechanization took an even greater grip on the economy the demand for engineers grew. Socially the results were interesting. A new species of working man, who was both mechanic and designer, and who, because he was indispensable, could command high wages, was creating a new aristocracy of labour. Some worked in engineering shops, some were attached as maintenance men to factories, some followed the semi-nomadic trade of the engine-driver, but all were men of the future. The first of the 'new model' trade unions was the Amalgamated Society of Engineers. Almost a breed apart, but equally essential to Victorian England, were the navvies, who having built the canals, went on to build the railways. Organized in gangs under their fore-men, and directed by the skilled surveyors and engineers who designed the permanent way, these men bored tunnels and cast up embank-ments. Some were mere labourers, others highly skilled, but all were hard living, hard drinking and careless of the death that was never too far away from their hazardous work. They too helped to transform the England of the past into the England of the future.

Too much concentration on what was new can be misleading. The older, domestically organized handicrafts still absorbed vast amounts of labour. Even in the great industrial towns factory workers did not necessarily predominate. Sheffield was full of small cutlers' shops. Birmingham specialized in small articles made of metal, buttons and buckles, japanned trays and wares of that type. Most of these were made by craftsmen, either working in their own homes or in small workshops. In such towns industries seemed to fit into the older social pattern without creating the bitter tensions of the textile towns. In the potteries also the dominant industry dictated its own pattern of society. Here Wedgwood son succeeded Wedgwood father, and under the personal control of the family, in Etruria, though not necessarily in other parts of the Potteries, many of the worst aspects of the industrial jungle were softened. The impact of mechanization and mass production varied considerably from craft to craft. In the Black Country nailers and chain-makers still worked in tiny unhygienic workshops in their own back premises. In every town and village the independent craftsman, often employing a couple of apprentices, still persisted. Each had its own blacksmith and shoemaker, milliners, dressmakers, tailors who still made individual garments for their customers. This was equally true of the new industrial towns and of London. Mary Barton was apprenticed to a dressmaker because her father did not want her to go into the factory, so was Fanny in Dickens's *Nicholas Nickleby*. Even as late as the early thirties there were more handloom weavers than there were factory workers in the combined cotton, woollen and silk manufacture. Though mechanical spinning had been adopted very rapidly by the cotton men, and rather more slowly by the woollen manufacturers, the power loom made headway much more slowly. It is often assumed that because a certain invention was patented at a certain date it was universally adopted, thus destroying in one sudden blow the old traditional skills. In fact this rarely happened. In their early stages many inventions were not efficient enough to replace skilled human labour. Cartwright's power loom was one of these. Considerable adjustments had to be made before it was a commercial proposition, and even when the breakthrough in cotton had occurred wool proved a less tractable material, and for fine cloth the hand loom was still needed.

Nevertheless indirectly the Industrial Revolution was responsible for the long-drawn-out agony of the handloom weavers which provides one of the most painful chapters in the social history of the nineteenth century and which is so vividly described in Disraeli's social novel *Sybil*. This was because the amount of yarn turned out by the factories in the last two decades of the previous century meant that weavers were in short supply and their wages soared. The result was that demand, combined with the continual increase in the population and immigration from Ireland, soon led to an over-stocking of the trade. After a few golden years, when the handloom weaver represented the aristocrat of labour, wages tumbled, though even by 1813 there were fewer than 3,000 power looms in operation. Indeed it may well have been that the cheapness of handloom weaving actually retarded the installation of more power looms, thus prolonging the agony of the handloom weavers, who could get work but only at starvation wages. They were a proud, independent breed of men, who hated to send their wives and children to work in the dreaded factories, though not to do so meant that the whole family was forced to live on a diet of porridge, oatcake, potatoes and skim milk, while the factory worker, when trade was brisk, could eat butchers' meat every day. In these years waves of despair and unrest swept industrial Lancashire wherever the handloom weavers congregated. After the widespread disturbances in 1808 a local magistrate told Spencer Percival that 'from the very low wages paid for weaving, the weavers are in the greatest distress, and quite unable in many cases to procure food'. (A. Aspinall, *The Early English Trade Unions* (1949), 97.)

Not every section of the labouring population can be fitted into the category of either factory or domestic worker. For instance the miners had a distinctive way of life and culture of their own. Though there was considerable variation between the pits in the different parts of the country, isolation, both cultural and geographical, was the general hallmark of coal-mining communities. Though Clifton was barely four miles from Bristol, and is now part of the city, the miners rarely came there and were feared as half-savage creatures when they did. The same was true of the mining village of Bedworth and the adjacent silk town of Coventry. Even Newcastle dreaded the influx of miners from the Tyne, on whose labours the prosperity of the town depended. Within the mining communities the social unit was still the patriarchal family. This was centred on the mine. Children were taken underground to act as trappers as soon as they were physically capable. In Scotland, in South Wales, and in some of the Lancashire and Yorkshire pits women, too, worked underground. Even where, as in the older pits in Northumberland and Durham, women were not employed underground, there was plenty of work for them on the surface. The work was dangerous and physically excessively hard but the miner lived well and expected to eat meat every day. When the northern collier was dressed in his best he wore white stockings, very tall shirt necks, very stiffly starched with ruffles, but, as one of them confessed, under all this splendour 'their legs and bodies are as black as your hat'. When asked if the women who worked underground washed, the answer was 'I do not think it usual for the lasses to wash their bodies; my sisters never wash themselves and seeing is believing; they wash their faces, necks and ears.' (*Report on the Sanitary Condition . . .* , 253.) Practices varied from coal field to coal field. South Wales miners, it was reported 'on their return from the pits in the evening strip to the skin and wash themselves perfectly clean in a tub of lukewarm water and wipe with towels' (ibid., 254). Victorian commentators reporting on this Welsh passion for cleanliness apparently did not feel that it was next to godliness because of the lack of conventional modesty shown by the women of the community who, when so employed, did not even trouble to shut the house door but, stripped to the waist, chatted cheerfully with any young man who might be passing. Mining villages had their own decencies and conventions, but they were not necessarily those of less isolated and specialized communities. When both sexes worked in semi-nakedness underground the sight of the human body was as commonplace as in a modern nudist camp. John Wesley had found many of his most fervent converts among the miners, but the unconverted were a rough, hard drinking set of men. One of the fascinating aspects of nineteenth-century social development is that communities which previously had been so cut off from the main stream of the labouring poor should begin to play so important a part in the early trade unions. In so doing they added a new, tough and independent element to the emerging working class.

Perhaps the most dramatic way of assessing the changes that had taken place in the structure of English society in the period under review is to contrast the England that in 1776 was on the verge of war with its rebellious American colonies with that which flocked to the Great Exhibition of 1851. In 1776 George III still possessed considerable political power, his ministers were drawn from the leading nobility, the House of Lords still exerted enormous power, both directly and through its influence over the members of the Commons. The Landed Interest still dominated both political and social life and the reigning monarch was nicknamed 'Farmer George'. Only a few cranks were advocating manhood suffrage, and when politicians spoke about 'the people', they meant only those who had a stake in the country, the property-owners of modest means. The idea that the labouring poor should concern themselves with the world of government, let alone take a share in the councils of the nation, would have seemed to most people arrant nonsense, and for this opinion there would have been not a little justification. Only the skilled craftsmen of London and a few of the biggest towns would have had the knowledge and judgment to exercise the franchise, and in comparatively democratic constituencies, such as Westminster, where the franchise was roughly based on a household qualification, many of them already had a vote. Nor in 1776 would these men have felt much kinship with the unskilled or semi-skilled manual worker. Society was still in the stage where status counted for more than income, when men gave deference to those placed above them in the hierarchy and exacted it from those below.

In 1851 the situation was very different. The purpose of the Exhibition was to show the world the extent of Britain's industrial achievement. Behind it lay three-quarters of a century of technological achievement. The people who flocked to it were largely those with an urban background, ranging from industrial magnates to working mechanics. Aristocracy, gentry, upper and lower middle class, intelligent working men all made the pilgrimage. Nor were its patrons confined to Londoners; excursion trains brought them from the provinces. The Prince Consort, who was one of its most enthusiastic promoters, wanted to use any profits that might accrue for the 'dissemination of a knowledge of science and art among *all classes*' (the italics are mine). In 1776 such a programme would have been a social impossibility. The political scene showed the same contrast. Though cabinets continued to be almost exclusively composed of peers, twice, in the person of Robert Peel, a manufacturer's son, and George Canning, the Crown accepted as its chief minister a member of the middle class. Canning was not even wealthy, though he married money, and his mother had been an actress. Even if not many of its members achieved cabinet rank, the growing insubordination of the lower classes had been sufficiently disturbing for the aristocratic Whigs to be prepared to accept the middle class as political allies and to enfranchise them in 1832. Henceforth politicians had to consider their views on many questions in which they had a direct concern. A Parliament utterly committed in 1815 to protecting the agricultural interest had repealed the Corn Laws in 1846, though it should be recognized that at least some agricultural opinion was no longer convinced of their utility. Nevertheless the Anti-Corn Law League was a middle class organization led by middle class men. Its success was a clear indication that the landed gentry and aristocracy could no longer impose their own policy on the nation as of the divine right of birth and land.

Though they had been less successful in protecting their interests against the rest of the community, even the working classes had made considerable progress. The organization of trade unions had given them experience in working for a common cause and driven home the need for class solidarity, at least among the new skilled artisans. For many of them, by the mid-century, their standard of living and education was at least showing signs of going up. By 1851 the nation was learning to handle the problems that an increased population, increased urbanization, increased technical efficiency and increased mobility had produced. The period of adjustment had been one of great suffering for many and of widespread tension, which had torn great rents in the traditional social fabric, but by the Great Exhibition it was clear that birth was giving place to money, status to class. This was evident even in the matter of dress. The poor and the rich wore clothes of very different quality, but in the style of their apparel the casual observer could no longer tell a noble from a prosperous business man, or a shopkeeper from a skilled mechanic, when they attended their place of worship on Sunday. Whether that place of worship were church or chapel would probably be a better guide to the class of the congregation in urban areas. Yet though the shape of things to come was becoming increasingly clear, much of the old remained. Half of England was still rural in its outlook and rural society had changed little. The sphere of the landowner's influence had shrunk but in the countryside he was still king. By the mid-nineteenth century English social development was running in two streams, urban and rural, one rushing tempestuously towards the future, the other still mirroring the past in its sluggish waters.

Chapter 5   The Climate of Opinion: Upper and Middle Class

To attempt to catch the climate of opinion of any age must always be a hazardous undertaking. When the age is one of rapid social and economic change, as was the period between 1776 and 1851, it is even more so. In 1776 only the opinions of the aristocracy, gentry, professional writers, bankers and merchants, and, to some extent, the tradesmen and craftsmen of the City counted. The majority of the middling sort and the mass of the labouring poor, as far as the written word was concerned, were largely inarticulate. The only means that the latter had of making their views known was to break into spontaneous riots. Where these were not spontaneous they were organized by their betters for political purposes. By the early years of the nineteenth century this was no longer true. The popular press, though hampered by stamp duties and often driven underground, had come into being. The growing urban working class could, and did, express, in terms that were often violent, its hopes and fears. In addition its new leaders were men of parts, whose weapon was the pen as well as the strike, and much that they wrote, private letters, manifestos, pamphlets, even autobiographies, survives. As a result it is possible to know, as never before, what ordinary men felt about the society in which they lived. Because these were the years of Disraeli's 'Two Nations' (*Sybil*), one can no longer write of one English climate of opinion. Though they impinged on one another and overlapped, two very different ways of thinking about contemporary problems, that of the upper and middle classes on the one hand, that of the working class on the other, emerged in the post-war years. Any attempt to assess the climate of opinion during these years means recognizing the common stock from which both sprung while according separate treatment to each. The dominating outlook was still that of the upper and middle classes, while that of the working class can often be seen as a reaction to it.

Any survey of either in a book of this size and character must be both limited to the essential ingredients that together moulded the way in which people thought, and superficial in its discussion of them. Nevertheless it should be possible to get a general overall picture. There are two useful guidelines through the labyrinth of super-abundant material. Mankind, though not all men, appears to possess two driving needs, the need to safeguard and further its own material interests, and the need to relate itself to the purpose of human exis-tence. The first is a matter for the economists, the administrators, the planners, and, for its implementation, the politicians. The second is the concern of philosophers and the churches. Because in a period of rapid change both questions are forced on men's attention, the climate of opinion during the vital years of the first Industrial Revolu-tion was much influenced by men like Adam Smith, Malthus, James and John Stuart Mill, Robert Owen, Jeremy Bentham and Edwin Chadwick, and by religious movements, both inside and outside the established church, of which the Methodists, Evangelicals and Trac-tarians were the most important. Between them these men and these movements made the England of 1851 a very different place from that of 1776.

The England that had set out to subdue its unruly colonists had not yet turned its back on 'The Age of Elegance'. Its characteristics were those that might have been expected from a long period of aristo-cratic domination. Style and taste were all-important. Architecture was formal, restrained and well-proportioned, lending itself equally to the magnificence of the great house and the quiet dignity of the urban street and square. Eighteenth-century painting was largely conditioned by an aristocracy and gentry conscious of the importance of the family and rooted in the countryside. The great artists of the time concentrated on portraiture and, to a lesser extent, on landscape. Hogarth had gone some way to meet the demands of a middle class purchaser but there was little of the genre painting of the earlier Dutch masters. In religion it was fashionable to be coolly rational. Enthusiasm was 'out'. Most educated men thought religion useful for the masses but themselves inclined to beliefs that ascribed to God their own rational approach to the universe and felt no need of a personal saviour. The clergy, from bishops to vicars, were appointed more for political or personal reasons than for religious ones. Patron-age was more important than prayer, spirituality at a discount and dedication rare.

Morally, the society of the day might be described as 'permissive', though in its upper ranks the permissiveness was not blatant, because the formal code of manners required that a decent outward seeming be preserved. Nevertheless elegance and style were a cloak for much that was brutal, cruel, coarse and lecherous. The amours of the Prince Regent were public knowledge. The Duke of Devonshire ran a *maison à trois*, openly sharing his favours with his beautiful Duchess, Georgiana, and Lady Elizabeth Foster. Yet outwardly the two ladies remained on amicable terms, with Lady Elizabeth's offspring born and brought up elsewhere. Undoubtedly there were many devoted wives and husbands in the highest circles, but they accepted those who ordered their domestic life otherwise with complaisancy, or at least without the censure of the Victorian world. The position of the courtesan is in itself illuminating. English gentlemen of wealth and fashion moved in two worlds, the world of wife and family and that of the demi-monde, where the reigning courtesan was queen. There was little secret about it and nothing to disgust the most fastidious man of fashion. A courtesan of the standing of Harriette Wilson was a woman of wit as well as beauty, as capable of intelligent and well-informed conversation as of giving sexual pleasure. Such women had their own box at the opera, where they held public court. Men delighted to drive with them in the Park, and considered it an honour to be known to receive their favours. They were very far removed from the prostitutes who touted for custom in the Strand. Genteel young women were shielded from all knowledge of this world until they married off; after marriage wives were supposed to turn a blind eye, even when they were not engaged in some more discreetly managed affair of their own. This non-recognition was easier to achieve because the invisible lines between the two worlds were never crossed.

Sexual laxity was not the only vice of fashionable Regency society. Gambling had assumed gigantic proportions. Card games of chance and games of dice were played in all the leading clubs for high stakes, which even when they did not ruin, for the loser of tonight might be the winner of tomorrow, produced an atmosphere of excitement and insecurity. Women were as addicted as men. The correspondence of the period is full of gossip about fortunes won and fortunes lost in a night, and of the ruin and despair that sometimes followed. Heavy drinking accompanied gambling and was, like it, an accepted part of life. Abstinence from anything that he wanted to do was the last virtue to be cultivated by the Regency gentleman! Underneath its veneer of good breeding the fashionable world was both tough and violent. This was the reverse side of the coin of courage. The absence of any anaesthetics made the pulling of teeth an ordeal few could escape and any kind of operation a nightmare. Later Grenville was to declare that 'wonderful as are the powers and feats of the steam engine, the chloroform far transcends them all in its beneficent and consolatory operations'. (Grenville, op. cit, vol. 1, 17.) Few readers, faced with a visit to the dentist or a serious operation, would be brave enough to dissent. But even the most gently nurtured high-born lady had no such consolation; she had to suffer like the poorest peasant. Women regularly faced death in or after childbirth. Many diseases had no cure; the tough survived to create a legend of the longevity of 'the good old days', the rest died. Wanton cruelty was accepted with something of the same acquiescence, not by everybody but by the majority, since they knew that pain could never be avoided. At public schools masters made no attempt to restrain the sadistic bullying of the little boys by their seniors. One popular practice was to hold some youngster in front of a blazing fire to see how long his ordeal could continue before he fainted with the pain. Later in his school career it was he who could do the roasting if it pleased him to see others suffer as he had done. Blunted by brutal treatment, taught to regard the infliction of pain as a form of amusement, it is not surprising that men and women beat their servants and thrashed their children, that husbands assaulted their wives, or that two of the most popular amusements were the prizefight, when men pummelled each other to pulp with their bare fists, and the cockfight in which the birds tore each other to pieces with beaks and sharpened spurs. It was an age shot through and through with violence. Physical suffering, and even death, were public spectacles. Men and women were whipped through the streets at the cart's tail; it was good sport to fling every kind of filth at helpless persons in the pillory; even after Tyburn days were abolished, hangings were still public. Even children were taken to watch an execution with the ostensible purpose of imprinting on their young minds that the wages of sin were death. Not everybody enjoyed such sights but few protested against them.

Indifference to the infliction of pain and sexual laxity were accompanied by a verbal coarseness and a frank, even humorous, acceptance of bodily functions which Victorian England was to find deeply shocking, and which remained outside the vocabulary of polite usage until its re-introduction on the English stage in the nineteen-seventies. Boyer's *Royal Dictionary*, which was specially designed for the use of young students wrestling with the intricacies of the French language, as late as 1803 gave the French equivalents of such terms as 'he is the crack-fart of the nation' and other colloquialisms that called for the use of such words as 'arse' and 'shit'. (F. K. Brown, *Fathers of the Victorians*,

19.) Cartoonists were equally uninhibited, portraying eminent politicians as 'making a motion in the little house' as well as moving one in the Commons, or caricaturing the Prime Minister as 'the bottomless Pitt' with an appropriate drawing. One can hardly imagine similar treatment being meted out to Gladstone. Yet if public opinion among those who shaped society countenanced much that was promiscuous, brutal and coarse, if it left men and women to gamble away their inheritance, it had certain robust virtues. The aristocracy and gentry were still the 'ruling classes' and as such they accepted responsibility, both national and local. If their philanthropy was directed rather to helping the deserving, who had fallen on hard times, and to making them useful members of the community once again, than to shielding the inadequate from the pressures of life, it was none the less genuine. Each individual was expected to stand on his own feet. Duelling had not yet become a dead letter; a man was expected to defend his honour with pistol and sword, and was despised if he did not. Castlereagh and Canning fought a duel with pistols, though this was considered somewhat reprehensible conduct between two ministers in the same government. Whatever else they might be, neither the aristocracy nor the gentry of Regency England were effete. Nor were they uncultured. Men who fought cocks and gambled at White's bought pictures, built stately homes and improved their estates. Fox might be a gambler, the younger Pitt too fond of the bottle, but both were able politicians and each in his own way a dedicated patriot.

It is fascinating to speculate on how far the middling sort were influenced by the views and practices of their betters. Snobbery was a potent social force; the wealthy City merchant had long tended to invest in land and to gravitate to the ranks of the landed gentry. In the smaller country towns there was considerable contact between the local gentry, who were often engaged in one of the professions, and the better-off members of the business community. Mrs Bennet's sister, the rather vulgar Mrs Phillips in *Pride and Prejudice*, married to a small-town attorney, occupied this middle ground. As far as their purses allowed, the middling sort copied the gentry in the furnishing and designing of their houses. London fashions also spread, first to the bigger provincial towns and then to the smaller ones. Circulating libraries were bringing the latest novels within the reach of middle class women, national and local newspapers were helping to create a common political awareness and cultural outlook. Philanthropy also brought about a sharing of experience and more contact between the upper and middling ranks. In the organizing of charity schools, and later Sunday schools, for poor children, in setting up hospitals for the sick poor and of lying-in charities, both the gentry and the middling sort were active.

Nevertheless there were deep divergences between them. The middling sort were the money-making section of society, and while the making of money has its own vices they were not those of either the fashionable world or the hard drinking, sporting landed gentry. The prosperous shopkeeper and tradesman lived in a substantial house, his diet was generous, his clothes of good quality. On Sundays he and his family were well turned out, but display, for the mere sake of display, was regarded as folly. A solid tradesman's family should not spend its substance aping the gentry. Gambling jeopardized resources; drunkenness consumed time and depleted energy; witty beautiful ladies of pleasure, the 'muslin brigade', belonged to a different way of life. As among their social superiors, the family was a tight-knit unit but what bound it together was not land but business, and business was often a matter of personal relations. The opportunities for open infidelity were less, and in any case bad for the harmonious running of a family business. Even the wealthy merchant, banker or manufacturer was rarely tempted to fritter time and money on fashionable amusements, though Jorrocks did go hunting. Inevitably there were many backsliders among the middling sort, men who idled, men who gambled and drank, men who womanized, but by their equals they were regarded as black sheep rather than as gilded gallants. What society allowed to a gentleman and what to an honest merchant, shopkeeper and tradesman were very different.

In the eighteenth century the tone of society had been set by the ruling classes. One of the most interesting developments of the early nineteenth was the way in which the social lead, in so far as it influenced national attitudes, was gradually transferred from the aristocracy and gentry to the middle classes. This is a statement that must be made with reservations. Class distinctions remained, and so did snobbery. Outwardly, as we have seen, the elegant life of the great houses and the fashionable life of London went on with little change. So did much sexual laxity. But outward permissiveness disappeared and accepted standards changed. Men no longer flaunted their mistresses in public; language grew more restrained; religion acquired a new importance. Fundamentally English society was accepting middle class standards and the gap, which had been wide in the eighteenth century, was closing. The reasons for this are complex and no two historians are likely to agree as to the precise weight to be given to each. Material factors were important as the new manufacturing class came to provide a greater share of the nation's capital and, with increasing self-confidence, came to lay more stress on the values that had helped them to do so. After the passing of the reform bill in 1832 they had a recognized stake in the political affairs of the nation; Parliament found itself increasingly discussing topics that concerned the new world of industry. Moreover it was middle class writers and thinkers who began to produce blueprints for the future, setting forth their views on such vital topics as the production and distribution of wealth, and the type of education needed to fit men for the society of the future.

The original impetus that was to transform 'merry England' into Victorian England seems to have been a religious one, though without these more mundane interests it might well have become a spent force before the moral transformation at which it aimed had been achieved. Even when the spiritual temperature of the established church was low there had always been some men of dedication and fervour. Such a one was John Wesley. His ministry, however, had been largely confined to the uninfluential and the poor. Charles II is reputed to have said that Calvinism was no religion for a gentleman. Most eighteenth-century gentlemen had reacted in the same way against Methodism. Nevertheless groups of serious Anglicans were desperately conscious of the need to rescue society from the abyss of infidelity and carelessness into which it seemed to be plunging and which they attributed, perhaps too exclusively, to the lack of a vital religion. Religion, they argued, was not a matter of outward observance; it did not consist even in the living of an outwardly decent life; it must be of the spirit. This was the doctrine that men like Henry Venn, the vicar of Huddersfield, preached to his northern congregation, that the ex-slaving captain John Newton proclaimed in his London parish, that Isaac Milner, President of Queens' and Dean of Carlisle, and Charles Simeon, Vicar of Holy Trinity, were teaching to the undergraduates of Cambridge. Because the movement remained within the established church, which Methodism, despite Wesley himself, had failed to do, evangelicalism seems to have made most headway in its early stages with the better-off members of the urban middle class. Men of the type of John Thornton, who had made a fortune in the Russian trade and whose house at Clapham became the centre of a group of like-minded people, later to be nicknamed 'the Clapham sect', responded to its offer of a personal religion. Many young Cambridge men reacted in the same way. Laxity can grow boring; a call to personal righteousness will always make an appeal to some whom the ordinary demands of daily life fail to satisfy. Whether this evangelical movement, with its rigorous examination of conscience, and its insistence that grace is a seamless garment, so that the idle pleasure, the thoughtless word, brings with it consequences not only in this world but in the next and that therefore conduct, even in trifles, must be examined and regulated, would have obtained the grip that it did on Victorian England had it not been that other circumstances enabled it to 'get off the ground' must remain one of the 'ifs' of history. The excesses of the French Revolution convinced the upper classes of the need for a religious revival. Both the evangelicals and the polite world believed that the laxity, drunkenness and idleness of the lower orders represented a threat to the nation though their angle of approach was different. The evangelicals represented these failings as the outward sign of inward depravity. Therefore because the poor had souls to be saved they must have sound doctrine preached to them, they must be protected from the more obvious of their worldly temptations by making them no longer available. The more worldly-minded view was that vice reduced both the will and the capacity for honest work and that, without the labour of the poor, the national economy would collapse. George III's ministers were in complete accord with this point of view. In 1787 the Proclamation against Vice and Immorality which included sabbath-breaking, blasphemy, drunkenness, obscene literature and immoral behaviour, was issued. Next year, it was followed up by the formation of a 'Society for Enforcing the King's Proclamation against Profaneness'. This first society was not exclusively, or even mainly, evangelical; gradually, however, its evangelical members increased their grip on it and it was reconstructed as 'The Society for the Suppression of Vice'. Not everybody approved of it. Sidney Smith in the *Edinburgh Review* castigated it as a band of snoopers.

Meanwhile the tentacles of evangelicalism were spreading and its teachings were beginning to percolate among the well-born and wealthy. A notable recruit was young William Wilberforce. Wealthy and a gentleman, he stood as a matter of course for Parliament and was returned for Hull in 1780. He was a friend of Pitt's and moved in the best circles. Like Wesley short of stature, he was gay, witty and a most delightful companion. Even before he was drawn into evangelical circles neither vice nor malice had any attraction for him; he was friendly, warm-hearted and kind. In 1784 he visited the Continent, taking Isaac Milner with him. At that time he was unaware of Milner's religious fervour because he also was 'full of levity' on all but serious subjects. In every way he proved a delightful and stimulating companion. It is wrong to think of many of the early evangelicals as grim, dour men, frowning on every pleasure and leading austere lives. They lived in the style to which their place in society entitled them. Wilberforce was a friend of the Prince Regent and often dined with him at Brighton. Because they did not affront society they were able to influence it. Had they withdrawn from the company of drunkards, gamblers, lechers, society would have regarded them as cranks and passed by on the other side. Instead the Clapham sect demonstrated that a man or woman could be an evangelical Christian and remain someone whom it was not embarrassing to know. By speaking seriously on serious topics, and by the uprightness of their private and public lives, they won over many people to their beliefs. Those who were not won over at least behaved with decorum in their company. Even the Regent assured Wilberforce that 'he should never hear a word at his table which could give him a moment's pain'. He kept his word; both the Prince and Wilberforce were gentlemen. (F. K. Brown, op. cit., 60.)

This attitude on the part of the polite world was fostered and encouraged by that very remarkable woman, Hannah More. Originally a younger member of Dr Johnson's bluestocking circle, after Garrick's death she became increasingly serious in her outlook. Among her friends was the evangelical admiral, Sir Charles Middleton, and his wife, and through them she was drawn into the Clapham group. In 1787 her long friendship with Wilberforce began. Hannah More's great asset was a skilful and persuasive pen. A year later she produced her *Thoughts on the Importance of the Manners of the Great to General Society*. Its tone was serious but conciliatory in that she refrained from launching indiscriminate charges of major laxities and vice. Instead she pointed out the responsibility of the great for setting a good example to the lower orders, calling upon the people who regarded themselves as the leaders of society to lead it back to true religion and virtue. Two years later she followed this up with a volume entitled *An Estimate of the Religion of the Fashionable World*, in which she pointed out that mere conventional religion was inadequate. It was not enough to be 'a decent good sort of a person' practising the humanistic virtues. What was needed was a concentration upon God, a determination to win eternal happiness by so ordering one's life in this world that every action turned on His will. Her books and Wilberforce's *Practical View of the Religion of Professed Christians* ran into many editions. They were among the best-sellers of the day and exerted a profound influence on the upper and middle classes. They were reinforced by sermons, by public meetings, and above all by the setting up of societies for almost every moral cause. Even when the founder members were not evangelicals the latter soon infiltrated. They were always prepared to work with any Christian body to do the work of Christ. Societies for good workers were no nineteenth-century innovation, but the skill with which evangelicals organized them and the scope of their propaganda made them pressure groups of a new and formidable kind, so introducing a new factor into the formation of public opinion. The movement even had its own newspaper, the *Christian Observer*, founded in 1801, and edited by Zaccary Macaulay, the father of the historian.

By the end of the French wars 'virtue was advancing on a broad, invincible front' (G. M. Young, *Portrait of an Age*, 4), though the impetus behind the advance was not solely religious. Infidelity and revolution were closely associated in men's minds and the simmering discontent and half-concealed violence of the lower orders seemed to threaten social stability. At the same time there was a vague superstitious feeling abroad that the success of the godless French might be due to the divine wrath with Britain's own laxity. This hangover from an earlier, less rational age persisted even after the war had been won. In 1831 William IV called for a national day of fasting and humiliation when cholera swept the country, hoping to appease the Angel of Death. One aspect of the advance of virtue was the insistence placed on the observance of the Lord's Day by the evangelicals, who left as their legacy to posterity the 'English Sunday'. By preaching, social pressure, and legislation they sought to impose this even on the ungodly. To do this they endeavoured to remove them from temptation through the activities of a new society: 'The Society for the Due Observance of the Lord's Day', founded in 1831. Two years later Sir Andrew Agnew, a founder member, asked leave to introduce a bill into the Commons which would have made any meeting for gaming or betting, any wake, fair, hunt, bull-baiting, cockfighting, shooting and, more elastic still 'any pastime of public indecorum, inconvenience or nuisance', illegal. There was precedent for such legislation, but Sir Andrew's bill would have gone further. It was designed also to prohibit the consumption of alcohol in hotels, except for bona fide travellers, the hiring of carriages except by clergymen and doctors, the sailing of ships to another British port, or even, if the ship were over 200 tons, to a foreign one. Even public speeches and lectures were to be prohibited. It is significant of the swing in public opinion that leave to introduce this extreme bill was only lost by six votes; later many of its provisions did become law. Strenuous attempts were made to stop Sunday trains; when in 1844 Queen Victoria actually travelled on one to fulfil a public engagement eyebrows were raised; when an accident took place on a Sunday it was hailed by strict Sabbatarians as the direct result of divine displeasure. In 1850 a further success was achieved when the Sunday collection and delivery of letters was prohibited, but after only two months of this inconvenience the business world revolted and it was restored. Similar, but vain, attempts were made to stop the publication of Sunday newspapers, but all efforts to get permission for the Great Exhibition to be opened on Sundays failed, although that was the only day on which many people could have seen it conveniently.

By that date English society had undergone a moral revolution, at least as far as its upper and middle ranks were concerned. England had been presented with a new pattern of family life in which morning and evening prayers and regular church or chapel attendances on Sunday were *de rigueur*. Swearing and cursing were no longer fashionable. Dress became more restrained and modest. Dancing and the theatre were looked on askance by many, who took literally the notice 'To the Pit'. Family life was expected to be happy, with husbands faithful, wives dutiful and children obedient. This did not necessarily mean that it need be gloomy and dull. Many pleasures were considered not to imperil the soul. Music round the piano was enjoyed; reading aloud was cultivated; sketching and embroidery were recognized hobbies. Country walks and the study of botany were encouraged. Novels such as Charlotte M. Yonge's *The Daisy Chain*, illustrated this ideal of a united family where serious discussion of religious topics was no barrier to laughter and gaiety on less solemn occasions. Such novels were widely read. To a modern reader they seem to drip with religion and morality but to contemporaries they seemed to reflect what was best and most admirable in family life. Charlotte Brontë, herself the daughter of an evangelical parson, makes Helen Burns in *Jane Eyre* a pattern of religious faith and Christian resignation and, though she allows Jane herself rebellious thoughts as a child, she and Rochester only find happiness when they submit themselves to the will of God.

How far this apparent permeation by religion of everyday life is evidence of a genuinely religious outlook it is difficult to know. Social pressure is a tremendous force. Many people find it easier to accept, with inward reservations, rather than to rebel openly. Nevertheless there is plenty of documentation to show that for many people religion had become an integral part of daily living and that they tried to order this in accordance with what they believed to be the divine will. The happy, religious Victorian family was not just a figment of the novelist's imagination. Even if it had been, its popularity would still have borne witness to the ideal for which people were striving, and to the topics which interested them most. Nevertheless the emphasis placed on religious observance and on morality was productive of some less desirable side-effects. Because the eighteenth century had been 'natural' in its attitude to bodily functions and bodily appetites, while underneath the elegance and formality of fashionable life sexual licence had been accepted, the evangelicals had seen spiritual life as one long struggle between Grace and Nature, with Nature in the role of the tempter. The case of the cured alcoholic provides a useful parallel. For many the cure lasts only as long as they do not allow themselves the indulgence of even a single drink. If the old sins were to be avoided there must be nothing to re-awaken the old desires. 'Lead us not into temptation' was often, for reasons that had only too strong historical justification, the prayer that lay behind the excessive prudery that came to replace the former excessive licence. Legs became limbs. A wife submitted to her husband's demands as a duty: no 'nice woman' could confess to sharing his pleasure. A woman of refinement would be embarrassed if seen entering the W.C. by a man. In many such subtle conventions woman's supposed delicacy was used to check the grossness of the male. In her presence he had to conform to the conventional idea of a Christian gentleman. It is not, perhaps, surprising that the nineteenth century saw a proliferation of clubs, pubs, and brothels.

In following Hamlet's advice to his mother, 'assume a virtue if you have it not', the evangelical clergy hoped that by a systematic cultivation of good habits the seed of true religion might smother the tangle of worldly weeds that threatened to choke it. There were dangers in such a policy designed to help the 'weaker brethren'. Expelling Nature with a pitchfork tends to bury rather than root out the more persistent weeds. Outwardly the majority conformed; indeed many were so conditioned to the stringent social code that it never occurred to them to do otherwise. How many rebelled secretly we do not know. A few rebelled openly, but the price exacted by their own conscience and by society was a heavy one. Others confined themselves to some emotional half-way house. The contrast between the *ménage à trois* of the eighteenth Duke of Devonshire and the complicated relationship of John Stuart Mill, Harriet Taylor and her husband is a comment on the changing morality of contemporary society. In the first case there was no pretence that Lady Elizabeth was not the Duke's mistress, in the second until her husband's death the liaison was almost certainly purely an emotional one; even then eyebrows were raised when the couple went about together without Mr Taylor. If the soil was congenial for the cultivation of virtue it was equally congenial for that of hypocrisy. This remains one of the cardinal charges made by posterity against Victorian England, where respectability had become the acid test of social acceptability.

When the early groups of the evangelicals started their campaign for the regeneration of society they were only too conscious of how little the established church, of which they were members, was fitted to play its part in the struggle that lay ahead. It was not only the abuses of absenteeism and pluralism, not even the hunting parson that troubled them. In their eyes it was the clergymen 'of a more decent cast' who were the greatest danger because they might lead people to suppose that a purely conventional religion could lead one to grace. In 1817 Charles Simeon inaugurated the Simeon Trust for the purpose of buying up advowsons (the right to present to a living) when these came on the market in order to ensure that in those parishes at least 'pious parsons' were appointed. What could be done in this way was limited and the majority of the clergy continued to be at best merely 'of a more decent cast'. The forces that drove the church to put its own house in order or, perhaps more accurately, drove Parliament to do so, were political rather than religious. By the thirties the church was being attacked on two fronts. It was thoroughly disliked, if that is not too weak a word, by both the Dissenters and the parliamentary reformers. For this there were substantial reasons. Though the former had been freed from their political disabilities in 1828 they still had substantial and very genuine grievances. They had to pay the great tithe to the rector and the small tithe to the vicar unless these had been commuted. They had to pay for the upkeep of the nave and the churchyard, a duty that was demanded from all parishioners who were householders. They could only be married legally in church and legally register the birth of their children there. They could not take a degree at either Oxford or Cambridge. The reformers were also furious with the bishops because of their opposition to the Reform Bill. Clerical opinion was fearful of the effect that it might have on the composition of the Commons, particularly as both Dissenters and Roman Catholics had been enfranchised. As a consequence the majority of the bishops had voted against the Bill when it had been debated in the Lords. The result was popular, organized and violent protest. It is sometimes forgotten that this is not a modern phenomenon of the sixties and seventies of the twentieth century. In Bristol the mob broke into the bishop's palace; in Carlisle it burnt an effigy of the bishop in the marketplace; even the Archbishop of Canterbury had the windows of his carriage broken with brickbats by a hissing, jeering crowd that pelted him with cabbage stalks! Nor were the ordinary clergy immune. The windows of the vicar of Sherborne were broken and his cellar sacked.

This wave of unpopularity sprang from something deeper than a political crisis. It was a manifestation of the changing climate of opinion, which the evangelicals had played their part in creating, but which sprang also from the feeling that the church, as the eighteenth century had known it, was becoming something of an anachronism in a changing world where the social structure of the past was increasingly coming under the critical fire of radical opinion. Non-residence went hand-in-hand with pluralities. When the Dean of Carlisle could hold, in addition to two other parishes, the fashionable living of St George's Hanover Square, while poor curates had to struggle along on a pittance, it was difficult to stifle criticism.

The combination of radical reformers and disgruntled Dissenters, who were often the same people, filled the clergy with alarm lest in a reformed House of Commons their enemies might combine to carry a bill disestablishing the church. This particular fear proved groundless, but in the teeth of clerical opposition some measures were introduced by politicians anxious to mollify criticism before it got out of hand. Peel during his first short ministry had set up a committee of inquiry to go into church revenues and as a result in 1836 the Ecclesiastical Commission was appointed. At last the church had a body able to review its economic problems impartially and to suggest remedies. It was able to lop off some of the revenue of the wealthiest bishoprics and to distribute the money more equitably. It also secured a ban on pluralities, a necessary reform in view of the fact that, in 1831, 2,268 of the clergy had held two livings or more. In future, unless the parishes were less than two miles apart, the beneficed clergy could hold only a single living. Something was also done in 1836 to deal with the grievances of the Dissenters. Arrangements were made to commute the tithe (see pp. 65–6) and provide for the solemnization of marriages in Dissenting chapels, and for births, marriages and deaths to be officially notified to a civil registrar. This had wider than mere religious importance. For the first time there was an official, as distinct from a somewhat unreliable parish register, record of every person's date of birth, which was to be a great legal convenience. There were, however, limits to these concessions. The church rate was not abolished and continued to be a source of bitterness. The campaign to allow Dissenters to take degrees at Oxford and Cambridge, though carried on vigorously, had no success. However, University College, London, was non-sectarian, which to some extent reduced the hardship for non-Anglicans.

The successful propaganda of the evangelicals stole much of the limelight, but there were other potent forces influencing the climate of opinion in Regency and Victorian England. Many people found their fulfilment not in religion but in the new Romantic movement. As the eighteenth century drew to its close the architecture, painting and poetry that had marked the High Georgian period began to lose its appeal. Horace Walpole's house, Strawberry Hill, was an architectural extravagance in the new Gothic style. Men began to turn to a new medieval past, which they invested with a quality of romance that, at least for the non-historian, it has not quite lost even today. It was seen as the age of faith and chivalry. This new sensitivity to the past was reflected in a vogue for the relics of antiquity, a taste which expressed itself in the adornment of parks and gardens with ruins that were as sham as they were picturesque. Their purpose was not to fulfil a material need but to evoke an emotion. After having been banished from polite society, emotion became once more fashionable. In literature the same romantic and often fantastic approach was to be found. Historical novels became popular and those of Sir Walter Scott replaced the racy comments on contemporary society that had characterized the works of Smollett and Fielding. Exaggerated tales of horror and suspense, of which Horace Walpole's *Castle of Otranto* published in 1765 was a harbinger, poured out of the circulating libraries and proved a fruitful source of income for the new genre of lady novelists. Mary Shelley first published *Frankenstein* in 1818. Not all women read them avidly and at least one female novelist, Jane Austen, poked delicate fun at the whole trend in *Northanger Abbey*. The poets too were swept away by the same torment. Scott took as his theme the ballads of the Border and *Marmion* was a great success. Byron's wandering hero, Childe Harold, thrilled Regency female hearts, a thrill enhanced by the author's classic beauty, open-necked shirts and aura of erotic disreputability. Wordsworth, Keats and Shelley found a different outlet for their emotion in a new discovery of Nature and a new appreciation of its wonders from the dancing daffodils to the soaring skylark. Like the melancholy Jaques, the Lakeland poets found 'sermons in stones, and good in everything'.

This feeling for the past had its religious manifestations. From the late twenties, and becoming marked in the early thirties, a group of young Oxford dons developed a new approach to the authority of the church. The leaders of the group were Keble, whose book of verse, *The Christian Year*, was published in 1827, Hurrell Froude and Henry Newman, both tutors at Oriel. The novelty of their approach lay in the fact that by repudiating the right of a secular authority such as Parliament to meddle with church doctrine they went behind the Reformation and appealed to the authority of an earlier, universal or catholic church, basing their case on the teachings and practices of the early fathers. These views were given publicity in a series of tracts under the title of *Tracts for the Times*. The first was published anonymously in 1833 as part of the campaign denying to Parliament any right to legislate for the church. Its sponsors were often known by the singularly ugly label of the Tractarians. As by this time evangelicalism, with its narrow personal approach, had spent some of its early force, many people found their appeal to the past, the breadth of their outlook and the high claims which they made for the English church in tracing its continuation and its authority back to the apostolic succession attractive. Nevertheless there was still much of the old anti-papal feeling in the country; to many people the word 'catholic' still meant Rome. This led to misunderstandings. Newman, the author of many of the Tracts, was at the time of writing a convinced Anglican, though later he embraced the Roman Catholic faith. Even as an Anglican he disliked the term 'Protestant', which he used as little as he could. For him the Anglican church was part of a Catholic church. This resulted in many people believing him to be a crypto-Romanist. Many people felt that their suspicions had been justified in 1845 when he was received into the Roman church, in which he became a cardinal in due course. In spite of his defection the Anglo-Catholic movement survived and became a potent force in Victorian England. This return to the past was reflected in the foundation of the Camden Society at Cambridge in 1839, with its interest in church architecture, church furniture and ecclesiastical ritual, interest which dovetailed with the Tractarians' sympathy for the pre-Reformation church. Of wider than purely religious importance was a general revival of would-be Gothic architecture made fashionable by the young architect

Pugin. Today the many Victorian churches built in the Gothic style bear witness to the popularity of this revival, but the most imposing pile of all was dedicated not to religion but to politics. When the old Parliament building was burnt down in 1834 it was rebuilt in Gothic.

Though Victorian public opinion, at least among the middle and upper classes, stressed the importance of religion as an ingredient in a healthy and stable society, the modern tendency to regard that society as self-righteous and smugly complacent is far removed from reality. True there was a deep pride in its achievements and in the technological lead which its industry had given to the world, but there was an equally deep unease as to the future paths along which this progress might lead the nation. Nor, at a time when traditional habits and modes of living were crumbling on every side, could it have been otherwise. Circumstances were forcing thinking men to challenge the old values and examine afresh not only religious truths but the whole structure of society. If the older ruling classes, the aristocracy and the gentry, were content with the world they had known, the growing class of capitalist employers and the swelling ranks of professional men were not only critical of it, but aggressive in their criticisms. It was particularly the professional men who were probing, asking questions, and providing their own answers to them. The age was one of intense intellectual curiosity and activity. Such questioning tended to focus on a set of related topics concerned with the shape of the economy, the efficiency of public administration, the distribution of political power and the type of education most likely to produce the kind of citizen that the shape of the new society was demanding. All these questions could be loosely grouped together as being of general utility, and the basis on which solutions were being sought was the greatest good of the greatest number. The men who were discussing them also aimed at destroying abuses by getting to their roots. Hence the blanket terms of Utilitarians and Philosophical Radicals that were used to describe the men who thought along these lines, though these terms covered much deeper and more original thinking than so brief a generalization is able to suggest.

Circumstances, partly of their own creation and partly the result of changes in the composition of society, gave the Utilitarians and Radicals the necessary platform from which to promulgate their views. One hesitates to use the term 'middle classes' too freely and too loosely; nevertheless as the national non-agricultural resources of Britain were developed, more and more ways of making money by non-manual activities were created. The urban middle class grew with them, so creating a reading public interested in just those topics that were exciting the smaller world of the intellectuals. They therefore supplied a reading public for a well-informed and critical Press. The *Gentleman's Magazine* in 1824 commented on the fact that a century ago few could have discerned that periodicals 'would have become the most eligible method of diffusing instruction equally among all classes. Difference of style may confine a work to a certain degree of society, but it is the peculiar advantage of magazines that they embrace all'. (December–June 1824, vol. xciv.) Economic factors also helped. New methods of producing paper and cheaper, more efficient, printing machines made it possible to produce larger editions of larger pages at a price that put them within the regular reach of persons of moderate incomes. Much of the impetus behind this literary output had come from Edinburgh, where the university, unhampered by religious tests, had attracted some of the most brilliant minds of the day. In 1802 the foundation of the *Edinburgh Review* provided the critics of the old order with an influential mouthpiece. To oppose these views the *Quarterly Review* was started to defend the values of the past. But eventually ambitious men gravitated to London. James Mill, who was to become the friend of Bentham and the father of a still more famous son, arrived there in 1802 to gain his livelihood by his pen. It was not, however, until 1824 that he and his friends succeeded in launching a new quarterly, the *Westminster Review*, which aimed at the dissemination of radical views. When this began to lose its edge, having fallen into unsatisfactory editorial hands, the Mills and their radical friends then sponsored the *London Review* in 1845. All these were serious papers, interpreting definite views of politics and society, full of authoritative articles and weighty book reviews. In them the problems and abuses of contemporary society were continuously being placed before a public that read not for amusement but for solid information and enjoyed the cut-and-thrust of argument.

To men prepared to base their case on argument, education was a matter of fundamental importance. Whereas the aristocracy and gentry had been content to accept a knowledge of the classics as the most suitable education for a gentleman, men of business had long been aware that something more in tune with the practical realities of life was necessary for the sons of men not born to rule. The fact that many of them were not members of the Church of England, and were therefore excluded from the endowed schools and from Oxford and Cambridge, had stimulated their thirst for education. Standing as they did on the brink of a new world, and almost drunk with the prospects that science seemed to hold out to mankind, the early educationalists had a pathetic belief that men could be trained by correct educational methods to be rational, and that once men had grasped what was the right and just thing to do that they would so act. All that was necessary, therefore, was to find the best way by which men could be trained to think correctly. As early as 1749 David Hartley, in his *Observations on Man*, had indicated the possibility of there being a science of the mind, and thereby had opened up the possibility that, like other sciences, this too had definite laws which, correctly understood and applied, would have the desired result.

Because they believed that the purpose of education was to fit men to become useful members of society, the emphasis of their teaching was to be scientific rather than classical. Growing minds, they argued, must be trained to understand and appreciate the wonders of the world around them. They were also to be taught to apply their knowledge to the practical world of industry. Accordingly they were to be instructed in chemistry, geology, mechanics, astronomy, geography, and to have some knowledge of mineralogy, electricity and optics; in short, they were to have some acquaintance with any science that would help them to understand the world in which they lived. Nor were literature and foreign languages to be ignored, though there was no room in this programme for fairy tales, the supernatural or the fanciful. Teaching methods also were to be revolutionized. Instead of learning by rote, aided by the birch, the young were to be led on by interest and an awakened curiosity. As far as possible they were to discover things for themselves and, a forerunner of the modern 'project' method, to be provided with simple materials to enable them to study mechanics by making models, and chemistry through easy experiments. Children were to be encouraged to collect stones and flowers in order to give reality to mineralogy and botany. Because the Utilitarian school believed that men were activated by a desire to seek pleasure and avoid pain, education was to be associated in the minds of the young with pleasure. Physical punishment therefore was to be avoided and children persuaded, not coerced, into learning. Minds were to be developed, not crammed. In all this there was an overriding optimism. Education correctly applied must produce good men, and good men would insist on a good society. Education, it was argued, would of itself produce a better world. In this creed there was no room for a mystic Christianity; men would be moral because they had been trained in the social virtues, not because they had been saved by the blood of Christ. Indeed to the new-style educationalist much of what the Church stood for was harmful. It buttressed the social inequalities of an earlier society and hampered the freedom of men's minds. Joseph Priestley was himself a Unitarian, as were many advanced thinkers. The education which they wanted for the ruling class was scientific and secular, which, if followed rationally, as indeed they believed by its very nature it must be, would lead to a new Utopia.

Men holding such views could hardly fail to sympathize with the early aims of the French revolutionaries in so far as they seemed to be striving for a more rational form of government and society. During the war they were branded as Jacobins but among the middle class intellectuals, men like Bentham and James Mill, this secular and scientific approach to education continued to make progress. It had its triumph in the founding of University College, afterwards in the University of London, as a degree-granting body that imposed no religious tests and examined in such subjects as engineering, medicine, mathematics, political economy, law and modern languages, as well as in philosophy and the classics. At last an English institution existed to cater for young men of middle class backgrounds and secular approach. Thomas Hardy's Jude the Obscure might have been more successful had he applied for admission there. This secular and modern approach to education had little impact on the traditional pattern of the great public schools, with their mixture of classics, bullying and nominal Anglicanism, to which the majority of the gentry sent their sons, unless they were tutored at home. Yet even here the shape of things to come had been foreshadowed by Dr Arnold of Rugby. A genuine educationalist, he had gradually gathered round him a set of young and enthusiastic masters, prepared to teach their pupils instead of flogging them into a repetitive familiarity with the classics. But his most important contribution to education was to remodel the pattern of behaviour expected from his boys. Bullying, bad language, drinking were to go; instead they were to be trained in the responsibilities of a Christian gentleman. When Arnold became headmaster in 1828 Rugby had been similar in outlook and practice to any of the other minor public schools. When he left it in 1842 it had become the prototype for the future. It is interesting that many of its pupils were drawn from well-to-do middle class families, who, without pretensions to gentility themselves, wished their sons to receive the education of a gentleman. In 1810 Sidney Smith had considered that in spite of their many defects the public schools still provided this, but, as the newest ideas on the scope and purpose of education began to make headway, as places of education they were overtaken by the new proprietary schools. Generally their promoters were a group of interested and wealthy businessmen anxious to secure an efficient and modern education for their sons. The subjects taught were to be in line with modern thinking and the teachers well paid. In the forties there was a crop of them; Cheltenham in 1841, Marlborough in 1843, Rossall, to cater for Lancashire, in 1844. Today the term 'public school' is used loosely to describe both endowed and proprietary schools, but their origin and early history are very different. With these schools and the addition of some good private schools by the middle of the nineteenth century the middle classes had moulded that part of the educational apparatus of the country in which they were personally interested to serve their needs.

During the years in which a new pattern of education was evolving middle class men had been growing in self-confidence. Increasingly they were coming to consider themselves as the most valuable section of society, providing as they did both the brains to run industry and the capital with which to finance it, as well as the solid morality with which to permeate the classes above and below them, thereby imposing their standards on the nation as a whole. To some extent the middle class owed their sense of superiority to the writings of the philosophers and economists, themselves an articulate group of professional men. If one major factor shaping the climate of opinion of Regency and Victorian England was religion, the other stemmed from their writings. An early and significant clash between the defenders and the critics of the old order was that between Edmund Burke and Tom Paine. The former's *Reflections on the French Revolution* postulated a view of society that to many people was becoming more outmoded every year, as the old 'ruling classes' seemed to stand more and more for selfish rather than national interests. In sharp answer to it Paine's *Rights of Man* made articulate the aspirations of ordinary men to share the responsibilities and privileges that hitherto had been regarded as pertaining only to those who had a stake in the country, in other words to men of property. Pain's arguments found more acceptance with working men than they did with the propertied middle classes, to whom they seemed to open the door to a revolutionary attack on the structure of society that went too far for their liking. The doctrine preached in the *Rights of Man* threatened to undermine the great law of subordination. The new industrialists had no more desire than the old landowners to share power with the mass of their workers.

The middle class point of view with regard to the distribution of political power is admirably illustrated by James Mill in his *Essay on Government*. In theory he accepted the concept of democratic government, because he believed that representative government was the only way to secure good government. He was equally convinced that the wide distribution of voting power could only work if the mass of the voters were prepared to be guided by the wisdom of the 'middle ranks'. With this reservation he made a trenchant attack on the old privileged society which still dominated the political scene when his *Essay* was published in 1820. His attack made admirable sense to the entrepreneurial class. The shortcomings of the existing mode of government were obvious to them. So were the shortcomings of society, and they argued that before either could be shaped more to their liking it would be necessary for them to secure the control of the legislature. Though the end product at which they aimed was different, these views were shared by working class politicians, organizers like Place, writers like Cobbett and demagogues like Orator Hunt. For workers and capitalists alike the road to Utopia lay through the securing of the franchise. Untried remedies are apt to be seen as universal panaceas, and this was no exception. Such views did much to form the day-to-day climate of opinion and to bring out the essential antagonism between a ministry that accepted as right and proper the society of the past and those growing sections of society which no longer found it adequate for their needs. Men's politics were increasingly becoming dependent not on their connections but on their class.

The economists made a considerable contribution to this growing consciousness of class. They were the repositories of the wisdom of the new age, not less so because what they wrote could, like statistics, be made to support diametrically opposed views. To understand therefore the way in which men argued about society and discussed its problems some acquaintance with what the leading economists had to say is a *sine qua non*. Each wrote against the background of his own age. Each concentrated on what seemed to be its most pressing problem at the time of writing. When Adam Smith wrote *The Wealth of Nations* (1776) the mechanization of industry and the urbanization of the industrial worker had hardly made any dent on the society about which he wrote. His advocacy of Free Trade did not envisage the Britain to which it was later to be applied. In advocating the removal of the stranglehold of economic regulation he aimed at freeing commerce from the narrow vested interests of merchant groups in order to make it serve the wider interests of the nation. He wanted to make existing society more efficient and could hardly have imagined the circumstances in which his teaching would be applied in conditions outside his terms of reference. When Malthus wrote his first *Essay on Population* he too was concerned with a pressing contemporary problem. At the time when he wrote the question as to whether the population was increasing or decreasing was being hotly debated, as until 1801, there were no official census figures available. Malthus argued that it must increase inexorably until the increase forced the majority, that is the labouring poor, to the verge of subsistence, because by its very nature population multiplied more rapidly than the resources of food needed to maintain it. War, disease, due to semi-starvation and vice, were, he wrote, the grim forces that alone kept the two in equilibrium. In later editions he modified his views to the extent that he now argued that this appalling and endlessly repetitive situation could be controlled if men would refrain from marriage until they were in a position to maintain a family, in the meantime following a conduct strictly moral. This, he assumed, by lessening the number of men and women, would increase the demand for labour, so leading to better wages and a higher standard of living for the labouring poor who, because they would no longer be pressing on the means of subsistence, would not be forced to take subsistence wages by the competition of an over-stocked labour market.

Malthus was analysing a fundamental problem of contemporary society; he was not criticizing its structure or the distribution of wealth within it. He thought of the labouring poor as functioning within the accepted social hierarchy. Nor did he grasp the fact that the merging technological changes and the more efficient use of land and natural resources were capable of putting off the catastrophe that he foresaw to some indefinite period as far as Britain was concerned. The effect of these limitations was to give him an even more profound influence on contemporary thinking because his readers also believed that disaster was just round the corner. His writings provided an armoury of weapons for all those people who for one reason or another thought the Poor Laws ought to be either abolished or made tougher. Many people blamed the Poor Laws for the dreaded population increase, asserting that they encouraged improvident marriages and large families. By helping an unmarried woman to keep her illegitimate children, opponents of parish relief argued, it encouraged immorality and more unwanted babies. In their eyes the total effect of the granting of poor relief was to make the improvident poor still more improvident and so eventually to increase rather than alleviate poverty.

Most middle class ratepayers would have agreed with Malthus, but it was David Ricardo whose writing provided the new capitalists with their best self-justification for their value to society. A Jew who had made a very large fortune in a surprisingly short time on the stock market, Ricardo was encouraged by that middle class champion James Mill to publish his *Principles of Political Economy* (1817). His avowed aim was to enquire into the laws 'which determine the division of the produce of industry among the classes who concur in its foundation'. Basically his treatise was an attack on the landowners and an apologia for capital. The background of his thesis was strictly contemporary. During the war much marginal land had been taken into cultivation which was only profitable when prices were high. If men were ready to pay rent for poor land, he argued, they were prepared to pay a higher rent for better land and the difference between the two came to the landlord in the form of an unearned increment. According to this theory of rent the whole of the surplus of the soil, apart from the modest profits needed to induce men to rent and cultivate land, went to the landlord, who was a mere parasite battening on the other two producers of wealth, capital and labour. In that case they had no right to a specially privileged position in society. To Ricardo and his followers the capitalist was the king-pin of the economy. This was especially true of the industrial entrepreneur, whose function it was to supply the means of production, gauge the market, employ labour, take risks and at the same time face competition from which the land-owner was exempt. These views were welcomed by the manufac-turers because they highlighted their usefulness and threw into sharp relief the distribution of political power that gave to the parasitical landowners a control denied to the class who were largely responsible for the creation of wealth from which the latter were benefiting.

The middle class received a further injection of moral solidarity from Bentham's writings. If men were to be judged by their utility to society then they believed that the middle class must be placed high on the ladder of merit. It was they who produced wealth; it was they who, by accumulating their profits instead of spending them on per-sonal gratification, added to the capital of the nation. This in its turn produced still more wealth. It was they who furnished the country with its professional men, its educationalists, its scientists. To do these things was to perform a moral act, whether the individual were a Christian or a freethinker. Morals in this sense were no longer the prerogative of the religious. Indeed in many ways Victorian morality, with its emphasis on the old Puritan virtues of frugality and hard work, was as much the product of the Utilitarians, who provided the social justification for these qualities, as it was of the evangelicals. From the Benthamites also came the stress on efficiency, on examinations for professional competence rather than reliance on the patronage of the past. It was from them that the small group of professional civil servants was recruited—men like Chadwick, who gave the state a new competence and blueprints for dealing with an industrial, capitalistic world, that marked its conquest of the past by the fanfare of the Great Exhibition. By then the middle classes had imposed their own standards of thought and behaviour on upper and lower classes alike. The fashionable world might merely keep its amours under cover, the great cities were still full of gambling dens, brothels and gin palaces, but 'keeping up with the Joneses' now meant keeping up in respectability as well as in the solid appurtenances of material well-being. For many people the strain was too great with the result that they were almost forced into the hypocrisy that is one characteristic of Victorian England. Because widespread pockets of every kind of poverty and misery still existed many fenced themselves in against compassion by appealing to the teaching of the economists that labour must find its own market level, that a beneficent competition must eliminate the weak and inefficient for the benefit of the greatest number, steeling themselves by the belief that everyone could by his own exertion raise himself above the line of poverty and crime. It was comforting for the successful to believe that failure was the reward of lack of effort and moral fibre. The popularity of Samuel Smiles's *Self Help* is symptomatic of Victorian England.

Even some women were beginning to wonder what they could do to improve their position in society. Harriet Taylor wrote bitterly: 'All that has yet been said respecting the social conditions of women goes on the assumption of their inferiority. People do not complain of their state being degraded at all . . . they complain that it is *too much degraded*.' (Quoted in St John Michael Packe, *The Life of John Stuart Mill* (1954), 125.) Traditionally women had been thought of as second class citizens, incapable of managing their own lives and controlling their own property, though history and reality had often given the lie to this assumption. Nevertheless it was a man's world, in which women were supposed to protect their interests by influence and charm, not by unbecoming claims to equality with men. Until a woman married she was subordinate to her father. If a **working girl,** she was part of the economic unit of the family; if a lady, she remained under her parents' roof, obeying her father and inferior to the sons. In theory, at twenty-one she could hold property and marry without her father's consent, but this independence was only possible for a woman of property. As Jane Austen's Emma observed, 'a single woman of good fortune is always respectable'. These were the lucky few. There was no tradition that daughters, whose parents could keep them, should earn their living; indeed with the state of female education, and the limitations which Victorian masculine opinion imposed on them, there was very little that a middle class girl could have undertaken in the way of paid employment. Women were 'delicate females'; they were not supposed to soil their hands; they must never frequent places where coarse language might sully the purity of their minds. Music, painting, embroidery, great attention to their toilette, the reading of innumerable novels, the oversight of the servants and, as a sop to religion and social responsibility, a little condescending 'good works' was supposed to fill their days. To this must be added visiting, gossip and the delights of shopping. Their business, and that of their mothers, was to find a husband; a husband at least brought with him the status of a wife and a house of one's own. As Charlotte Lucas reflected when she accepted the odious Mr Collins, 'Mr Collins to be sure was neither sensible nor agreeable ... But he would still be her husband. Without thinking highly of either men or matrimony, marriage had always been her object: it was the only honourable provision for well educated young women of small fortune, and however uncertain of giving happiness, must be their pleasantest preservation from want' (*Pride and Prejudice*). The alternative was to become an unwanted old maid. The census returns for 1851 show how genuine this fear might be; 24.86 per cent of the female population under the age of 30 were unmarried, 17.89 of those under 35 and 11.88 of those over 50.

A middle class woman who remained unmarried, who had no fortune, and whose parents, for some reason or another, could make no provision for her, had three possibilities before her. She might become a governess: she might earn a meagre living with her needle; she might, like Miss Mitford the author of *Our Village*, rely on her pen. When Miss Matty, the delightful old maid in *Cranford*, faced by the loss of her income caused by a bank failure, decided to open a little shop in Cranford she was conscious of the social daring of her venture. Ladies did not keep shops. Yet the bankruptcy of a father or the failure of a bank were all too frequent in the business jungle of the early nineteenth century. Because the general standard of education was low, and no training was required, most young women so situated became governesses, even though later, like the Brontë sisters, they turned to writing. Generally speaking this was a heartbreaking and thankless life. Often their employers treated them as superior servants, and gave them little backing against troublesome or naughty children, while by the servants they were often ignored and held in contempt. Miss Weeton, whose diary is so revealing, wrote bitterly: 'A governess is almost shut out of society; not choosing to associate with servants, and not being treated as an equal by the head of the house or their visitors, she must possess some fortitude and strength of mind to render herself tranquil or happy.' (Weeton, op. cit. 62.) Clare was luckier in her relations with Lady Cumnor in *Wives and Daughters*, but she was clever enough and pliable enough to ingratiate herself with the family. It is illuminating that her youngest ex-pupil, Lady Harriet, described her as 'not very wise certainly; but she is so useful and agreeable, and has such pleasant manners, I should have thought any one who wasn't particular about education would have been charmed to keep her as a governess'.

Yet marriage was not always a happy escape. As Miss Weeton was to discover, the position of a married woman was in some ways even more one of bondage. In law she became her husband's chattel. Unless legal settlements had been made before marriage, all her property passed to her husband, who had a right even to any money she might earn. Everything she had was his, even her children, to whom, if he pleased, he might deny access until 1839 when the Infants' Custody Act allowed a woman of irreproachable character to petition the Lord Chancellor for a hearing before a special court. An absolute divorce, with the right to re-marry, could only be got by a private Act of Parliament, though for adultery and cruelty a wife might obtain a separation order from the ecclesiastical courts. Without this a wife remained a chattel. A husband was entitled to exact obedience, and physical ill-treatment would have to be considerable to justify outside interference. A husband was permitted to lock up a recalcitrant wife, or even to turn her out of doors. Most marriages, it must be conceded, were outwardly placid and many very happy. Most women accepted the rôle assigned to them. Even the rebel Mrs Norton, Lord Melbourne's friend, though she fought with all her strength and ingenuity against the law that had taken her children from her, declared: 'The wild and stupid theories advanced by a few women of "equal rights" and "equal intelligence" are not the opinions of their sex. I (with millions more), believe in the natural superiority of man, as I do in the existence of God.' (Quoted in W. F. Neff, *Victorian Working Women* (1929), 239.) Mrs Norton's tribulations at the hands of a brutal husband are well known; as a prominent figure in London society she had many friends, and in addition she had the compelling pen of a professional writer, but her story is in no sense unique.

In many ways it can be paralleled by that of the uninfluential Miss Weeton. Tired of being a governess, she was unwise enough to marry a certain Mr Aaron Stock in 1814. He owned a small factory in Wigan and eventually did well. She might have been better advised to have married 'an old respectable farmer' who had taken a fancy to her. Indeed she confessed that 'If he were but an old gentleman, instead of being nothing but an old man I really think I would have given him a hint to make an offer' (Weeton, op. cit. 104), but class barriers were too strong. Governesses did not marry farmers. It will be remembered how the managing Emma would not let her little protégée contemplate a union with a respectable local farmer. Mr Stock probably married Miss Weeton, who had saved and bought cottage property that brought in some £75 a year, for her money. The marriage was not a success, though it had its happier moments; a daughter, Mary was born in 1815. But by November 1816 Mrs Stock was writing to a friend: 'My husband is my terror, my misery, I have little doubt he will be my death' (ibid., 159). Two years later she was writing: 'Bitter have been the years of my marriage, and sorrowful my days'. On 5 January 1818 she wrote: 'Turned out of doors into the street. In the anguish of my mind, I broke out into complaints; this was my only fault.' She then went to her brother who tried to patch up a reconciliation but, as Stock handed over all domestic authority in the home to a daughter by his first wife, the situation was soon as bad as ever. When permitted to sit in the parlour Mrs Stock was not allowed to speak to her husband, and if she complained she wrote 'I am threatened to be turned out of doors'. By 1819 things had reached a climax. Poor Mrs Stock declared that she had been beaten 'almost to death' and that the doctor had said that 'the bruises would have mortified if I had not been so extremely thin'. Later she wrote: 'I was threatened with being sent to a Lunatic Asylum, only for asking for food' (ibid., 176). Then apparently her husband got her arrested on the ground that she struck him; had her friends not arranged bail she might have been sent to the house of correction. Finally she got a deed of separation, her husband allowing her £50 a year, which was about what she had brought to him on marriage.

Even then her troubles were not over. She was not allowed to live within 2½ miles of Wigan and was permitted to see her daughter Mary only three times a year, which nearly broke her heart. Obstacles were put in the way of even these meetings. Again and again the unhappy mother wrote pitiful letters begging to be allowed to see her child. On 16 April 1823 she pleaded: 'More than a year has passed since I saw my only darling child' (ibid., 216), and again in July: 'I again intreat you that I may see my child. Why am I thus debarred the natural rights of a mother?' (ibid., 228). The end of the story is obscure, but apparently when Mary was older the mother and daughter did contrive to come together again. Mrs Stock's story could have been that of any unhappily married early nineteenth-century wife. Doubtless there were faults on both sides. Having been used to controlling her own income, Mrs Stock confessed, 'My principal ground of complaint is being kept so totally without money, at times when he is angry with me' (ibid., 159). There is little wonder that the wives of difficult husbands practised submission and guile to avoid a similar fate; the majority of less successful marriages were in all probability more like those of James Mill and of Carlyle, who appeared to ignore their wives' wishes or rode roughshod over them. But one cannot generalize in matters of personal relationships, whatever the law may be. Mr Taylor, the husband of John Stuart Mill's platonic but devoted mistress, showed his wife Harriet the most wonderful understanding and sympathy, helping the three of them to survive an almost impossible emotional situation. But though a handful of intellectuals, predictably including John Stuart Mill, were in favour of legislation to improve the legal position of women in society, public opinion (and this included the Queen) as a whole was either indifferent or hostile. By 1850 sufficient interest in the question had been fostered to secure the appointment of a royal commission on divorce, but there was not enough impetus behind it to produce results. Nevertheless it was a sign of changing times that the matter had got so far.

In this brief survey it has been impossible to do more than indicate the major changes that had taken place in upper and middle class attitudes and values between 1776 and 1851. It would probably be true to say that the majority of people accepted what they called 'progress' as inevitable and beneficial. But as to what was meant by progress in more specific terms, and as to how it was to be obtained, there was wide divergence. Some people saw the hope of a society cleansed of its sins and abuses in a revival of religion. Others saw it as the fruits of a rational and moralistic education. Within these two schools of thought there was every kind of diversity and many clashes of viewpoints as each group fought for its own particular objective. Humanitarians wanted a sympathetic administration of the Poor Laws, wanted protection for young children employed in factories. Economists argued that this programme was either useless or positively harmful. People who believed sincerely in the need for some provision for educating poor children were in bitter rivalry as to whether that education should be controlled by the established church alone. Dissent and Anglicanism divided those sections of the population who cared for either into opposing camps; freethinkers called 'a plague on both your houses'. Even among the propertied classes attitudes varied enormously according to locality and to religious belief or disbelief. Only an overall impression is possible and to every generalization some exceptions can be found. It is easy to forget that 'history is about chaps' and that 'chaps' vary greatly and are not even consistent in their own views and behaviour.

Yet when all this has been said some general features of English society, at least as far as the upper and middle classes are concerned, remain. It was far more an urban society than it had been, with all the change in values that this implies. It was also more homogeneous in outlook in so far as evangelicalism and the ethos of the new capitalistic society had provided a new framework for men's minds. It was more politically conscious, particularly after the fight for the Reform Bill, an awareness fostered by the growth of a responsible Press. Issues such as Free Trade and the repeal of the Corn Laws aroused widespread interest. In all these spheres the industrial, capitalistic middle class had shown that it could produce its own leaders and organize its own political campaigns. It could not meet the Landed Interest on equal terms. Society was also more humane, striving consciously for the good. By 1851 flogging had been abolished in the army. Tyburn day had gone. The laws had been overhauled and the death penalty reserved for only the most serious of crimes. Something, though not enough, had been done to make the prisons less brutal and less unhealthy, largely as a result of constant pressure from the Prison Discipline Society. The aim now was reformation as well as deterrence, hard labour, not rotting idleness. Among the upper classes duelling had ceased to be the gentleman's method of defending his honour. In sport cricket was replacing cockfighting. Outwardly violence was disappearing and being replaced by moral compulsion. Though many people fell far short in performance, Victorian society believed in the moral value of effort, that 'life is real and life is earnest' and that God helps those who help themselves. Psychology, as the modern world understands the term, had not yet come to confuse their sense of right and wrong. Man was still the master of his own destiny. They expected and respected achievement and the Great Exhibition was a fitting monument to the things that they thought worthwhile. It is symptomatic of their outlook that they refused to open it on Sunday and that when it was moved to its final home at Sydenham there was a last-minute flurry to furnish the male nude statues with fig leaves, lest the delicacy of Victorian womanhood should be affronted.

Chapter 6   The Climate of Opinion: Working Class

The 'brave new world' appeared a very different place to the proper-tied and non-propertied sections of the nation. The working class world was not uniform but, like the upper and middle classes, composed of many strata. Working class men's reactions to the society in which they lived were also not uniform. These depended on their income group, on the nature of their employment, and on their locality. The difference between a skilled London craftsman and a Dorset farmworker was, in its way, as great as that between a member of the House of Lords and a prosperous shopkeeper. The Dorset labourer was not without his skills, but between him and the Londoner the gap of experience was so wide that they might have inhabited different planets. Yet both, though they could not communicate, shared a common mood of disillusion and resentment. To the average member of the middle class technical invention spelt progress and still further opportunities to enlarge the productive capacity of the country. For the craftsman it could as easily spell insecurity and redundancy. The cropper threatened by the gig machine, the weaver menaced by the power loom, the agricultural labourer faced with the competition of the threshing machine, saw part if not all of their livelihood being swept away. The worker's capital was his skill. The industrialist could switch his resources from one form of investment to another. The working man, tied by his settlement to stay in the parish where alone he had a legal right to poor relief should he need it, might find employment there, and certainly employment at a comparable wage, impossible to find. The result was a hatred on many people's part for the machine, though even writers such as Cobbett argued that the machine was not the basic cause of the low wages and widespread destitution in the first two decades of the nineteenth century. The alternate booms and slumps of the war and post-war periods caused more unemployment than the competition of the machines.

These years were full of bitterness, which waned when trade was good and built up again with each depression. The Lancashire weavers, petitioning for a minimum wage, declared that a man working a twelve hour day could only earn 9s a week and out of this he had to make deductions that amounted to nearly a quarter of this sum. One Bolton weaver, John Honeyford, declared that, after similar deductions, his remaining pay was only 7s 4½d. In July 1818 a captain of the Oldham Militia told that very unsympathetic magistrate, Colonel Fletcher, that the condition of the weavers was 'extremely depressed'. In the Black Country, with the falling-off of wartime demand, unemployment was rife. It was the same story in the countryside. Here declining profits meant that marginal land went out of cultivation and everywhere farmers tried to reduce their wage bills. Ratepayers were clamouring to cut poor relief. Working men and women everywhere were faced with either cuts in wages or unemployment. Even those whose present position seemed secure never knew what lay round the corner. Some craftsmen, such as engineers, were able to swim with the tide and even improve their standard of living, but for most people it was a struggle for much of the time and for some a struggle for all of the time. Even the skilled craftsmen of London, men who worked for a consumer market, and whose skill was not threatened by the new-fangled machines, found that the capitalist was getting a grip on his trade and that he too was becoming a mere wage-earner.

Resentment was increased by the fact that much of the misery appeared to be man-made. It was the manufacturer who hired and fired, who decided what wages he would pay, and who seemed to live in comfort while his workpeople starved. The reality was more complex. Master and man were alike involved in the birth pangs of the new urban industrial society, and the employer had much less power to ameliorate harsh economic conditions than the people he employed believed. What made the situation even more unbearable in the eyes of the latter was that the Government appeared to side with the bosses. In the past the forces with which the labouring poor had had to contend had been less obviously due to human selfishness, and authority had seemed less partisan. When in the past through a failure of the harvest prices had risen to famine levels the rural poor had at least understood why there was so little grain. Moreover the men who profited from their misfortunes were local men, men who bought up the cheese or grain and re-sold it in more profitable urban markets. These were men who could be, and often were, manhandled by angry crowds. Though rioters ran the risk of being hanged or transported, the gentry on the whole were kindly disposed to those hit by the price of bread and often sold some of their own grain below the market price or organized some sort of *ad hoc* relief fund. The King and his ministers were believed to be benign, and what went wrong was attributed to local profiteers and not to them. Increasingly from the closing years of the eighteenth century this more traditional view of social relationships was replaced by a growing antagonism between working people and 'Them', namely the propertied classes and the Government.

The outward and visible sign that Authority was against the workers was the passing of the Combination Acts in 1799 and 1800. The gist of them, stripped of the contents of the separate clauses, was a blanket prohibition of combinations, or to use the more modern term, trade unions, to force employers to pay greater wages or shorten hours. Even to belong to a combination carried with it a penalty of three months in the common gaol or two months in a house of correction with hard labour. It is true that combinations between masters to reduce wages or increase hours were also declared illegal, but the penalty for them was a £20 fine, not imprisonment. Moreover such combinations were almost impossible to detect when they could take the form of a group of businessmen discussing mutual problems round a dinner table in a private house. It is also true that the policy embodied in the Combination Acts was not new; throughout the eighteenth century the masters in specific crafts had obtained legislation to prevent their journeymen combining in this way. In addition 'conspiracy in restraint of trade' was an indictable offence in common law, carrying with it the penalty of three months' imprisonment. All that the Combination Laws tried to do, or so it was hoped, was to streamline and make the earlier policy more easily applied. Nevertheless, by nailing their industrial policy to the legislative mast the Government was proclaiming the course which it intended to follow.

In so doing it was not deliberately sabotaging the chance of the mass of the people to improve their material position. Ministers considered that they were acting in the interests of the nation as a whole and not merely in those of the employers. Adam Smith had taught that economic regulation by the State was a stranglehold, which in the past, in so far as it had been the result of successful pressure by a small group, had often been the case, and that all men must be allowed to follow their best interests freely. When the Lancashire cotton weavers, reduced as everybody admitted, to desperate straits, in 1808 petitioned Parliament to pass a minimum wage bill the reply was: 'They are of the opinion, that no interference of the Legislature with the Freedom of Trade, or with the perfect Liberty of every individual to dispose of his time and his labour in the way on the terms which he may judge most conducive to his own interests, can take place, without violating general Principles of the first Importance to the prosperity and happiness of the community' (*Report of the Select Committee on the Cotton Weavers' Petition*, 1808). What ministers failed, or refused, to realize was that the individual manufacturer in an overstocked labour market was in a strong bargaining position against the individual workman with a wife and family to support. What seemed to them sound economic doctrine seemed to the working class sheer favouritism and rank injustice.

There were, however, still Acts on the statute book which had fallen into complete disuse but which the working class leaders, who were beginning to emerge from the ruck of discontent, thought might be pressed into service. These were part of the great Elizabethan code of industrial relations, the Statute of Artificers of 1563. One clause empowered the magistrates at quarter sessions to fix wages 'according to the plenty or scarcity of the times'. The other prohibited anyone from following a variety of occupations, including weaving, who had not first served a seven-year apprenticeship. This, if enforced, would have dried up the pool of untrained and half-trained men and boys on whom the manufacturers drew. To petition for their enforcement was not an unlawful combination; men still had the right to organize to present a petition to Parliament, or to enforce the law. Even so the Government found the position embarrassing and in 1812 and 1813 both clauses were repealed. Later the conviction that all interference on its part would be both futile and dangerous was strengthened by Ricardo's Wage Fund theory. This laid down that only a certain proportion of the national income could be paid out in wages without damaging future production and that this proportion was a fixed one. The only way the workers could get more was by increasing the size of the cake; then their slice, but not their proportion of the whole, would increase. In other words, harder work and more productive effort was the answer to poverty, not higher wages, which in the end benefited no one.

For the first twenty years of the nineteenth century industrial strife was endemic. Few areas and few trades escaped trouble; the Home Office was flooded with accounts of strikes and violence. The cause was economic rather than political. The workers were not interested in political reform as such; they wanted clothes and food for their families. As one Manchester correspondent declared, 'there is a point beyond which human nature cannot bear'. For many people during these years that point had been reached. Others, fearing that they might be reduced to the same level, turned on the new machines and destroyed them. In 1811 and 1812 the rather elementary economic warfare adopted by the French and countered by the British Orders in Council had cut foreign markets to a minimum. In warehouses goods piled up and unemployment mounted. When a man could get work it was at the lowest wages. If he could not there was nothing but the parish between him and starvation. This was the background of the Luddite riots, so called because the rioters were supposed to be organized and led by a secret leader, King Lud. His main followers were the stockingers or framework knitters and the shearsmen or croppers. The main areas of disorder were Lancashire, Yorkshire, Nottinghamshire and Cheshire. In an attempt to cut costs and tap a wider market the master hosiers were switching over to making cheaper goods that could be turned out by semi-skilled or female labour on the broad frame, thus cutting the amount of work available for the skilled men who worked on the narrow frame. As the majority of these frames were owned by the masters who rented them out to the framework knitters, they were easy targets for attack. Organized bands went round breaking frames where these were being worked by unqualified labour at cheap rates.

The case of the croppers or shearsmen was different. They were highly paid craftsmen employed in shearing the cloth, but like everyone else connected with the textile trade, they too were feeling the pinch of a fall in demand. When the Yorkshire manufacturers attempted to cut costs by introducing the new mechanical shearing frames the croppers were in an ugly defiant mood. Mobs assembled on the moors at night with all possible secrecy. Soldiers were posted inside the threatened mills and fired on the attacking mobs. Some mills were burnt down and one manufacturer, who had expressed his wish to ride his horse up to its girth in Luddite blood, was murdered. Charlotte Brontë has enshrined in *Shirley* memories of the troubled days. Miss Weeton too has preserved something of the atmosphere of Yorkshire as viewed by her employers, writing in her journal:

> Though Mr and Mrs A. are extremely cautious in what they
> say on the subject I can discover that they feel very serious
> uneasiness respecting the Luddites, and they may well! having
> been fired at in their bed and an intimate acquaintance

(Mr Horsfall) murdered, their terror will be some time ere it subsides. Even since the assizes commenced, Mr Ratcliffe's house has been fired into, I have just heard, by some unknown hand. He has been a most active magistrate and by his means principally have the ringleaders been discovered and apprehended. (Weeton, op. cit., 73.)

It was, however, symptomatic of the general alarm that her employers stopped keeping a manservant in the house because it was rumoured that male servants were often in league with the Luddites.

The importance of the Luddite movements lies in its consequences. In their public statements ministers were explicit in attributing every symptom of working class violence to overt revolutionary intentions. How far they were justified, or even honest, in this view it is difficult to know. The possession of hindsight can be of doubtful value to the historian by making fears that were all too genuine at the time seem ill-founded in the light of subsequent events and fuller evidence. In those areas where the rioters were strong the threat to authority seemed near at hand and concrete; mobs were demonstrating, property was being attacked and it was easy to find a national revolutionary plan behind what were sporadic events. The government at Westminster, with the war against Napoleon on its hands, could only spare a modicum of attention for domestic troubles. Nevertheless the ministry showed itself to be solidly behind the manufacturers and upholders of the sanctity of property. Frame-breaking was made punishable by death, spies were used to ferret out dissatisfaction, magistrates were encouraged to hunt out and apprehend plotters, and soldiers were put at the disposal of the local authorities. Nothing was done officially to alleviate the misery that had given rise to unrest. This was not so much out of indifference as because the economists were convinced that there was nothing that government could do. The result was to shake the faith of labouring men in the justice of the society of which they were a part. Hitherto, at least among the uneducated poor, there had been a deep-rooted belief that, although their immediate masters might use them ill, if the King and Parliament knew of their grievances and sufferings, their rights would be protected. The Luddites were not innovators; if they broke machinery it was because they wanted to return to traditional practices. If they rioted for food it was to force dealers and shopkeepers to charge the accustomed prices. That new economic forces were making it impossible to put the clock back was something they could not grasp.

All they knew was that their rulers had failed them and that their employers were exploiting them. Men's reactions to this situation varied with their background. Men like Hardy and Place, who read widely and thought long, and Londoners, living at least on the fringe of the political world, were not aiming at overthrowing existing society by force. They had no intention of staging their own version of what, often inaccurately, they thought that the revolutionaries had done for France. But they were revolutionaries in the sense that they had been forced to realize that they could no longer rely on the gentry to protect their interests, and that only when some share of political power had been secured by them and their fellows could such protection be achieved. But to the great mass of the population these desperate years brought not a programme for the future but a sense of overwhelming bitterness. Though the Combination Acts were considerably less effective than the Government had expected, merely driving the workers' activities underground, their existence was a constant reminder of the antagonistic attitude of society towards their aspirations. When working men were transported, or hanged, for acts of violence, or imprisoned for combining to secure a living wage, they began to realize that 'if they did not hang together they would hang separately'. Though the Combination Acts were repealed in 1824 (a repeal modified by new legislation in 1825—after that date it was no longer a criminal act to belong to a combination to raise wages or shorten hours) the methods by which they could enforce their claims were still largely illegal. Resentment remained and it was in these years that wage-earners became increasingly conscious that whatever their trade or locality they shared a basic community of interests. With this realization the birth of a class society was well under way.

It is not surprising that the working class began to look elsewhere for remedies. This caused a split in their ranks and considerable difference of opinion. The earliest leadership came not from the cotton operatives of the north, or from the croppers of the west and Yorkshire but from the small master craftsmen of London. These men were highly intelligent and self-educated with something of a metropolitan outlook. The remedy to which they looked was therefore political, believing that the way to improvement lay through parliamentary reform. Their following was largely drawn from the craftsmen of London and their first bible was Tom Paine's *Rights of Man*. Later William Cobbett's *Political Register* provided them with a platform for their views. In the fight for the Reform Bill the Radicals at Westminster were glad to have them as allies. Though Hardy, an original founding member of the London Corresponding Society, had been tried for sedition in 1794, both he and Francis Place were men who eschewed violence and believed in negotiation and political pressure. But for most of the working class this programme had no appeal. They wanted something more immediate, more drastic, and looked to violence rather than to reason to improve their position. If society had to be overturned to give them their rights, they had no aversion to overturning it. Life had done little to indoctrinate them against violence; it was part of the everyday world around them. Violent death was an ever-present hazard in mining communities. Many factory workers had been strapped and beaten when children in order to keep them awake at the end of a twelve hour day. Drink was one of the alleviations of life, and drink led to fights. Prison life was brutal, death or transportation in overcrowded, unhealthy ships was the penalty for many offences for which their consciences could not condemn them. To them the Law was something that prevented them from obtaining their rights rather than something that protected them and for the Law they had little respect. So there were always some men ready to advocate desperate courses. Such attitudes were far from being universal. In the prosperous times of the late eighteenth century the more skilled weavers had been a highly respectable body of men, their houses were well furnished, their standing apparently secure. Even as late as 1818 their conduct was described as 'so proper and orderly that the strongest sympathy is excited towards them in every feeling mind' (Aspinall, op. cit., 251). It was falling earnings and near-destitution that turned them into rioters when no other course seemed open. Fear did the same to the croppers. But in bad times it was the men of action who swayed their fellows, not the men of resignation. Indeed one reason for the unpopularity of the Methodists was that they advocated patience and non-violence. In the first two decades of the nineteenth century the climate of working class opinion is best judged by the spread of illegal combinations and the amount of machine-breaking that took place.

There were enough scattered incidents to show that the workers were in the mood to take the law into their own hands. Because combinations to discuss wages and hours were unlawful until 1824, in order to guard against betrayal men who joined were 'twisted in' by the swearing of horrific oaths pledging them to secrecy. Not all the men who joined did so voluntarily. Persuasion was often backed by threats as to what might happen if a man stood out against his fellows. If manufacturers brought in blackleg labour in the course of a strike, the reaction of the local workmen was again violent. The intruders were beaten up, and on a few occasions the terrible weapon of throwing vitriol to maim and disfigure was employed. Not content with destroying machines some extremists burnt, or tried to burn down, the mills of unpopular manufacturers. Even murder was not entirely ruled out. The central plot of *Mary Barton* is the story of an honest man and a good workman who was so driven by lack of work and a conviction of being exploited that after an angry emotional meeting of his comrades, when the lot fell on him, he shot and killed his employer. In the forties this was not an incredible thing to happen, but even more significant was the fact that Mrs Gaskell did not see John Barton as a villain, but as a victim of circumstances which in themselves were not unusual. Incitement to violence was even more common, as witness some verses written to chastise some rowdy opponents of Orator Hunt when he visited Manchester in 1818.

> Ye sneaking coward crew,
> Touch him—and blasted be the hand
> That graspeth not a vengeful brand
> to rid our long oppressed land
> Of reptiles such as you
>
> Then vengeance shall no longer stay,
> The mighty flood shall break away,
> Our purse proud tyrants' vanity
> Shall to the earth be cast.
>> (Robert Walmsley, *Peterloo: The Case Re-opened* (1969), 47)

Religion seems to have done little to act as an antidote to violence. A common misbelief about the past is that religion played an important part in the lives of the masses. This is a doubtful assumption and needs clarifying. The pattern was different in town and country. For the poor, religion was a by-product of the social and political system. It was enforced on them from above for their own good, and even more for the good of society. In the seventeenth century religion was dictated by politics; people, rich and poor alike, could be fined for not attending public worship on Sunday without a valid excuse. With an acceptance of a limited toleration the pressure was social rather than political but, in squire dominated country parishes the villagers were expected to attend. For most of them it was not an unwelcome obligation; the Sunday service was also a social occasion where, once the service was over, friends met and exchanged news and gossip. The spiritual benefit conferred depended on the personality of the parson. Sermons could be nonexistent, brief, read or mumbled, while their contents were often above the heads of a country congregation. On the other hand, some resident clergy saw that the children were taught their catechism, sometimes instructed them in reading, and inculcated the habit, if no more, of going to church. In rural areas this tradition died hard. For country people the church calendar was closely intertwined with the seasons of the year. The plough was blessed on Rogation Sunday, hirings took place at Michaelmas, Easter and Christmas were seasons of rejoicing when even the poor got some crumbs of good cheer. Harvest Home was celebrated in the parish church, the patronal festival might be marked with a fair or feast. Moreover in isolated districts superstition and religion were often closely mingled, producing some very odd and un-Christian results. The cross was a useful weapon against witchcraft and spells.

In London and the big towns the situation was different. In the middle ages the churches, as their size and number indicate, had been sufficient for all to come to mass. But by the eighteenth century an increase in the urban population had been accompanied by a decrease in faith, and in the money that faith produces to build new churches. This lack of churches, serious though it was in some rapidly developing districts, was probably not the reason why the urban poor ignored them. Church was not a social occasion for them. Poverty too often meant lice and unwashed bodies that stank. Even when poor men or women were reasonably clean their clothes still contrasted sharply with those of the middling sort, who made up most of the congregation. Moreover there was no one to see that they came to church; no one to drive, persuade or welcome them. The chapels were little better, at least in London and the bigger towns. Wesley's work had been done largely among the labouring poor, but the converted, turning to a sober and disciplined way of life, had tended to prosper. Wesleyan congregations therefore came more and more to be composed of the lower middle class, who felt themselves alien to the class below them, on whose way of life they had turned their backs. This was true of Wesleyan congregations everywhere. In the mining villages, where he had done so much of his preaching, the chapel was a potent social force holding the community together and marking it off from the Anglican gentry of the countryside. This was particularly the case in Wales. But the Methodist Conference often appeared to be more interested in Foreign Missions than in efforts to revive religion in the towns. The Primitive Methodists did a little more, but they were not a large body. The Congregationalists had a Home Missionary Society, organized in 1819, but its funds again were small. The majority of their members were middle class. The bastion of religion in the new industrial towns was therefore largely manned only by Roman Catholic priests who concentrated on the immigrant Irish.

The countryman when he first came to a town continued his church-going habits for a time. Joseph Arch recalled that his father, an ex-agricultural worker, used to attend, but his environment and the lack of pastoral care discouraged his children from following their father's example. Until the Tractarians came to feel that their duty lay there, working class parishes, many of which were deplorable slums did not appeal to the gentry, who largely made up the beneficed clergy. Moreover the working man often had a grudge against the gentry. As we have seen many of them were magistrates and as such concerned with prosecutions for the breach of the Combination acts. The more dynamic of the working class were frequently freethinkers, an attitude that enabled them to reject the social implications that had become part of the traditional outlook of both the Anglicans and the Methodists. Ministers, worried by the volume of anti-government feeling that was running like a forest fire through the working class, were inclined to attribute it to the lack of religion among the masses. They therefore tried to counter it by subsidizing the building of new churches, and by endowing new benefices in populous districts. Certainly the new churches remained half-empty. It is revealing of current social thinking that because these churches were intended for working people they were built as cheaply as possible. Nor were they adequately endowed, which meant that pew rents had to be charged, which meant that eventually such congregations as they attracted were drawn from the middle class and not the people for whom they had been intended.

It is not surprising that the amalgam of religion and social deference that the Anglican clergy preached failed to influence working class thinking. Literary propaganda was equally ineffective. At the close of the eighteenth century Hannah More, whom Cobbett described as 'that prime old prelate in petticoats, that choice tool of the borough-mongers' (William Cobbett, *Political Register*, 29 May 1830, vol. lxix, c. 710), had lectured the poor as well as the rich on the error of their ways. In 'Village Politics' she attacked the subservient influence of Paine; in 'The Way of Plenty' she remonstrated with the poor on their extravagant habit of eating white bread and butcher's meat, which forced them to demand higher wages, when they could have fed their families equally well on broth made from vegetables and sheep's head or on a mess of rice cooked in skim milk. The tone and assumptions of these Cheap Repository Tracts, as the series was called, are a measure of the wide gulf that separated the 'haves' from the 'have nots' at the turn of the century. So was the bland assumption that the poor would receive their teachings with gratitude and deference. 'The Shepherd of Salisbury Plain' portrays, with an unction that repels the modern reader, the archetype of what the upper ranks thought a poor man should be. The shepherd never complains; whatever pleases God pleases him. His dwelling is of the humblest, one room up and one room down, his family's clothes are patched and patched again; their Sunday dinner consists of potatoes, some coarse bread and a pitcher of water, whereupon the small daughter exclaims at their good fortune in having both enough potatoes and the salt with which to season them when other people are so much worse off. When to test their principles the visitor, who tells the story, suggests that the small son be sent to the beer house down the road to bring back a jug full, neither father nor son will profane the Sabbath by being seen in a beer house on that day. The wife, though crippled with rheumatism because of the dampness of their cottage, expresses her thankfulness to God that He has left her with the use of her hands so that she can still patch the children's clothes. It is easy to regard such tracts as the nauseous fruit of mere hypocrisy. The frightening and revealing fact is that they were not. When evangelical writers declared that it was in the genuine interests of the poor for their starving souls rather than their starving bodies to be fed, that is precisely what they believed. To put a person in the way of grace was to secure for him eternal happiness; merely to save his body might be to condemn him to eternal damnation. Cobbett's forthright comment was: 'The working classes of the people have a relish for no such trash' (William Cobbett, *Political Register*, 5 April 1817, vol. xxxli, c. 417). It is against this background that Karl Marx's dictum that religion was 'the opium of the people' should be understood.

The workers had, however, a very considerable relish for education. Cobbett, in the same article, declared they 'understand well what they read; they dive into all matters connected with politics; they have a relish not only for interesting statements, for argument, for discussion; but the powers of eloquence are by no means lost upon them'. Their early leaders were self-educated. The range of their interests was wide. They burned to understand the problems of the society of which they were members. They wanted something solid into which to get their teeth; political economy, philosophy, mathematics, in particular, attracted them. Such erudition was acquired the hard way. Even the solitude of the new-style prison cell was seized upon to improve their minds. Little formal schooling was available and then it was a question of saving a few pence to buy books, one at a time, and forcing themselves to comprehend their contents after a day of heavy toil. Even the candle by which to read them could place an additional burden on a fully stretched budget. Later, the novelist Charles Kingsley was to describe the cost in effort and health that his hero Alton Locke paid for his education. There was little that the mass of the workers could do to further the cause of their own education without some middle class help. Nevertheless many of them made gallant efforts to see that their children learnt the rudiments of reading and writing before they were old enough to go to the bleach fields or the mill. My own grandfather, William Edge, recording his own childhood wrote that his parents must have been very poor at the time of his birth, paying less than a shilling a week rent for their 'Living Place and Loom place'. Nevertheless they sent him to a small school near by.

> I do not now remember whether I paid three half pence or two pence per week. The school was only a part of two cottages the School Master living in one of them and the few that went would only make him a few shillings per week by no means a living as that school Masters of those days might be anybody that had a little means but required a little to supply the needful of Life and its Necessities. Lads of those days may forget a many things of their Boyhood History. But a few if any will never forget the school master's Cane, for they never knew when they would get it nor how they would get it. This same day school was used as a Sunday School under the Church of England (private family papers).

Many children got the rudiments of reading and writing in Sunday school, or from a village school run by the squire, who in return expected his small scholars to read improving tracts and the tales of Mrs Trimmer and Hannah More. Upper and middle opinion was deeply divided as to the desirability of providing the manual workers with more than this. The traditional view, still held by many, perhaps the majority, was that if working men were educated they would no longer be prepared to do the manual work that society required of them; they would no longer be content with their place at the bottom of a deferential society. The theories of the radicals forbade them to hold such views. Education, they believed, was necessary for the harmony of society. If men were trained to think rationally, and this they believed was the main purpose of education, then it followed that the workers would accept the middle class analysis of industrial society, and would realize that in the long run their interests and those of the capitalists were the same.

The earliest experiments in cheap but effective education for the children of the poor are associated with the names of Joseph Lancaster and Andrew Bell. Joseph Lancaster, a Quaker, started a school in the Borough Road in southeast London in 1798. The number that came showed the latent demand; it also overwhelmed his slender resources. To cope with the flood of children he fell back on the monitorial system, instructing the older and brighter children, who then each took a group and passed on what they had themselves been taught. The idea was not new. Dr Andrew Bell had been working along similar lines but had received less publicity. By 1807 there were forty-five Lancasterian schools in various parts of the country. Lancaster was an inspired teacher but he was not a business man, and by 1811 his schools were taken over by the Royal Lancasterian Institution, which in 1814 became the British and Foreign School Society. The middle class were taking over. On the committee there were some well-known names, Wilberforce, Romilly, Thornton and James Mill. The teaching was undenominational, though many of the committee were Anglicans. Strict churchmen were not content to leave this new type of educational institution to an organization which did not give an Anglican content to its teaching. Therefore they in turn founded the National Society for promoting the Education of the Poor in the Principles of the National Church. Within their limits both societies did something to help the working man become more literate, and in 1833 Parliament voted grants to both of them. Their activities were, however, little more than a drop of education in an ocean of ignorance. Brougham calculated that between their inception and 1810 perhaps some 100,000 children had, at one time or another attended a Lancasterian school. In 1820 he made his first bid to secure a national system of education, but the attempt was premature and failed.

The first section of the population for whom a minimum of education was legally prescribed were the child workers in the cotton mills. Though the first aim of the 1833 Act was to prevent children being worked hours detrimental to their health, the second, as Leonard

Horner, one of the first inspectors appointed under the Act, pointed out was to 'give time for the children to receive a suitable education, and to insist that their education shall not be neglected' (M. W. Thomas, *The Early Factory Legislation*, (1948), 7). Accordingly the Act ordered every child to attend school for two hours each working day, and in order to ensure that they did so each child was to present a certificate to that effect before it could be legally employed in the following week. Beyond this the onus remained with the parent to find a suitable school and to pay the necessary fees unless the factory owner, as some of the better ones did, provided a teacher and a school room on the premises. In most industrial towns the only schools available were lamentable, being at best overcrowded and ill-ventilated; a Preston surgeon told Dr Playfair that 'It is by no means an uncommon thing, on entering public [i.e. Church or National] schools, to observe children carried out in a fainting state, and the visitor, who feels the contaminated state of the air on entering it from a purer atmosphere, cannot be astonished at the occurrence' (*Report on The State of Large Towns*, 392). The state of the small cottage schools was even worse. They were often to be found in courts or dirty lanes, even in cold and damp cellars. In Preston out of thirty-five cottage schools examined only one was in a dry and airy situation. In one case the school was kept by a small shopkeeper, who crammed thirty-six children into one small room above it, which she had to leave every time a customer arrived. Preston's schools were not worse than those elsewhere. In Liverpool one cottage school was reported as being 'in a garret up three pairs of dark broken stairs, with 40 children in a compass of 10 feet by 9, and where on a perch, forming a triangle with the corner of the room, sat a cock and two hens! Under a stump bed immediately beneath was a dog kennel, in the occupation of three black terriers, whose barking, added to the noise of the children . . . was almost deafening. There was only one small window, at which sat the master, obstructing three fourths of the light it was capable of admitting' (ibid.). The standard of the Manchester schools was apparently somewhat better, but it is surprising in such conditions and with such teachers that anything was learned at all. Nevertheless Edward Ashton, a prominent Lancashire manufacturer, gave it as his opinion that 'factory children are better educated than children in other parts of the country; certainly better than the children of agricultural labourers' (Nassau Senior, *Letters on the Factory Acts* (1837), 49). This favourable opinion may have been based on the children in his own mill, for whom he ran a good school.

Many adult workers were desperately hungry for teaching that would deepen their understanding of the changing world around them. It was to meet this need that George Birkbeck a, young professor of Natural Philosophy in Glasgow, started a series of lectures on elementary science for local mechanics. The response was tremendous. Eventually, in 1823, this Mechanics Class grew into the Glasgow Mechanics' Institute. In the same year similar proposals were made for London. The moving spirits behind it were largely middle class Radicals. The original suggestion had come from Robertson, the editor of the *Mechanics' Magazine*, and his assistant editor, Thomas Hodgskin, was active in promoting the movement for Mechanics' Institutes. These were intended to be run jointly by middle class sponsors and working class members, the latter to be limited to men who worked with their hands. It is significant that though the latter were to be in the majority on the committee, two-thirds of which were to be drawn from them, the officers were predominantly middle class. Cobbett viewed the enterprise with ambivalence. He subscribed £5 towards the funds as a mark of his respect for the working classes, but warned them: 'Mechanics I most heartily *wish you well*; but I also most heartily wish you will not be *humbugged*, which you most certainly will be, if you suffer anybody but REAL MECHANICS to have anything to do in managing the concern' (William Cobbett, *Political Register*, 15 November 1823, vol. lviii, c. 436). His fears were justified. The curriculum covered not only science and mechanics, but also economics and politics, and the latter, under the inspiration of Thomas Hodgskin had what today would be described as 'a left-wing slant'. The result was that Hodgskin and his dangerous views on the conflict of interest between capital and labour, views which were in direct contrast to those of Mill, were gradually squeezed out. The movement for Mechanics Institutions, as they were then called, spread rapidly in the provinces; many an inscription over some dingy hall today bears witness to the workers' thirst for knowledge. They did indeed provide much that was needed in the way of mechanical and scientific information. But antagonistic economic doctrines and socialistic criticisms of society were carefully controlled by their local middle class backers. This did not mean that Lord Brougham and his Radical friends were, as Cobbett would have implied, wolves in sheep's clothing. They genuinely believed in education, Brougham declaring that reading 'was the surest way to improve our character and better our condition'. He campaigned for the abolition of the tax on paper as tax on knowledge; he was anxious to provide clear elementary textbooks on almost every subject of interest to contemporary society. In 1826 he was instrumental in the foundation of 'The Society for the Diffusion of Useful Knowledge', and next year its publications, *The Library of Useful Knowledge*, began to issue sixpenny books twice a month. In 1829 this was followed by *The Library of Entertaining Knowledge*, designed to lure non-readers into developing the habit. It was because they attached so much importance to education that they were anxious that the working man should not be misled by faulty theories of society. The middle class Radical was to be the judge of what was 'useful' and 'entertaining' knowledge.

These publications at least provided working class readers with books that were neither pious tracts nor political polemics, and were the means of disseminating a great deal of valuable information in a clear and interesting form. In attempting to assess the climate of opinion of the working class in the earlier decades of the nineteenth century, it is important to remember that there was a genuine market for this type of reading matter. Men wanted books that were solid in content and serious in purpose. Their attitude was indeed very similar to that which accounted for the popularity of the quarterlies with middle class readers. There was also a mounting demand for very different reading matter from their more politically motivated members. In eighteenth-century England there had always been some craftsmen, particularly in London and the bigger towns, who had been interested in something outside their immediate day-to-day existence. But these men had read the same papers as the rest of the reading community. Now they were beginning to want a popular press which would give voice to their aspirations and their views of society. This was in itself a startling commentary on the change that was taking place in British society. This does not mean that the skilled crasftman of the past had no interest in the politics of the day. Foreign visitors to eighteenth-century London had been surprised to find artisans in coffee houses reading the news sheets; after 1760, when the provincial press grew rapidly, it was not unusual for journeymen and craftsmen to gather in some tavern to hear the latest issue read out by a literate colleague. But in 1776 the press was divided by political, not class differences; it was either ministerial or opposition.

By the beginning of the nineteenth century a new type of publication, directed specifically to working class readers, was beginning to appear comprising both news sheets, dealing with and commenting on current affairs from the angle of the workers, and pamphlets, periodicals and books. This situation was highly distasteful to the government, particularly after 1793, when they believed that the social stability of Britain itself was endangered by the new ideas of liberty, in a non-traditional sense, equality and fraternity, that were causing such havoc across the Channel. To them it seemed a matter of the first importance to prevent the spread of such ideas in this country. This is the natural reaction of any country at war wherever there is an ideological element in the conflict. It was the attitude of Britain towards Nazism and Fascism between 1939 and 1945. But to the critics of contemporary society, attacking a traditional structure that no longer seemed adequate to meet the needs of the majority, the right to the public expression of their views was vital. The mass of the people always tend to be inarticulate, to feel their grievances rather than to be able to analyse them and suggest lines of actions to improve their condition. This is the work of the thinking minority, and if they cannot get their views through to what has been called 'the silent majority' there is little hope of their criticism becoming effective. Eighteenth-century governments had used the laws against seditious libel to prosecute the opposition press. Men were free to publish but they had to take the consequences. In 1792 the risk had been somewhat diminished by Fox's Libel Act which left to the jury what had hitherto been the function of the judge, namely the decision as to whether what had been written amounted to seditious libel or not. In this lay at least one safeguard for the prosecuted author and publisher. Juries, particularly in London, often refused to convict men prosecuted by the Crown. Even this, however, was only a limited safeguard. In times of emergency the Habeas Corpus Act was suspended and men accused but not convicted could be kept in gaols whose conditions were enough to deter any poor person who had not the wherewithal to buy the alleviations that money could bring. The government's most effective everyday weapon was, however, financial. Newspapers were liable to stamp duty, which originally had been levied for fiscal purposes, and to issue or sell an unstamped copy was an illegal act. The amount of this duty had increased steadily. This would not have been unreasonable at a time of mounting inflation if the object of the ministers had not also been to stifle a working man's press by making the papers too expensive for them to buy. In 1815 the stamp duty was raised to 4d, just when other prices were beginning to fall after the end of the war. This meant that a newspaper now cost 7d and was well beyond the pocket of the wage-earner. From that date the struggle for the freedom of the press took the form of the grim and often heroic persistence of the publishers of the popular press to ignore stamp duty in the face of the determination of ministers to enforce the law by means of prosecutions. Authors and publishers now had to face the twin hazards of prosecution for seditious or blasphemous libel, and that of publishing and selling unstamped newspapers. In 1819 the duty was extended to periodicals. It took great courage and devotion to run the risks involved. That so many working men and women were prepared to do so is a tribute to their determination to alter the traditional balance of society.

If one were forced to ascribe to any single fact the great increase in the number of readers drawn from 'the lower orders' after 1790, that fact must be the publication of Tom Paine's *Rights of Man*. Paine had the eighteenth-century facility of writing lucid prose and of presenting his arguments with a clarity and apparent logic that made it possible for an untrained mind to grasp their essentials. This simplicity also helped to disguise their impracticability in matters of detail. He made everything sound so irrefutable. The gospel that he preached, like Rousseau's thesis, that man was born free but was everywhere in chains, was both revolutionary and intoxicating to a generation of readers who were beginning to resent those chains. To the authorities the whole contents of both Part I and Part II, as well as a subsequent volume on the Age of Reason, were seditious and blasphemous. His arguments were directed to all the unprivileged members of the community, not merely to the lower orders; Part I was largely an attack on the monarchy, the constitution and the landowning aristocracy. It was Part II, with its recital of the wrongs of the mass of the people and its suggestions for social justice, that struck a chord of reality among artisans and labourers, and made them Paine's most fervent disciples. It has been estimated that by 1793 200,000 copies had been sold. Up and down the countryside magistrates reported that everywhere artisans and journeymen were reading an abridged edition that sold for 6d. Where men either could not afford to buy this pamphlet, or were unable to read it, little groups, rather like the classes of the Methodists, clubbed together to buy it and met to discuss it. Paine, who thought it safer to retire to France, was tried in his absence and convicted of seditious libel, and his books were banned. In 1795 the ministry followed up its anti-Paine campaign by procuring a law that extended treason to the written or spoken word. The battle for a free press had started.

Paine's books continued to circulate in semi-obscurity and in 1793 Daniel Isaac Eaton published what proved to be a premature journal aimed primarily at working class readers. As a reaction, one of many, to Burke's phrase 'the swinish multitude', it was at first called *Hog's Wash*, but later its title was changed to *Politics for the People*. In a hierarchical society the title alone was a challenge. In 1796 the threat of a series of prosecutions for publishing Paine's books forced him to flee to the United States. At home a mixture of government repression and popular pro-war and anti-Jacobin feeling made the general climate of opinion unfavourable to further experiments of this kind. After a spate of pamphlets and shortlived periodicals working class criticism of society was driven underground for a time. The man who revived it was William Cobbett. He already had a vehicle to hand for his opinions in the *Political Register* which by a quirk of fate he had started as an anti-Jacobin and Tory paper with government approval in 1802. By 1806 Cobbett had gone over to the Radicals, launching an attack on what he called 'The Thing', and which comprised all the corruption and stupidity of the political contemporary machine, the equivalent in terms of modern journalism of 'The Establishment'. His readers at this stage were largely middle class Radicals who could afford to pay 1s 0½d for his paper. In 1816 he widened his appeal by *An Address to the Journeymen and Labourers* which he republished as a 2d pamphlet, arguing that as it contained no news it was exempt from stamp duty. This was the beginning of his famous *Two-Penny Trash*. In face of government hostility, after the suspension of Habeas Corpus in 1817 he too retreated to America, from where he continued to publish his *Political Register*. In his absence Jonathan Wooler filled the gap with his *Black Dwarf*.

The government reacted strongly against this new wave of criticism from below, a wave whipped up by the economic distress of these postwar years. Between 1817 and 1821 there were 131 prosecutions for defaming the King and his ministers, and for seditious or blasphemous libel. Journalists, and booksellers like the working class Carlile (1790–1843) declared defiantly from Dorchester gaol 'If one web be destroyed, a few hours work will spin another stronger and better than before' (G. D. H. Cole and A. W. Filson, *English Working Class Movements*, 167). In the twenties the battle raged over the selling of unstamped papers. Carlile himself spent in the aggregate nine years in prison for his share in these illegal activities. A host of less well known people, including some women, were involved in the distribution of the 'the great unstamped'. As these could not be sent by post they had to be distributed by stealth by hand, an activity which not seldom led to a prison sentence. That the struggle was carried on until the government reduced the duty in 1836 to a more reasonable 1d, and, moreover, ceased to wage a campaign against the unstamped press, illustrates the debt which the press, no less than the churches, owed to the imprison-ment, if not the blood, of its martyrs. Perhaps nothing shows more convincingly the tough mood of the working class during these testing years.

The immediate result of this popular press was the impact that it made on the outlook and programme of its readers. This was not to incite them to use direct violence to redress their grievances. Indeed Cobbett came out strongly against it, trying to convince the enraged Luddites that machine-breaking was no answer to their problems. What working class journalists did was to familiarize their public with the corruption and unfairness of the society in which they lived. They asked such questions as: 'Provisions fall and down come the wages of journeymen and labourers; and why in the name of reason and of justice, should not the salaries of the Judges and the pay and allowances of all others in public employ come down too?' The misery of the poor Cobbett declared was due to 'the sum taken from those who labour to be given to those who do not labour'. To him it was of vital importance that people should understand the causes of their distresses as a preliminary to the search for a remedy. In his pre-publication blurb to his monthly pamphlet *Two-Penny Trash, or Politics for Working People* he stated his policy to be 'to show the working people *what are the causes* of their being poor; *what it is* that in spite of their ingenuity, industry and frugality, makes them unable to provide in a suitable manner for their wives and children'; declaring that his motto would be:

Yes, while I live no rich or noble knave
Shall walk the world in credit to his grave.

His periodical, he promised,

shall strip the thick mantle from political hypocrisy; it shall lay hypocrites and oppressors *bare*, and shall leave them to be dealt with as justice shall dictate; it shall inculcate industry, sobriety, conjugal fidelity, paternal care, and tenderness, fillial affection and duty, honesty towards employers, due obedience to the laws, devotion to the country, and *inextinguishable hatred* against its worst enemies, *those who wallow in public plunder*. In short, it shall contain matter which, once got into the head of a working man, will remain there for the whole of his life. (William Cobbett, *Political Register*, 30 November 1816, vol. xxx, c. 561).

The attack on the distribution of wealth received powerful reinforcement from what might be called the 'left wing' economists. The middle classes had based much of the justification for their control of this wealth on the writings of Ricardo, in which he stressed the contribution of the capitalist and the parasitical nature of the landowners. 'The Devil', it is said, 'can quote Scripture for his own purpose.' Working class champions discovered that the theoretical armoury of their opponents contained useful weapons that could be turned against their middle class adversaries. Both considered the landowner to be a parasite, but to the industrial urban worker the entrepreneur was even more the living embodiment of all the injustice from which their class suffered. It was he who paid inadequate wages for long hours; it was he who governed their working conditions; he who cut wages or sacked redundant hands. Their sense of exploitation was bitter and deep, giving a moral content to their attack. Accordingly they took from the writings of the economists such dicta as suited their purpose. Adam Smith had stated that 'rent and profit eat up wages, and the two superior orders of the people oppress the inferior one'. (Quoted in Harold Perkin, *The Origins of Modern English Society, 1780–1880.*) A simplified version of Adam Smith's theory of value was to prove an effective weapon in the hands of economists sympathetic to working class aspirations, who twisted it into an assertion that it was the labour bestowed on the raw material that gave it its value and that therefore the profit, after expenses, which might or might not include managerial costs, morally should go to the man who had actually made it. Instead they argued that the workman was cheated out of all but a fraction, which came to him in the form of wages, of what was his just due. Some of Ricardo's writings also provided ammunition for attacking the middle class position. He too had stated that the value of the commodity was almost exclusively determined by the relative amount of labour employed in its production, though he was careful to qualify this statement to include the rewards of management and risk-taking. From these premises a group of economists were formulating a revolutionary socialism which argued the right of the manual worker to be the main beneficiary of the profits of his labour. Prominent among them was Thomas Hodgskin, who had taken an important part in promoting the Mechanics' Institute, and whose treatise *Labour Defended against the Claims of Capitalism*, published in 1825, put forward views which James Mill and his friends thought too mischievous to be encouraged. Two years later he published a volume on *Popular Political Economy.*

It was one thing to state the labourer's moral claim to the profits of his industry; it was another to devise practical methods for its realization. Here the contribution of Robert Owen was to be important. In the early days of his New Lanark experiment he had been more concerned in improving the working conditions in his factory and in producing the type of environment that would help his workers to become responsible and self-respecting than in devising schemes by which they might share in the profits of the manufactory. But his efforts to persuade his fellow capitalists to co-operate in his struggle to get an early Factory Act to improve conditions compulsorily had disgusted and dispirited him. From around 1818, when he published his *Address to the Working Classes*, his ideas were coloured increasingly with the ideal of co-operation rather than competition as the basis for production. Such ideas fitted in well with the labour theory of value. If society would not give the labourer 'a fair day's wage for a fair day's work' then the labourer should opt out of this unjust society. Instead he should co-operate with his fellows both to make and to distribute goods and so secure to the men who had made them, the profits of their labour. In 1821 *The Economist* was started to advocate this co-operative solution. The idea was attractive and the difficulties unrealized. In London experiments were set on foot to form co-operative groups of craftsmen and to provide machinery for the exchange of their products. Without some middle class backing and funds the scheme could not have lasted even as long as it did. Yet in spite of its short life the idea had enormous attraction for the bitter and bewildered working class, and in the wave of militant trade unionism of the thirties Robert Owen won nation-wide support for his Grand National Consolidated Trades Union, which once again aimed at the producers taking over the means of production on a co-operative basis. In the practical field little was achieved, but the widespread insistence on the labour theory of value, and the popularity of the Owenite literature indicate dramatically the climate of working class opinion and the desperate search to escape from what was felt to be an endless circle of exploitation.

No remedy was believed in quite so fervently as parliamentary reform. The effect of the present system was to concentrate power almost wholly in the hands of a few great political families, their friends and their dependents the wealthy merchants and bankers, though very many economically modest individuals did exercise the franchise. The forty shilling freeholder in the counties and the household qualification in some boroughs, of which Westminster is a well-known example, did allow some quite humble people to vote. Nevertheless essentially Parliament was an assembly of gentlemen and landowners. This had fitted the social structure of the past but was increasingly resented in the new capitalistic and industrial Britain. From the last quarter of the eighteenth century criticism had been mounting; the Whigs thought that the Crown was becoming too powerful through its control of patronage; theorists like Major John Cartwright began to argue the case for manhood suffrage, and before the outbreak of the French Revolution the idea of reforming the House of Commons by striking at patronage and extending the franchise was in the air. The first attacking force, if one can use that phrase, was composed of Whig theorists, like Sir Francis Burdett and his colleagues, supported by the middle class, who wanted a share in shaping the policy and legislation that affected their interests, and reinforced by working men such as Thomas Hardy and Francis Place, who had been inspired by the writings of Tom Paine. The philosophical Radicals both believed in the theory of manhood suffrage and wanted to mobilize the pressure of public opinion that working class support would give them. But they did not visualize working men in Parliament, nor expect them to take a share in moulding policy when the vote had been won. Their rôle was to back up the middle class and accept their leadership against privilege. This was not the intention of working class leaders. They realized that in the fight for the vote they must work with the middle class as allies, and they tried to moderate their own more violent wing, but they had no intention of taking directives from above for ever.

The hopes that they did entertain were extravagant; the twentieth century was to prove that in the long run they were viable. As early as 1793 *Hog's Wash* was exhorting its readers: 'Be ye, therefore, increasingly employed in endeavouring to procure a fair and equal representation, in parliaments of a proper duration. When that is obtained your other grievances may soon be expected to cease.' (Cole and Filson, op. cit., 57.) What they did not, and could not, have foreseen, was that it would be for a very different working class in a very different world, and at a very distant date, that this prophecy would begin to be fulfilled. So, for the first three decades of the nineteenth century, they permitted extravagant hopes, hopes that were encouraged by working class journalists who understood little of what went on in the corridors of power and who believed that it would be an easy task for the new brooms to sweep them clean from the debris and corruption that had been allowed to accumulate there. Cobbett, in an article addressed to labourers 'on the subject of parliamentary reform', asked a string of rhetorical questions, beginning with: 'Will a reform of Parliament give a labouring man a cow or a pig; will it put bread and cheese into his satchel instead of infernal cold potatoes; will it give him a bottle of beer to carry to the field instead of making him lie down upon his belly to drink out of the brook; will it put upon his back a Sunday coat and send him to church, instead of leaving him to stand lounging about shivering with an unshaven face and a carcass half covered with a ragged smock-frock, with a filthy cotton shirt beneath it as yellow as a kite's foot?' The questions go on and on, giving incidentally a revealing glimpse of the hardships and aspirations of the country labourer, until at the end Cobbett declares: 'The enemies of reform jeeringly ask us, whether reform would do these things for us; and I answer distinctly that IT WOULD DO THEM ALL!' (Cobbett, *Political Register,* vol. lxxii, c. 4.)

When public opinion was being organized to support the Whigs after Lord Grey had become Prime Minister in 1831 and the reform programmes' practical politics, Francis Place and his Radical middle class friends founded the Political Union, which, though with some opposition, included working men on its committee. Among its avowed aims was 'To watch over and promote the interests, and to better the condition of the INDUSTRIOUS AND WORKING CLASSES', as well as to 'obtain a full, free and effectual Representation of the People in the Commons' House of Parliament'. In spite of these impressive sentiments the Union's actual working class committee men were all moderates who had been carefully vetted by Place, so as not to antagonize his middle class allies. Papers such as the *Poor Man's Guardian* suspected it of window dressing.

Reform was the slogan under which their Press had taught labouring men to fight. The violence of the eighteenth century was by no means a thing of the past; the traditions of the mob, given licence by their superiors to plunder and destroy for political reasons, was by no means dead in the big towns. The result was ugly scenes of riot in Bristol and other large towns when the Lords threw out the Bill. At Derby the gaol was broken open, at Nottingham the old castle was burnt out, at Bristol some 110 persons were killed, wounded or otherwise injured, though, as in the case of the Gordon riots in the previous century, some of these casualties were the result of plundered cellars, the contents of which had made the rioters too drunk to escape from burning buildings. Not all those who shouted for 'Reform' were Hampdens!

The passage of the Reform Act marked the final severance of the middle class Radicals from the great mass of the working class. For the latter it was, apparently, the negation of all their hopes, and the distrust and contempt that they had for their former allies was bitter and lasting. Instead of taking steps to lessen their grievances the re-formed Parliament passed the Factory Act in 1833 and the Poor Law Amendment Act in 1834. To the working man both seemed to make his position worse rather than better. As a result of the Factory Act (see chapter 8) he was likely to be confronted with a drop in his children's earnings without any compensating shortening of his own hours of work. The new Poor Law represented a constant threat to incarcerate him and his family in the workhouse, and once there to separate husband and wife, parents and children. Not for nothing were the workhouses known as Bastilles. No measure was more hated by the entire working population throughout the century. Whatever merits it might have were not visible to them. As a result, the working classes showed a new determination 'to go it alone', and to rely on their own actions to improve their position. Nevertheless, though the working classes shared a common aim in the creation of a more tolerable society, in which a man would get a fair day's wage for a fair day's work, and in which he would not be faced with the perpetual fear of wage cuts, unemployment and hunger, there were great differences of opinion as to how this objective could be obtained. In spite of their bitterness and disillusion the skilled craftsmen and artisans of London were sufficiently in touch with political realities to know that revolutionary attempts to overthrow existing society could never succeed and that however unreliable their middle class Radical allies had shown themselves to be in the past they were still indispensable. The new breed of factory operatives and the despairing workers in the decaying industries, believing that they had been sold down the river by these erstwhile allies, were resolved to have no further dealings with them. If righting their injustices involved revolution as a last resort they were prepared to use violence, believing, as the London men did not, that such tactics would succeed. In the thirties and forties therefore it is hardly possible to generalize about the climate of opinion of the working classes as a whole, as even a cursory examination of the main working class movements in the two decades demonstrates.

With their belief in the efficacy of political action shattered, working men redoubled their efforts to find an economic weapon with which to protect their interests, either by contracting out of capitalistic society and organizing production on a co-operative basis, or by reshaping their unions into a weapon to fight exploitation. In the provinces the campaign for amalgamation of the unions reached a crescendo of euphoria between 1833 and 1834 with the formation of the Grand National Consolidated Trades Union. This combined Owen's dreams of co-operation with the creation of a gigantic engine of working class solidarity and was designed to change the social order and provide a rival to the Parliament at Westminster. Faced with the opposition of the employers who broke the Builders' Union with a lock-out, and of the government, who prosecuted the Tolpuddle labourers for swearing an illegal oath, this ramshackle conglomeration of trades had no chance of success. By the end of 1834 the high hopes of using the forces of organized labour to secure a juster society had followed those once entertained about the Reform Act.

Nevertheless the common mood of resentment remained and was to find even more dramatic outlet in the Chartist movement, which once again was to demonstrate the many-sidedness of working class thinking. The London group, men like William Lovett, who drew up the original draft charter, were politically minded. They had taken an active part in the fight for parliamentary reform and later, after the collapse of the dream of creating a new Utopia, either through co-operative action or national strikes, had failed, Lovett and his friends formed a small and select Working Men's Association in 1836. As always these and like-minded men had looked to the achieving of political power by persuasion as the only viable method of securing the welfare of the working population. Out of their deliberations emerged the six points that were later to form the People's Charter, namely manhood suffrage, vote by ballot, payment of members, annual Parliaments, no property qualification for members and equal electoral districts. This is not the place for an account of the Chartist movement, which dominated working class politics until 1848, but its broad outlines, and even more the reasons for its ultimate failure illustrate the many crosscurrents that shaped working class thought and emotions during these years. Once again there is the illusion of unity in the programme of the Charter and the reality of diversity in the means advocated to further it. In spite of the fact that three national Charters were presented to Parliament in July 1839, in May 1842 and in April 1848, and that Chartist conventions met to discuss policy, the national movement was little more than a grouping of smaller local ones, each inspired by local grievances and local economic conditions. Even its leadership for most of the time attempted to speak with two voices. The London and to some extent the Birmingham Chartists believed in moral force, but in the north, badly hit by a series of trade depressions, hunger and the talk of violence went hand in hand. The question of relations with the Radical middle class continued to bedevil the movement as the moral force men argued the need of working with them while the physical force wing rejected them fiercely. These two wings were further divided by their attitude towards the Anti-Corn-Law League, the northerners seeing it as no more than a manufacturers' device to lower wages, while the more intellectual Londoners argued that what benefited the economy of the country must in the end benefit the workers also.

Chartism, like the earlier working class movements, failed. In 1848 it spluttered out like a damp squib because, whatever the sufferings of the masses, society was not ready for its remedies. The middle class had no need of working class allies and had no intention of diluting its share of political power, while the working classes were too divided to achieve much more than sound and fury. Nevertheless the Chartist movement, with its rallies, its conventions, its press, for instance *The Northern Star*, and its fiery leader, Feargus O'Connor, did much to consolidate both middle class and working class self-consciousness by dramatizing both the mistrust between them and their different reactions to the economic problems of a new industrial society. As Professor Asa Briggs has said, 'Chartists and their opponents belonged to two nations, but they were the creatures of the same age'.

By the opening of the Great Exhibition the period of grandiose plans and extravagant hopes was over. The failures of the previous decades had convinced practical men that less ambitious but more humdrum organizations might achieve more solid results. What followed was the gradual re-organization of individual unions of skilled workers, with emphasis on educational activities and on benefits, and with a subscription high enough to provide them with funds on which they could fall back. None of this would have been possible if the economic situation had not also improved. The first desperate years of transition were over. Both masters and men had learnt to live with the capitalistic system, which now was seen to have advantages as well as evils. A flourishing agriculture, combined with free trade, had made food cheaper; the hated machines had ended by making consumer goods cheaper. Even the mistrusted reformed Parliament was beginning to tackle conditions within the factories, so that in practice the working day for all operatives would be ten, not twelve, hours. Steadier employment, some rise in real wages for many working in the new industries, and shorter hours were all helping to create a new working class image. As the standard of food and clothing went up, workers adopted the same standards of respectability as those which were already the mark of the lower middle class and the white-collar workers. This newly emerging pattern of working class life cut the better paid workers off from the mass of the less skilled or less organized. Most trades still worked abominable hours, faced seasonal unemployment and received no legislative protection; this was to be the work of the second half of the century. Housing was still appalling, food adulterated and, for the great mass, educational opportunities dismal. There was still much casual labour, with all the uncertainty it produced. Ignorance, violence, bitter poverty, gin and crime produced the same vicious circle for thousands of the urban poor. Habitual drunkenness was a normal ingredient of town life and men, women too, reeling down the street or sprawled in the gutter, common sights. Therefore between the casual or unskilled labourer or the docker and the engineer or factory operative the gulf was deep. As the latter climbed out of the slough of misery that still engulfed the former, the sympathy and understanding, even the sense of exploitation that had once bound them together, faded. Mayhew's London, with all its squalid details, represents one stratum of the mid-nineteenth century, the members of the newly Amalgamated Society of Engineers one that was totally different. There were still 'two nations', but their components were different by 1851.

Chapter 7   Constitutional and Administrative Adjustments

The combined interaction of the population explosion, ever-increasing industrialization and its by-product, urbanization, confronted nine-teenth-century Britain with some tremendous problems. The funda-mental one was the changing nature of society as it was gradually transformed from one of 'order and degree' to one of class. This raised basic problems concerned with the control of political power. The secondary problems, which had to be resolved against this back-ground of change, were formidable enough in themselves. There was the problem of destitution and the need to reshape the Poor Law to meet new conditions. There was the problem of what today would be described as 'industrial relations', the need to fit the human factor into this new world of mechanization, to secure working conditions that were tolerable from the point of view both of the individual and of the health of the nation. There was the nightmare problem of disease-ridden towns and a soaring death rate within them. There was the problem of education. How were the new masses to be equipped to take their place in a new technological society without new ideas ripping it into opposing sections? There was the practical problem of law and order. Was it any longer possible to run the gaols on a basis of *laissez faire* and private profit for the gaoler or to solve the problem of crime by a policy of the gallows? Could society be protected any longer by these methods? Would the growing humanitarian and utilitarian element among thinking people be content with this human and economic wastage? Different problems affected different sections of the people in different ways. The traditional rulers were concerned primarily with the challenge to their hitherto dominating position both socially and politically, and with the need to protect their interests. The new-type industrialists and the middle class had different interests to push. Corn laws and traditional shackles on trade were repugnant to them; they looked for a new commercial code and a new capitalistic freedom. The growing ranks of the professional men were critical of a society that muddled through, a society where birth counted for more than efficiency, where education relied on flogging and where drains were constructed to run uphill. The mass of the workers, torn from their traditional roots, were making new demands and claiming a new position in society. Everything in the first decades of the century seemed to be in the melting pot.

This put a tremendous strain on government and on the fabric of political life. How far could it be considered competent to meet it? Sooner or later, through evolution or revolution, the constitutional and political arrangements of any society must be in rough alignment with the structure of that society and with the distribution of economic power within it. Until the closing decades of the eighteenth century the British constitution had roughly fulfilled these conditions. Though the King retained more power than is sometimes realized, ultimate control was in the hands of Parliament. No minister could carry on the King's government for long who did not possess its confidence. The composition of Parliament therefore was the key to political power. Membership of both houses remained firmly in the hands of the aristocracy, the landed gentry and the Anglican church, even though not all its members came from these privileged groups. Men of ability, such as Edmund Burke, provided they had the right patron, were to be found there, men of wealth, prominent merchants and influential bankers who bought an estate, married into the gentry, or even the aristocracy, and adopted the way of life of a gentleman were not excluded by invisible social barriers. Nevertheless the typical member of the Commons was the country gentleman.

This corresponded to economic reality. As we have seen, at the close of the eighteenth century land was still the greatest source of wealth, next in importance came finance and trade, to which industry was largely subservient. This situation was reflected with surprising accuracy in the House of Commons. Each county returned two knights of the shire. These men were commonly regarded as the most independent members of the House. Though their nomination was normally arranged between the leading county families, they were in no man's pocket and to represent the county was a coveted honour. The majority, however, were returned by the boroughs, 432 out of a house of 558 on the accession of George III in 1760, and 465 out of a membership of 658 after the Act of Union with Ireland. The methods by which they were chosen were therefore of the greatest importance. Here again historical accident had been moulded to conform to social and economic realities. Franchises varied in their details from borough to borough but fell into five main categories. Only one of these, the potwalloper or household franchise, could be described in any sense as democratic. The other four could be manipulated either by important local landowners or by financial and commercial magnates who had the money to do so. In this way an assembly of landowners was diluted to secure a roughly balanced representation of the most important national interests.

Industry was less well represented. This was partly due to its organization, or rather to its lack of it. The woollen industry was scattered geographically and the clothiers and linen drapers too dependent on the merchants for working capital and markets to act as a whole. This was equally true of the early cotton manufacturers. Coalmining and the making of iron were largely tied up with the landowners, who controlled both the raw ore and the coppice wood on which the iron masters depended for fuel. Moreover, apart from the brewing industry, which was heavily capitalized and wealthy enough to be represented in the Commons, most industries were local and small-scale, supplying goods to limited markets. In many the small master was still the dominant figure, and such men did not aspire to go to Westminster. Their instrument was the parliamentary petition. Master craftsmen who could not control their journeymen, Spitalfields weavers suffering from French competition, or indeed any craft that found itself in difficulties which it believed legislation could cure, petitioned the House. Industry was not voiceless, in general it could rely on some local M.P. to put its case there, but its voice was that of a petitioner, not that of a legislator. Its minimal representation in the Commons was also due in part to the fact that a not easily defined proportion of the more substantial manufacturers were not members of the established church and, because no man not willing to receive communion according to the rites of the Church of England was eligible to become a member of a corporation, as such were excluded both from borough influence and from taking a seat in the House.

In 1776 to most men a Parliament so constituted seemed a perfectly workable and reasonable assembly. Apart from a few cranks like Major John Cartwright, who advocated manhood suffrage, the idea of virtual representation held the field. The franchise was not a matter of arithmetic, of calculating how many voters each M.P. should represent but of having a stake in the country. As we have seen, each man, however humble, was considered to be a part of some 'interest', and therefore if each 'interest' were represented that was all that was necessary. But in the new society that was taking shape this argument no longer seemed valid to critical minds. Reform was not merely a matter of manipulating the composition of the Commons to make room for a new 'interest'. This had been done before and could have been done again. It would have solved very little if more manufacturers, men such as the elder Peel, had been returned for pocket boroughs, because society was increasingly no longer divided vertically into 'interests' but horizontally into classes. Virtual representation, as far as industry was concerned, was becoming more and more difficult to defend. It was still true that in towns such as Birmingham and Sheffield, where the small master and the small workshop still were typical and the relationship between master and man was still personal, apparent identity of interests remained, but in the great cotton towns the situation had changed. Here the split between capital and labour was a reality. The manufacturers might argue that their interests and those of their workers were identical, that both depended on the prosperity of the industry; the economists, mostly middle class in outlook if not in origin, might agree, but the workers facing long hours, cuts in wages and unemployment when trade was slack, thought otherwise. The middle classes, whether manufacturers, or professional men, were also becoming increasingly aware of the anachronistic quality of a legislature in which the Landed Interest was predominant, and were in no mood to play the part of a subordinate 'interest' in that House. Moreover behind the general dissatisfaction of the new for the old lay something very like a moral repudiation. In the past Parliament had functioned smoothly because patronage and influence had been accepted as part of its pattern. Now, as more men came to criticize the privileged hierarchical society of the past, these things in themselves seemed wrong and a Parliament that depended on them in need of reform. Increasingly the old arrangements were discredited in men's eyes, not only because they failed to give due weight to their material interests, but because they outraged their sense of what was right. By the time that George IV became king Parliament no longer met the needs of the nation.

There was another sense in which the traditional machinery of government was inadequate for contemporary needs, though this was less generally recognized. Hitherto government activities had been limited to raising money to finance a simple administration, whose main responsibilities had been confined to conducting foreign policy in time of peace, organizing the fighting in time of war, and keeping law and order at home. It had been a national government in the sense that it was concerned only with the wider aspects of national policy. Local government it had left to the lords lieutenants, the justices of the peace and the corporations, except when it had been involved in some local issue through the petitions presented to it. Occasionally, at the instigation of individual members, it had appointed a committee to investigate some particular abuse or scandal, as when General Oglethorpe had raised the question of the plight of poor debtors, but in general, apart from the Poor Law, it had concerned itself very little with social or economic problems. Even when it did, as in the case of the Poor Law, it confined itself to providing a legislative framework while leaving the administration and interpretation to the local authorities and the courts. Government of this kind therefore required very little in the way of a trained and professional civil service. A handful of clerks sufficed for the manning of most departments with a few able men who were quasi-administrators and quasi-politicians to direct them. Between administration and politics there was as yet no hard and fast line. Indeed it would be true to say that the need for more control had hardly been envisaged and any interference on the part of the central government in the affairs of either the counties or the boroughs would have been fiercely resisted. As a result government had no special sources of information beyond that available to its members as individuals and no machinery for obtaining it. Only towards the end of the century, in 1793, did the newly formed Board of Agriculture appoint the well-known agricultural writer Arthur Young, and after him William Marshall, to carry out a series of surveys. With so little administrative machinery, and so little accurate information, government was quite incompetent to deal with the intricate issues which were facing contemporary society. When it came to such problems as destitution and poor relief, crime and punishment, the state of the factories or the filth of the towns, it was dependent on the private investigations of men such as Sir Frederick Eden, or John Howard or Dr Perceval of Manchester, otherwise generalizations had to serve for statistics and prejudices for policies. Before any of these problems could be tackled at a national level means had to be found first to secure reasonably accurate information and then to work out administrative methods by which policy could be implemented. Neither in outlook nor in resources was the unreformed Parliament fitted for the tasks that lay ahead.

With the end of the war criticism and pressures began to build up. Though the aims of the reformers were different, and often conflicting, they were at least united in their attack on the overwhelming power of the aristocracy and landed gentry in Parliament. This was brought sharply home to them with the passing of the notorious

Corn Law in 1815 which, in order to protect the agricultural interest, forbade the importation of corn until it reached the price of 80s a quarter. Its effect on the price of bread has been debated by the economists, but to the urban worker, often struggling to survive in the face of a depression which brought with it underemployment and even unemployment, and to the manufacturers anxious to keep wages down, it was a clear demonstration that when the landowners believed their own vital interests to be at risk they would use their control of Parliament to get the necessary legislation to protect them. It was equally plain that so long as they retained this control there was no legal way to stop them. The conclusion was clear: only those classes adequately represented in Parliament were safe from this type of exploitation.

The unreformed House of Commons in reality was far less impervious to outside pressures and to the problems of a changing society and economy than its detractors admitted. Though the immediate post-war governments had regarded the underswell of discontent among the masses with alarm, and though, in the face of the dictums of the economic pundits, ministers had believed themselves helpless to alleviate the distress which lay behind it, Parliament had made genuine efforts to understand what was happening. Its principal probe was the select committee of either house. In response to some petition presented to it, or arising out of a debate, it became increasingly usual to appoint a select committee made up of a dozen or so members who had either special knowledge of, or a special interest in, the subject under discussion. These men examined witnesses and prepared a report which they presented to the house in question. It was not, by modern standards, a reliable method of investigation. Witnesses were not on oath. The questions asked were often amateurish, revealing all too clearly the preconceptions of the questioner, and much of the evidence that they elicited was vague or hearsay. Often the selection of the witnesses interviewed was unbalanced and weighted, both geographically and psychologically. Nevertheless the range of topics discussed by such select committees illustrates the early interest which both houses displayed in the problems of a society under strain, even though the solutions that they produced were minimal. Included among the subjects examined before 1832 were the case of handloom weavers of the west, the case of labourers in husbandry, the combination laws, the state of the prisons, the use of the death penalty, the policing of London, the education of the 'lower orders' in London, the state of children employed in cotton factories and, inevitably, the mounting poor rates. In addition to these more purely social issues much parliamentary time was consumed in considering how to adapt the Navigation Acts, the laws of trade and the financial system to meet the needs of a changing economy. Though in the first two decades of the century the results of much of these deliberations were small, after the death of Castlereagh the ascendancy of men such as Huskisson and Canning and Peel was marked by the adoption of policies more in line with progressive contemporary thinking.

In the sphere of commerce and industry even before the French wars the newer type of industrial capitalist had never been as devoid of influence in protecting his interests as the parliamentary reform lobby for propagandist purposes tended to imply. As early as 1785 the newly formed Chamber of Manufacturers had organized so formidable a flood of petitions to the Commons against Pitt's proposals for Free Trade with Ireland that his bill was substantially killed, having been so modified that it was no longer acceptable to the Irish Parliament. By the nineteenth century an articulate and increasingly prosperous middle class was able through the use of the Press, of pamphlets and of petitions to exert considerable influence over public policy in matters that concerned it closely. Huskisson's legislation on the navigation laws, and the steps that he took to provide more rational commercial regulations, were in accordance with, if not directly due to, their wishes. Nevertheless, the middle classes considered that influence outside the House was no substitute for authority within it. For the mass of the people, who lacked even this influence, a reform of the existing system seemed even more vital. To secure this two things appeared essential. One was an extension of the franchise, the other a redistribution of seats. The right to vote depended on historical accident, not on any rational or uniform rule. Even before 1832 some working men, those for instance who were somehow possessed of a forty shilling freehold in the counties or were householders in a so-called potwalloper borough, where the ability to boil one's own pot on one's own hearth conferred the right to vote, exercised the franchise, but as a class they were voteless. The complaint of the middle classes was not that they were voteless, indeed in the boroughs they predominated, but that the qualifications differed so greatly from borough to borough. In some only members of the corporation could vote, in others this right was extended to the freemen. In yet others it was restricted to the occupants of those houses still liable to pay the old medieval rate of 'scot and lot' or to certain ancient tenements, the 'burgage tenure'. The results of this haphazard system were that men of equal wealth and standing in the borough might, with respect to the franchise, be on a very different footing. In addition, where the right to vote was confined to comparatively few the opportunities for patronage were ever-present. This could lead to boroughs falling under the influence of a local landowner or a financial magnate. Nevertheless middle class reformers would have been content to have accepted some type of economic qualification if it were uniform and would have put men of comparable status on the same footing, and provided that most middle class males had a reasonable chance of attaining it. Only some form of manhood suffrage would have given the working class the political power for which they were fighting. Any enlargement of the electorate, it was argued, must do some good in that it would diminish the influence of the boroughmonger and lead to a more independent House of Commons. To have reformed the franchise within the existing boroughs would only meet part of the problem. Most of them had been given their charters when both wealth and population had been concentrated in the southern half of Britain. Now the new wealth and the additional population were concentrated in the midlands and the north. As a result towns such as Birmingham and Manchester were of too recent growth to have parliamentary representation. There was at the very least therefore a good case for the redistribution of seats that would give more adequate representation to this new wealth.

Nevertheless earlier demands for reform, whether they had been sponsored by politicians (the younger Pitt was active in this field in the seventeen-eighties), by theorists such as Cartwright, by demagogues such as Wilkes or later by newly conscious working leaders, such as Orator Hunt, had been met with a black wall of apathy or fear. But by the eighteen-twenties the demand was being pressed by elements that were too important and too numerous to be ignored. Parliamentary reform might have been delayed much longer had there not been political as well as social and economic reasons for yielding. The Whigs had been out of office too long and while in the political wilderness had gathered some radical allies, men like Sir Francis Burdett and 'radical Jack', the Earl of Durham. Even men of a more moderate cast of mind, like Lord Grey, were conscious of the defects of a parliamentary system that had kept them out of office so long. They had no desire to count heads or to abandon the theory of virtual representation. But they did want the elimination of what they had come to regard as corruption. They did want elections to be less under ministerial control. Moreover they were conscious that in the newer type of middle class they had potential allies. Now that the middle classes possessed so much of the national wealth there was no break with tradition in the idea of taking them into the councils of the nation: it had long been a tenet of government that property deserved representation. There was also the further advantage that to accept them as allies would be to deprive the populace, which was considered the real danger to property, of their potential leaders.

Ministers like Peel saw the necessity of making at least some concessions, and the first group to benefit from this mounting pressure were the Dissenters. Throughout the eighteenth century they had been campaigning quietly but persistently for the removal of the disabilities which the Test and Corporation Acts had placed upon them. In this campaign they had received a measure of assistance from the Whigs, largely because the country gentlemen had been either Tory or independent in their attitude towards politics while the Whigs, who had dominated government for most of the eighteenth century, tended to seek allies among the commercial and banking elements in society. They were never prepared to risk the opposition of the established church by pressing the claims of the Dissenters too far, but, by passing periodic and unsensational acts of indemnity for those Dissenters who had assumed office without first receiving communion according to the rites of the Church of England, they had made it possible in practice for Dissenters to take part in local government. This semi-backstair assistance was as far as the Whigs were prepared to go. Anglicanism was still an important factor both politically and socially and most Anglicans were still opposed to granting equal constitutional rights even to non-conforming Protestants, while the idea of doing so to Roman Catholics came up against a long tradition of mistrust. Nevertheless politicians were finding it increasingly difficult to shelve the question. The early nineteenth century had seen a considerable increase in the number of Dissenters. Many of these were men of substance, whose influence in borough elections could be politically useful. Moreover there was some split in Anglican opinion itself. Many evangelicals were prepared to overlook differences of theology and organization between fellow Protestants who were equally committed to keeping the Sabbath holy and to observing the same strict moral code. They were therefore not unsympathetic to the Dissenting bodies. Some politicians were also conscious of their potential usefulness as political allies in the battle that was obviously approaching over parliamentary reform. In 1828 Lord John Russell, no mean politician, took up the cause of the United Committee, which was composed of Baptists, Congregationalists and Unitarians, and was leading the campaign for equal rights. In February he introduced a bill in the Commons to repeal the Test and Corporation Acts as far as Protestant Dissenters were concerned. Neither Wellington nor Peel liked this breach with tradition but they accepted it as politically expedient and the measure was passed. That it did pass was a testimony to the changes that were taking place in contemporary society. Dissenters were now in a better position to secure the removal of their other grievances and to defend their interests, for it will be remembered that in the matter of tithes, the payment of church rates, the solemnization of marriages and the registration of births these were still considerable.

Peel and Wellington had hoped that by agreeing to remove the constitutional grievances of the Dissenters they would isolate the Roman Catholics and so frustrate similar demands on their part. In this they failed. Sir Francis Burdett had for some years been campaigning on their behalf within the House, and had introduced a bill as early as 1823. When in 1828 he sponsored another bill it is symptomatic of the changing character of the Commons, even before the Reform act, that this measure passed by six votes. The Lords, however, threw it out, and there the matter might have rested for years if it had not been for the situation in Ireland. In England itself the Roman Catholics were not a strong lobby. Those ancient families who had refused to give up the faith of their fathers had for the most part settled for inconspicuous security, managing their estates and living peaceably with their neighbours. Unlike the Dissenters, economically they were neither important nor part of the modern middle class world. The masses of the Irish, who came looking for work in England, and who were popularly regarded as being a burden on the poor rates, were no argument for extending civil rights to their co-religionists. After the Act of Union, which had added Irish members to the House of Commons and some Irish peers to the Lords, the Irish electors could not be ignored. The current position was that Irish Catholics could vote for the representatives that they sent to the Parliament at Westminster, but could not stand as candidates themselves. By 1829 the activities of Daniel O'Connell had produced an impasse. It was clear that Irish Catholic voters would only vote for Roman Catholic candidates even though the law would not allow them to take their seats when duly elected. To avoid what must have become an intolerable situation Wellington and Peel gave way and Roman Catholics were freed from their civil disabilities in 1829.

Next year brought the reformers their opportunity. The death of George IV, which necessitated the holding of a general election, co-incided with the bloodless revolution that drove Charles X, the last Bourbon king, from France. This fanned the demand for reform. Wellington, the prime minister, was stoutly opposed, and said so in terms that were militarily blunt but politically unwise. By now all the opponents of the old system, radical, middle class and working class, were prepared to act in concert. Wellington resigned and Lord Grey came in pledged to reform. The long struggle for the bill belonged to political rather than social history, but no social historian can ignore either the wildly exaggerated hopes that it aroused or the wave of mob violence that swept the country when it was known that the Lords had thrown out the bill and that the decisive vote against it had been that of the bishops. The only thing that seemed vital to a semi-hysterical public was the bill, the whole bill and nothing but the bill. Muffled bells mourned its defeat and towns were delirious with joy when finally it passed.

When the storms and the fury, the hopes and the fears had died down the first Reform Act provided yet another illustration of the old dictum that the more things change the more they remain the same. Grey and his colleagues had regarded it not, as historically it was to become, as the first step towards democracy, but merely as a recognition that the middle classes had created new forms of wealth in the shape of industrial capital, and that as property owners they had a stake in the country. Joy therefore soon turned to disillusion among the working classes, who had expected much and found them-selves no wit the better for all their exertions. Moreover they had now lost their allies. The middle classes had been bought off and the Whigs were adamant against any further tinkering with the composi-tion of the Commons or any extension of the franchise. That they had never intended any radical break with past traditions is clear from the fact that they still assumed that the rôle of the lower house was to represent interests rather than heads. The way in which the seats were redistributed is proof of this. Though the smallest boroughs, and those most likely to fall victims to corrupt practices, were disen-franchised, many small ones were still allowed to send members because they were regarded as representing some special local interest. In other ways also this so-called progressive Act demonstrates how very slowly the basic pattern of society was changing. Roughly all that it did was to confer the franchise on the male occupier of a house rated at £10 or more a year in the boroughs, and to the £10 copyholder, the long lease holder and the £50 tenant-at-will in the counties. The result was that most middle class men with a fixed abode were now entitled to vote.

These changes made remarkably little difference to the composition of the Commons which remained, as it had been before, an assembly of well-to-do gentlemen. For this economic factors were partly responsible. Though the grosser forms of corruption had been eliminated, or at least made more difficult, standing for Parliament was still an expensive business. The property qualification remained, though after 1838 this was extended to include personal as well as landed property, and the absence of payment for members meant that a man needed an adequate private income, as well as the necessary leisure for the performance of his parliamentary duties. The rich industrialist who could afford these expenses was often too engrossed in his business to spare the time and energy, though some thought it worthwhile to do so. The reason for the paucity of middle class members was not, however, purely economic. It was also social. The landed gentry had always constituted the ruling classes and most voters still preferred it this way. Given a choice between a captain of industry and a gentleman of means, outside the great manufacturing towns the majority would have voted for the gentleman. Even Dissenters seem to have voted for Anglican gentlemen rather than for new men of their own persuasion. Nor would the payment of members, advocated by the Chartists, have altered the situation substantially. It was commonly thought, and with some justification, that the man who was financially independent was more likely to be politically independent also than the man who, as a career politician, had to rely on office for an income. Had Macaulay been possessed of private means he would not have abandoned his political career for a well-paid post in India.

Nevertheless though the composition of the Commons was remarkably unchanged the business and the tone of the house were not. To some extent members may have been conscious of the importance of the middle class voters in towns such as Manchester and Birmingham, Liverpool and Leeds, Sheffield and Bradford where they could swing the elections, but the basic reason for members' change of attitude was their realization that society itself was changing and producing new problems. Contemporary writers were constantly harping on the fact that Britain was living in an age of transition.

Parliament did not pass a spate of social legislation between 1832 and 1867 because the middle classes were enfranchised but because poverty was overwhelming the countryside and the new towns were an ever-growing hazard to health. This impulse to legislate did not necessarily come from ministers, who were often only too content to leave ill alone. The first half of the nineteenth century was a general period of soul-searching and questioning. Influential periodicals such as the *Edinburgh Review* and the *Quarterly* provided a stream of long and detailed articles on the social and intellectual problems of the day. Leading newspapers devoted much space to parliamentary debates. The interest in such questions as the use and abuse of child labour, the unsatisfactory character of the Poor Laws or the continuation of agricultural distress was not new in 1832. As we have seen most of the social legislation of the thirties and forties had already been the subject of parliamentary debates and enquiries in the twenties, or even earlier. Though such debates in the Commons were often distressingly ill-attended, Lord Ashley, afterwards the philanthropic Earl of Shaftes-bury, once had to confess that he had not even known that the employment of children in factories had been debated in a previous session, there were a handful of men in the Commons who took such problems very seriously. Robert Peel the elder, one of the few captains of industry who were also members, was approached by Robert Owen to raise the question of the employment of young children in factories and, though Owen later washed his hands of the campaign, blaming Peel for the way in which the bill had been mangled and postponed, Peel did at least see the 1819 Act onto the statute book. The combina-tion of the private member, who had not yet been shackled to the party machine, and a serious and well-informed public opinion outside Parliament, resulted therefore in much parliamentary energy being expended on social issues. Because of this the impact of the Industrial Revolution on central government was deep and lasting. As G. M. Young has put it, the temper of the Commons was moving from Humbug to Humdrum. Facts and statistics were replacing oratory.

The difficulty was to find some method by which the facts could be disentangled from the passionate advocacy of interested parties. Some useful work had been done by select committees, particularly in drawing attention to abuses, but members had neither the time nor the expertise for a thorough investigation into any intricate problem. The solution, which was finally adopted in 1832, was to appoint a royal commission, composed of eminent men, who were empowered to hear evidence and to submit their report, based on it, to Parliament. The form of such a commission was flexible, both with regard to numbers and methods. Sometimes the main body sat in London and relied on questionnaires and on assistant commissioners' personal reports. Sometimes the commissioners made their own on-the-spot investigations. In theory such commissions were impartial bodies, interested only in discovering the true facts, but, because men who had the necessary experience and interest in social questions were in short supply, in practice they tended to be composed mainly of Benthamites, sharing common ideas on administration and shaping their recommendations in such a way as to give effect to them. Yet whatever their defects royal commissions proved the best method that had hitherto been devised for collecting and co-ordinating the essential information on which subsequent policy could be based. Much of their work was well done and even today their reports make excellent and graphic reading, providing social historians with a wealth of detail on the grimmer sides of nineteenth-century society that is invaluable.

It was in this atmosphere that the modern state began to take shape. Traditionally Englishmen from every rung of society had believed passionately in individual liberty and local independence. Now nineteenth-century society was faced with a conflict between older beliefs and newer necessities. The basic situation was that the new living conditions called for new social habits. The countryman who kept a pig or two in a sty near his house, or who piled a manure heap outside his door, was threatening his neighbours with stench, or creating more than the normal hazards to health which such rural customs generated. Even the pollution of streams remained a minor evil when the few cottages along their banks housed only a handful of people. Country churchyards were not normally so full of freshly buried corpses that they poisoned the nearby wells. But in the new towns, when an ex-rural population did these things the consequences were disastrous. Yet there was little or no machinery by which such practices could be legally checked. Until the state was prepared to take upon itself the responsibility for both enunciating the general lines of policy and providing the administrative machinery with which to enforce them, society had to continue to feel the full force of unbridled change.

But for most people outside the metropolis Westminster seemed far away. The authority with which they came into contact was local, not national. In the enforcement of law and order communities were remarkably self-contained. In the past this had been inevitable. In the absence of any adequate system of communications linking the provinces with the centre, and in the absence of a trained civil service, the men who possessed local authority were forced to act on their own initiative and manage their own day-to-day affairs. In local government the parish and the county were the operative units. The parish, which had originally been a purely ecclesiastical institution, had long been taken over as an administrative one by the central government. This, at a time when every person was presumed to be not only a Christian but a member of the same church, was a reasonable arrangement, though later it caused bitterness among Dissenters. Parochial business was entrusted to a vestry of the ratepayers acting through the parish officers, namely the churchwardens, overseers of the poor and the constable. Of these the office of churchwarden was the most ancient and honourable. By custom one was appointed by the incumbent, the other by the vestry. The overseers of the poor, appointed originally by the justices of the peace, had come in practice, though not in theory to be chosen by the vestry. The constable, who had the most unpleasant duties to do, such as the apprehending of vagrants and of tipplers in unlawful places and at unlawful times, the whipping and passing-on of vagrants, was the dogsbody of the justices as well as the servant of the parish. It was a position no man wanted. All three had an official status that corresponded to their social importance in their own community. The churchwardens were drawn from the most substantial and respected farmers, the overseers from the lesser farmers, craftmen and, where they existed, shopkeepers. Constables were generally respectable labourers. All of them were amateurs who held office for a year and could be fined if they refused to serve. Between them they were responsible for the upkeep and maintenance of the church, the relief of poverty and the repair of the King's highway within the parish. For these purposes they were empowered to levy and collect a Church Rate, a Poor Rate and a Highway Rate. Gradually they were made responsible for collecting other rates such as the County Rate. All rates, however, had to be confirmed by two justices to whom parishioners who thought themselves unfairly assessed might appeal.

In this, as in other ways, the magistrates were the real controllers of local government. Their functions were both judicial and administrative. When they spoke for the county as a whole they sat in their corporate capacity at Quarter Sessions. As such they dealt with county administration and, with a jury, could deal with serious criminal

offences. But there were also many other matters, from signing removal orders for paupers to exercising summary jurisdiction on
minor offences which two justices, sitting in petty sessions, could do.
Many were the humble wrongdoers who were hauled before them by
the constable. Even a single justice could make his authority felt. His
was the responsibility of calling on a crowd to disperse, often known
as reading the Riot Act. Individual paupers could appeal to him over
the head of their overseer. At the head of the county stood the Lord
Lieutenant, who as the senior justice was the official keeper of the
county records, the *Custos Rotulorum*. As the King's representative he
could call out the militia. In practice it was he who recommended to
the Lord Chancellor the names of the gentlemen, whom he thought
suitable, both socially and politically, to serve on the Bench. The
justices were selected from the most respected county families; the
operative word was 'gentlemen'. Leading county figures, such as
Squire Osbaldestone, were almost automatically placed on the commission, and most of them considered it a social obligation to take
their duties seriously. Parsons, too, increasingly in the nineteenth
century served as magistrates. Not only was the local power of the
justices very great, they were also the channel of communication
between the provinces and the central government. Sometimes
ministerial views were conveyed by the Justices of Assize on circuit in
an address to the county, sometimes in periods of disorder and discontent individual justices made it their business to keep in touch
with the Home Office, sending in reports and asking for guidance.
This was particularly the case in the industrial counties in the early
decades of the nineteenth century when 'King Lud' was out and
strikes and demonstrations endemic.

   This system of local government by parish and county had evolved
when England was largely rural and it mirrored the social structure
and traditions of that age, when it was taken for granted that the
gentry and aristocracy would rule the county and the respectable
middling sort would run their own parishes. The influence of this
tradition on social and political development was important. Men
were forced to serve the community without pay, often to the detri-
ment of their own interests. They were supervised, watched and
bullied by their social superiors. Though every office, even the most
humble, carried with it some authority and some perquisites, there
was little mystique and no glamour about government. It was a
practical and often troublesome job that had to be done, not something
about which to theorize. It was the current belief that any man of

suitable status could serve his turn of office, and in thinly populated rural areas there were probably few who at some time or another were not forced to do so. Though they practised it only on a local scale, such men knew from their own experience that politics was the art of the possible and that without some standards of honesty and application the work of the community could not go on. This in itself was no bad training for subsequent democratic self-government. It also explains why centralization was so hated. Men who had managed their own local affairs time out of mind did not believe that strangers from Westminster could manage them better. The second consequence of this long tradition of local service by annual unpaid officers was an ingrained belief in the amateur as opposed to the expert, an ingrained belief that has not wholly disappeared even today.

Until the end of the Napoleonic wars this system worked reasonably well in the countryside. In the towns it had never functioned in quite the same way. Here, too, the parish was the basic unit of administration, but superimposed on it as the co-ordinating authority in the boroughs was the corporation, composed of the mayor and burgesses. Some boroughs had their own judicial officer, the recorder, and the mayor *ex officio* was a justice of the peace. The City of London had its own arrangements. Towns which were not corporate boroughs, as far as local government was concerned, were regarded merely as more thickly populated areas of the county with no other administrative machinery than that of the parishes of which they were composed to handle their affairs. Some, like Manchester, were still legally manors, managed by the traditional manorial authorities. The extent to which this system remained viable in the post-war period varied between town and country and between one area and another. Generally speaking, where there had been little change in the pattern of life, as in the purely rural areas, the parish officers and the county justices continued to function as they had always done. But in places where the population was concentrating, such as in villages where the framework knitters were congregating, or in those villages that were rapidly becoming industrialized and growing into towns, the strain on the machinery of the parish was heavy. Moreover, many of the problems of both administration and justice were either too big for the bench to handle, or lay outside the range of their experience and understanding. The industrial and political tensions in Manchester that culminated in Peterloo are a case in point. Even in the depths of the countryside from the thirties onwards the central government was undermining the self-sufficiency of the parish. In 1834 the Poor Law

Amendment Act transferred much of the management of the parish poor to the newly constituted Unions. The same Act also eroded the authority of the justices to approve rates or order relief on their own responsibility. In other ways, too, legislation nibbled at their powers; in 1835, for instance, they were deprived of their responsibility for the upkeep of the roads within the county. These limitations, however, did not seriously threaten the power of the landed gentry within the county. The justices were still the main source of law and order, Quarter Sessions still dealt with all offences except those reserved for His Majesty's judges. Even individual justices were still important local figures. In rural England, therefore, because the social pattern remained largely unchanged the parson and the squire dominated village life and the Bench ran the county.

In the towns, where the problems of the new society were con-centrated, the old system was breaking down, though both the local and central authorities were slow to grasp the necessity for change. Thus the Municipal Corporation Act of 1835, though it substituted a uniform pattern of elected councillors, nominated aldermen, and a mayor chosen by the council for the heterogeneous borough con-stitutions of the past, did so mainly for political reasons. It was a post-script to the Reform Act and was motivated by the hope of decreasing the possibilities of parliamentary corruption rather than by social pressure. Nevertheless its social consequences were important. It put the middle and lower middle classes in command of the borough in which they lived. All ratepayers, including such women as might qualify, were entitled to vote by secret ballot for the councillor who represented their ward. The 1835 Act, however, did not necessarily lead to the immediate enfranchisement of the masses of the working people within the borough, because the poorest householders were frequently exempted from the payment of rates, but it did provide a legal and democratic framework for the future development of urban life. It also provided a rough measuring stick for assessing the degree of local enthusiasm for urban improvements. The powers conferred by the Act were chiefly concerned with the responsibility of the council for corporate property, but it also gave councils considerable per-missive powers to provide other services and amenities without the expense of applying for a special Act of Parliament. In boroughs which were still in an economic backwater these permissive powers were little used. It must always be remembered that the council represented the ratepayers, out of whose pockets the necessary money would have to come. They had therefore a built-in resistance to expenditure, particularly as the councillors were likely to be less conversant with those parts of the town where the poorest inhabitants were huddled together and where conditions were worst. Where the eye did not see and the nose did not smell the need to take action, when to do so would put up the rates, tended to be ignored. The impulse to effective action was most likely to be found in cities like Manchester and Liverpool which, as one witness so graphically put it, could not sit back and allow themselves to be buried under their own excreta. It was in such towns that the middle class showed their capacity for drive and initiative in creating better urban conditions. Before the 1835 Act their main instrument had been the Local Improvement Act. This had been in effective use since the eighteenth century and arose from the practice of the wealthier and more influential townsmen approaching Parliament to obtain a local Act which would enable them to appoint commissioners with legal authority to raise money for the lighting and paving of streets, the removal of rubbish and the paying of a regular watch. Much progress had been made along these lines but the improvements had largely been confined to the better parts of the town where people who could afford to pay for these amenities lived. Moreover, this piecemeal legislation led only too often to administrative chaos, because there was no overall authority to mark out and co-ordinate the spheres of activities of the local improvement commissioners. Liverpool is a good example of the administrative confusion that could follow. When that city was examined by the Commission on Large Towns and Populous Districts in 1844 it was found that the paving and sewering of the streets was entrusted to a mixed body of fifteen independent commissioners and nine members of the corporation. The supervision of the draining of courts and alleys, however, was the responsibility of a committee of the corporation. Another quite separate committee attended to the cleansing of the streets. To add to this fragmentation of the public services the water required for both cleansing the streets and for the Fire Police, who were under the Fire Department, was controlled by the Water Department. Water used by ordinary consumers was provided on a commercial basis by two competing private water companies; in some cases both had their own mains running down the same street! Such a welter of authorities made the provision of the necessary services needed by any large town inefficient and expensive. Liverpool was by no means unique. That this state of affairs should have been so usual is revealing. It demonstrates the utter lack of experience that contemporaries had of the best ways in which to deal with the complexity of large-scale urban living. Nowhere is the impact of urbanization on local government more clearly seen than in these attempts of the largest towns to provide the machinery and the funds that must somehow be mobilized if large-scale urbanization were not to end in utter disaster. The first half of the nineteenth century mainly illustrated how not to set about this task. Yet, blundering and inefficient as many of these attempts were, headway was being made; by 1850 local authorities were carrying out duties and providing services that would have staggered their predecessors in 1776.

The Industrial Revolution, with all that went with it in the shape of an increasing and migratory population, posed special problems for London. Historically, its cores had been the old walled City and the city of Westminster. Gradually the intervening spaces had been filled up until by the eighteenth century the two had been joined to make one compact urban area. In the nineteenth century the old East End and West End of the town were spreading in every direction. First pleasant villas, standing in their own gardens, began to fringe the main roads that linked London with the outlying villages in a kind of superior ribbon development, as the gentry and well-off members of the middle classes moved to get away from the dirt and squalor of the centre. Next speculative builders commenced to build row after row of small terraced houses for the ever-growing population as people from the surrounding countryside flocked to the metropolis in search of the work that the rural areas could no longer provide for their increasing numbers. As a result the green fields, scattered villages and market gardens were replaced by purely urban conditions with all the problems of sanitation, housing and water supplies that were inseparable from intense concentrations of people. This created a situation in which what had become urban areas, facing the same problems as the industrial towns of the north, were as yet equipped only with the simple organization of the parish and the county with which to deal with them. The slowness with which the new machinery for local government was created in Greater London was no doubt partly due to inertia, but the application of new rational arrangements based on the newer conception of administrative expertise was delayed and made more difficult by the refusal of the City to alter its own traditional pattern of self-government. This was ancient, elaborate and defended by powerful vested interests. Yet geographically the City was part of Greater London which had engulfed it. There was also the further complication that most of the wealthy parishes in the West End had already obtained local acts which had allowed them to make improvements within their own boundaries. The result was that the metropolitan area draining into the Thames and facing very similar problems of urban sanitation was governed by the City Corporation, by seven commissioners of sewers responsible for draining, and by nearly a hundred boards for lighting, paving and cleansing, by commissioners for highways and bridges, turnpike trusts, commissioners of police, boards of guardians of the poor and commissioners of woods and forests, all of which had been superimposed over some 172 vestries of various types and sizes. Administratively it was a jungle. Yet to reduce this chaos to some sort of administrative order meant that the City would have first to give up its privileges and acquiesce in a new unhistorical uniformity. This it was unwilling to do. No government felt itself in a position to defy the City, with the result that not until the Metropolitan Act of 1855 was concerted action to deal with this unsatisfactory state of affairs possible.

The chief sufferers from this prolonged procrastination were the newer suburbs, parishes such as Lambeth and Battersea. Where the well-to-do congregated parochial machinery could be bypassed by means of a Local Improvement Act; at the very least the streets could be paved, lighted and cleaned. Where there were few or no wealthy parishioners the situation was very different. Here the parish had to manage as best it could with the antiquated machinery of the vestry and its traditional officers. Nor could it usually depend on the paternal oversight of public-spirited magistrates. The justices of Middlesex had long had a poor reputation. Nor were the parishes on the south bank such as were likely to attract well-to-do residents. Even in the eighteenth century they had housed the more insalubrious industries, likely to offend by their dirt or stench or vulnerability to fire risks. Round them clustered the dwellings of the poor, labourers, petty shopkeepers, beer house keepers. As more and more people flocked into London this type of development spread. In the new suburbs the inhabitants were made up of artisans, shopkeepers, and small industrialists, with a sprinkling of professional men, lawyers, doctors, schoolmasters, accountants and clergy. As public transport improved particularly with the arrival of the railways, many of them were clerks of every description who worked in the City, the white-collar workers who counted themselves as middle class, clinging on to a threadbare respectability. The poorest layer was composed of the casual labourers. Such areas were not necessarily poverty-stricken, though much poverty was to be found in them. Many parishioners were prosperous business men without any pretensions to gentility.

Much of the housing could be described as lower middle class. There was usually a reading public large enough to support a local newspaper.

Administratively the situation was ridiculous. A community by no means devoid of money and ability and numbering tens of thousands found itself having to cope with all the problems of urban living with the machinery that had grown up to meet the needs of a rural parish of a few hundred. Yet before 1834 the vestry, composed of ratepayers (few of whom mercifully troubled to attend or the chaos would have been even worse) untrained, unpaid and annual churchwardens and overseers were supposed to collect rates, relieve paupers, supervise the highways and generally conduct any parish business that might occur, with only the help of a paid vestry clerk. To Dickens they might be figures of fun, even scorn, but their position was in reality an almost impossible one. Some London parishes employed more help than others, having a paid assistant overseer and a paid surveyor of the highways; others, begrudging the money, muddled on. The burden was made easier after 1834 when the running of the workhouse and the giving of outdoor relief was taken from them, but what remained was onerous enough. The vestry had no control over the building and planning of houses nor over the initial construction of the roads that served them, but once these had been made, and had been in use for a year, the property owners could apply to the parish for them to be taken over. Roads once dedicated to the public in this way became the parish responsibility. An elected highways board rarely had the expertise to keep them in efficient repair and the expense could be a serious burden. In large parishes the collection of the rates was another burden and opportunities for peculation were numerous. Rather surprisingly, except in a petty way, this seems rarely to have occurred as a result of planned dishonesty, but muddle, confusion and mismanagement there certainly were.

One difficulty in parishes of this type was the lack of any genuine community feeling. This was something that disappeared with size. The church, once the centre of parish life, was regarded with indifference by its nominal flock and with active resentment by those parishioners who were Dissenters. Moreover most of the parishioners were a floating mass of immigrants who had no attachment to, or permanent roots in, the area into which they had drifted. Few men therefore brought much genuine spirit of service to their term of office, though more than might have been expected seem to have struggled to do their best during the year that they held it. There were exceptions. In some parishes, particularly where a select vestry, elected by the annual open vestry, managed the parochial business there was a very real danger that control might slip into the hands of a corrupt oligarchy. This happened at Bethnal Green which developed a species of 'boss rule' very similar to that of Tammany Hall in New York. In such instances the impact of the Industrial Revolution on the older self-contained and tightly knit parochial community is self-evident. But even without corruption the parishes were all but helpless in the face of the magnitude of the problems. Urban society had outgrown its traditional forms of government and to all intents and purposes in Greater London local government had broken down.

Surprisingly few people seemed aware of what had happened. But though ministers were still chiefly concerned with foreign policy, with the problems of overhauling the commercial system, and with the perennial task of raising money, and only turned their attention to social malaise when this seemed to threaten law and order, a group of men influenced by the writings of Bentham and their own practical experience were beginning to develop what can be described as an administrative outlook. To them the solution was not to be sought in attempting to revitalize the traditional framework of local government but in constructing new specialized bodies, staffed by full-time, adequately trained personnel. To such men it seemed futile to expect amateurs to have either the time or the experience to devise workable remedies for contemporary social problems, whether these concerned the poor laws, public health, the employment of children or the state of the prisons. What was needed was the innovating, rational expert. Their intention was not to take the control of local government out of local hands, but they did believe it to be essential that there should be some central full-time and expert body to work out uniform lines of policy, which should also be empowered to guide, and, if necessary, compel the local bodies to follow. Edwin Chadwick, partly through his dedication and partly through his relentless determination, has become very much the archetype of this new professional civil servant, and the subsequent legislation on all these topics bears the imprint of his mind. Local elected bodies were shorn of their powers at both ends. They were forced to accept directives on policy from some central body at Westminster and they were forced to entrust the day-to-day administration to paid and professional servants. The guardians of the poor had to act through the relieving officer and the master of the workhouse, local boards of health had to employ a clerk, a treasurer, an inspector of nuisances and a surveyor. They could, if they liked, also employ a medical officer of health. Both the latter officers could only be dismissed with the consent of the central board. This was intended to safeguard them against interested opposition, but the protection thus afforded was somewhat illusory as the fixing and payment of their salaries was left to the local elected board. Nevertheless the principle that local authorities must work through properly qualified full-time salaried servants was becoming a recognized practice in some important fields of local government. By the middle of the century, therefore, some intelligent steps had been taken to remove the heaviest burdens from the parishes, who in the process lost much of their administrative importance.

Slow though the initial progress had been, between 1830 and 1850 a genuine beginning had been made in bringing both the central and the local governments into line with the social and economic changes that had taken place since 1776, even though the fierce opposition of interested parties had confined the compulsory provisions of the Public Health Act to those towns where the death rate was particularly high, and had excluded London from even its permissive adoption (see chapter 8). Even from this limited application of the new administrative principles some interesting points emerge. The legislative changes had been the result of conscious pressure and conscious aspirations. Parliamentary reform had been achieved by the conscious pressure of the combined middle and working classes and could be described as the fruit of a widespread and popular demand, which in itself mirrored the changing structure of society. The pressures that produced the changes in local government were different and came largely from a small body of professional civil servants. Because the efficiency of the new type of local government depended less on the elected boards than on the salaried staffs, which they were forced to employ, a new problem was introduced into local government, which was to have considerable importance in moulding the society of the future, and later was to concern both the central government and, through it, the community as a whole. This was the problem of the rôle of the expert in a democratic society. How far were the wishes, probably prejudiced and uninformed, yet nevertheless the wishes of the majority of elected representatives of the community, be they local or national, to prevail when they came into conflict with professional opinion? How far was a society that prided itself on its freedom to be dragooned for its own good in the cause of efficiency? How far was the expert and the specialist to be allowed to shape future social development?

By the mid-nineteenth century the changes that had taken place both in central and local government were in rough alignment with contemporary society. The aristocracy and gentry still controlled Parliament, but they no longer thought it safe to ignore the opinions of the wealthier section of the middle classes. In 1851 it would not have been possible to pass the Corn Law of 1815. Though there had been innovations in urban areas, in rural England local government continued to function through the traditional machinery of the parish and the bench. As far as the landed gentry were concerned, this often meant merely exchanging one official position for another. In rural districts the justice of the peace often became one of the new guardians of the poor. In the towns, where the middle classes provided the upper layer of urban society, they controlled the instruments of local government, sitting on the elected boards of guardians and boards of health and representing the ratepayers on the new town councils after 1835. Only to the mass of the working classes was any effective share of government denied, though some superior artisans voted in parliamentary elections. That the majority should still be excluded reflects roughly their position in society. The hungry forties were barely over. Only slowly in the industrial towns were living conditions becoming more uniformly decent. The effect of the factory acts had not yet begun to shorten the hours of the adult male worker. The reconstruction of the early trade union movement was only just beginning. It was not until the fifties that there were sufficient numbers of respectable working men to convince their betters that as a class they too could be trusted with political power. As yet working people also took little share in local government. Even if a working man were technically qualified, his twelve hour day left him with little time even to attend a meeting of the vestry. What scanty leisure he had, unless passed in idleness and drink, he preferred to employ in the service of his chapel or his union, or in self-education or Chartist agitation. When he disapproved, as he most certainly did, of such legislation as the Factory Act of 1833, or the Poor Law Amendment Act of 1834, his instinctive weapon was the riot or the demonstration. The legal exercise of power, therefore, in nineteenth-century England was largely concurrent with the distribution of wealth and influence within that society. Considering the great changes that had taken place within the society between 1776 and 1851, that this should have been achieved without the revolution which seemed to threaten in the first two decades of the nineteenth century is a striking tribute to its inherent capacity for development and change.

Chapter 8   Legislative Experiments in Social Reform

That Britain escaped revolution during these difficult decades when both the economy and the social structure were under the strain of major changes was due, at least in part, to the fact that Parliament did, however reluctantly, attempt by legislation to ameliorate some of the consequences. Little of the new legislation was popular and much of it was pushed through by convinced minority opinion in the teeth of bitter opposition. Moreover the ship of state escaped capsizing quite as much because of the self-righting nature of the economy and the adaptability of the officers and crew as because of the legislative course that it followed. Nevertheless what was done charted the passage to the more stable and prosperous decades of the heyday of Victorian Britain.

It would not be strictly true to claim that the nineteenth century saw the beginning of social legislation in England. The Elizabethan Poor Law and the Statute of Artificers (1563) were the Tudor responses to an age of transition. But such statutes were infrequent milestones. During the following two centuries there was widespread acceptance of the existing social order, despite some criticisms in the seventeenth century from groups such as the Levellers; traditional abuses were hardly questioned and few people though it the duty of Parliament to remove them. The Tudor statutes had been aimed at reinforcing public order or strengthening English industry. Their purpose was not humanitarian and they were only indirectly concerned with improving social conditions in so far as they recognized that changing circumstances called for new controls. It was not until the nineteenth century that it came to be felt that the community as a whole had a responsibility for the minimum welfare of the individuals who composed it. This, when it happened, was a major social revolution. The first part of the nineteenth century is often conventionally described as 'the age of *laissez faire*' but this is not borne out by the spate of new legislation that marked these years, however much the nostalgic disciples of Adam Smith might wish that it were. Pushed by circumstances, Parliament was forced to interfere with the internal economy of the textile mills and the mines, with railway promotion, with banking practices and with the malodorous habits of the urban population. It was driven to reshape the Poor Law and even became dimly aware that perhaps something should be done to encourage the growth of literacy among the children of the poor. There was a new spirit of protest and of concern abroad which was to prove strong enough to break through both the inertia of the past and the vested interests of the present and to secure legislation that profoundly altered the status quo and challenged old assumptions, whether these were economic, social, political or constitutional. The mounting demand for reform that swept the country was literally a demand to re-form the old to meet the needs and the aspirations of the new.

In the social sphere the urge to attack injustice, abuse and inhumanity had many different origins. The evangelicals wanted to make society more moral, to teach children to read so that they could study the Bible and appreciate the Christian truths. Coupled with this was a genuine humanitarianism appalled by the impossibly long hours which young children had to work in factories and which left no time for education and moral training. Less disinterested protests came from the factory workers themselves who presented petitions to Parliament and organized demonstrations in support of shortening those hours to a bearable ten. Malthus warned against the dangers of over-population, the Abolitionists clamoured for legislation to put an end to slavery. William Cobbett railed against the 'tax eaters' and the Establishment. The followers of Bentham and the Philosophical Radicals crusaded, as we have seen, in the cause of efficiency, and looked for a society that should be run on rational lines. Left to itself, Parliament would doubtless have let sleeping dogs lie, but this chorus of voices woke so many that they all began to bark at once. The responsible press, particularly the quarterlies and monthlies, printed a stream of articles that showed up abuses or suggested remedies. A stream of petitions poured into Parliament and private members began to ask leave to introduce bills to promote their favourite causes. Very little of the legislation that followed was due to ministerial initiative and the number of members personally interested in social engineering was limited. Indeed it is probable that most of the House remained indifferent to social issues and were more concerned with such subjects as Free Trade and taxation. But there were enough men sufficiently interested to harry the cabinet into taking action.

However, they required very little pushing before they resolved to examine the working of the Poor Law. Nobody could be complaisant about the situation when apparently a considerable proportion of the labourers in the south depended on the parish to bridge the gap between earnings and subsistence if they were in work, and for their entire subsistence if they were not. This state of affairs was attacked on every side. Cobbett and his friends attacked it from the human angle, blaming the widespread rural misery on 'the tax eaters' and parish parsimony. Malthus blamed a too generous giving of parish relief for the terrifying increase in population because it removed the natural checks of want. The Economists stressed the rising cost of relief. In 1803 some £4,300,000 was spent on relief; by 1818 this had risen to £7,900,000. Then the amount began to fall until by 1824 it was down to £5,700,000. Next year this trend was reversed and by 1830–1 the sum had crept up to £6,800,000. This expenditure which represented 9s 9d per head of the population, fell disproportionately on the southern counties. Here some cases could be found that seemed to indicate that the poor rates were becoming such a burden on land that there was a danger of its going out of cultivation. Even if this extremity were not reached the burden of the rates, combined with the agricultural depression and low prices, often forced landlords to lower their rents. There was also a widespread impression that the agricultural labour force was becoming demoralized. Evidence for this was less clear, though individual instances were quoted of work-shy and insolent labourers. Moreover the agricultural riots of 1816 and 1830–1 (see chapter 3) were clear signs of rural desperation.

The truth was that nobody really knew what was happening or why. Each group put forward its own explanations and campaigned for its own solutions. In the hope of getting a clearer view of the situation Lord Melbourne appointed a royal commission to collect evidence and make a report to Parliament. Two years later, in 1834, it passed its report, which in its turn provided the basis for the Poor Law Amendment Act of that year. The main body of the commissioners, which included the economist Nassau Senior and the Bishop of London, remained in London and obtained their evidence by means of sending out a series of questionnaires to the parishes, following these up with visits of inquiry carried out by assistant commissioners, who were unpaid except for the reimbursement of their expenses. There were inherent dangers in this procedure. The work of the assistant commissioners was troublesome, time-consuming and unprofitable. This meant that only men with a genuine interest in the problem would undertake this work, and interested men rarely have an open mind. Moreover they were too few in number to do more than visit a sample of selected parishes. Normally these were where the breakdown of the traditional system seemed most obvious, and parishes where conditions were more satisfactory tended to be passed over. Even so, the commissioners were presented with a mass of information far too bulky to be included in the appendix of their report. Accordingly they selected what seemed to them to be the most significant evidence. Though they claimed that this was representative, subsequent critics, such as Blaug (see Reading List), have pointed out that the questions that the commissioners and their assistants asked were framed in such a way as to elicit the answers that they expected and that they placed far too great an emphasis on the evidence that seemed to support their own preconceived views, namely that the way in which relief was granted was leading to the wholesale demoralization of the labouring poor. For instance, a woman with several bastards was reported as saying that she had no intention of forgoing her pleasures in order to save the parish money! Cases were quoted of improvident marriages where the young couple went straight from the church to the overseer's house to ask for assistance. The neat cottages and patched tidy clothes of the independent labourers were contrasted with the rags and dirt of pauper households. Labouring men were accused of throwing themselves on the parish in order to be found work on the roads where the hours were less and the supervision slacker than for men employed by the farmers. These road gangs were reported to have declared that the 'poor were not to be oppressed with work' and to have threatened to duck an overzealous overseer who had tried to tighten discipline.

The commissioners were honest men with an unconscious built-in tendency to stress the evidence that appeared to support their own convictions. They did not manufacture evidence: the cases they quoted were genuine. How far they were also typical is another matter. In defence of the commissioners it must be conceded that when a man can secure from a public source, with little effort, much the same income as he could by his own greater effort, the possibilities of demoralization do exist. But recent research has pointed out that by 1832 the possibilities of large numbers being affected in this way were declining because the practice of making up wages for single people or small families had largely disappeared by then. What remained was the relief given to families with numerous children and was more like an early version of the family allowance. Then men were accused of spending their parish pay in the beer shop; today mothers are accused of spending their child's allowance on cigarettes or bingo. The poor themselves made a distinction between this bread allowance, which over a period of thirty years they had come to consider as their right, and going on the parish as a recognized pauper. Workshy people there always were, and probably always will be, but the conclusion that the rural working class as a whole were demoralized by parish pay is a conclusion open at least to considerable doubt. Indeed, even the assistant commissioner for Lancashire himself reported that he had found that the handloom weavers, who could no longer exist without some help from the parish, were a hard-working and most respectable set of men. Here the parish pay at times seems to have played the part almost of a re-training grant to tide weavers over until they could adapt themselves to factory conditions. There is evidence, too, that even among the rural poor there were many who by self-help and a desire for independence had improved their circumstances, though in general such instances were usually quoted merely to illustrate the way in which the Poor Law worked against such men, because farmers preferred to employ paupers whose wages were subsidized by the parish. There seems considerable justification, therefore, for believing that the 1834 Report exaggerated the extent to which the operation of the Poor Law had demoralized the working population. In the country life probably went on much as it had always done and the commissioners may have been too ready to attribute to the influence of the Poor Law rather than to more fundamental causes the existence of the unmarried mothers and illegitimate children which so aroused their moral indignation.

On the administrative side their criticisms were sounder, perhaps because it is easier to evaluate administrative than moral weaknesses. The English Poor Laws had been evolved over three centuries to meet conditions that were rapidly disappearing. Most of England had been rural and the corporate towns, if the problem of poverty had been pressing, usually contrived an administrative machine that suited their individual requirements within the framework of the existing Law. But for most communities the obvious unit had been the parish. Such an arrangement had suited rural England where people were well acquainted with their neighbours' affairs and characters, and where the number of persons to be relieved at any one time was small. This was work that unpaid, untrained and often illiterate men could do without it making too great inroads into their time during their years of office. When the numbers of those to be relieved grew, this system became increasingly unworkable even in rural areas, while in the crowded town parishes, with their rabbit warrens of slum alleys, it had all but broken down. Any kind of personal check was impossible. Both the report of the select committee of 1817 and that of the royal commission abound with descriptions of the unscrupulous devices employed by persons to collect relief to which they were not entitled. Apart from trickery there was another genuine difficulty. As towns became more and more divided by social distinctions, those parishes in which poverty was greatest contained the fewest wealthy ratepayers. Though legally there were provisions by which neighbouring parishes could be compelled to share the burden, in practice these were almost inoperable. Magistrates also, like the overseers whom they supervised, had no training in assessing social needs. As Chadwick cuttingly observed, a shilling was nothing to them and they had no criteria by which to judge a poor family's needs. In such conditions, both outdoor relief and that provided by the workhouse, where this existed, were inefficient and haphazard. Here there was great need for reform.

The Poor Law Amendment Act of 1834, which was based on the Commission's recommendations, is an important milestone in nineteenth-century social history. Earlier investigators had grasped the problem of over-dependence on relief, but the solution, or rather any solution sufficiently drastic to deal with it, had eluded them. Edwin Chadwick, who, because of his competent and thorough work as an assistant commissioner, had been promoted to be a full one, suffered from no such indecision of mind. The problem as he saw it was to break the connection between wages and relief, so that no able-bodied person could receive both at the same time. In this way a free labour market would be created, and the process of semi-pauperization made impossible. Few people would quarrel with his objective: it was an insult that what had been earned as wages should often be received in the form of poor relief. His solution, however, was over-simple. It took no account of the complexity of the problem and made no distinction between agricultural and industrial poverty. Indeed to read the report one might imagine that the new industrial towns and the factory worker hardly existed, so little were their problems either investigated or considered. Nor did the report face the problem of under-employment in the countryside. Briefly, Chadwick's solution was to refuse relief to any able-bodied person outside what has been described as 'a well regulated workhouse'. In order to cut relief off from families overburdened with children, it was explicitly stated that relief given for the child should be regarded as relief given to the parents. In the same way relief given to a bastard was to be regarded as relief given to its mother. Henceforth the able-bodied must make shift to keep themselves or go into 'a well regulated workhouse'.

These institutions were intended to act as a deterrent, not harsh enough to deter the desperate who otherwise faced starvation, but grim enough to deter anyone else. As the wages that a labouring person could obtain were often scarcely enough to secure a bare subsistence in food and shelter, the workhouse could not offer less. The deterrent element, therefore, had to take the form of severe internal discipline which made the workhouse more like a prison than a place of refuge and earned it the name of 'Bastille', in a generation that had not forgotten the French Revolution. The old workhouse had been dirty, overcrowded and often repugnant to the respectable poor, but discipline had been lax, the inmates not cut off from their friends and the outside world. The food, to judge by the diet sheets of the better run ones, was often more adequate than a labouring family could have afforded. Even the drunkard was not forced into abstinence. Moreover, there was no segregation of the sexes, and in many a good deal of promiscuity appears to have taken place. These are, admittedly, generalizations; much depended on the degree of interest that the local middle class and gentry took in the administration of the workhouse, and also on where it was situated. Country poorhouses were little more than a couple of cottages used to provide a shelter and last refuge for the destitute and the aged. Some of the larger workhouses were well run, but none of them had the antiseptic quality of the institutions envisaged by Chadwick.

In the new workhouses the sexes were segregated and the children provided with separate quarters. The intentions behind these provisions were moral. Sexual licence was to be stamped out and the young protected from contamination by the adult inmates, many of whom were semi-criminal, or diseased prostitutes. One hated consequence was the splitting up of respectable families who were forced by poverty and unemployment into 'the House'. Nothing was more resented than this enforced separation of husband and wife. Richard Ostler, perhaps better known for his campaign on behalf of the Yorkshire factory children, wrote a pamphlet with the lurid title 'Damnation! Eternal Damnation to the Fiend-begotten, Coarser Food New Poor Law'. 'I tell you deliberately', he wrote, 'if I have the misfortune to be reduced to poverty, That the man who dares to tear from me the wife to whom God has joined me, shall, if I have it in my power, receive his death at my hands! If I am ever confined in one of those hellish Poor Law Bastilles, and my wife be torn from me, because I am poor, I will if it be possible, burn the whole pile down to the ground.' (Quoted in Cole and Filson, op. cit., 334.) Such sentiments were common, as was also the belief that the purpose of this enforced chastity was to prevent paupers breeding. Rumours were even spread to the effect that workhouse bread was poisoned in the interests of a Malthusian reduction of the population! It is sometimes forgotten that threats of violence and subversive rumours are not entirely modern phenomena.

Though Chadwick was hated by the working class with a focused bitterness that has rarely been equalled, he was not wholly responsible for the conditions that prevailed in the new workhouses. His object had been to make the position of the able-bodied inmate less eligible than that of the poorest free labourer outside, but it had not been his intention to submit the aged and the infant poor to the same harsh regime. His original plan had envisaged separate establishments for the different classes of paupers needing relief. This policy would have been expensive to implement, particularly if suitable accommodation had had to be specially built. The result was that the boards of guardians, who were elected by the ratepayers of the new Unions into which the parishes had been grouped, merely adapted the existing workhouses to the new system. In these much of the sleeping accommodation consisted of dormitories which were unsuitable for married quarters. In extenuation the Poor Law authorities argued that people were only expected to remain in the workhouse for short periods, and that it was better that families should be split than that they should starve. Some cynical assistant commissioners even suggested that some aged couples might welcome separation from their life partners!

However unexceptionable the intentions of the Poor Law Commissioners, throughout the nineteenth century the workhouse was hated with a deep and bitter detestation. That fighting parson, The Rev. J. R. Stephens, declared in 1838: 'sooner than that wife and husband, and father and son, should be dungeoned, and fed on "skillee"— sooner than wife or daughter should wear the prison dress [this was an allusion to the fact that the inmates had to wear special clothes provided by the Union, their own often being ragged and filthy] sooner than that—Newcastle [where this particular speech was being made] ought to be, and should be—one blaze of fire, with only one way to put it out, and that with the blood of all who supported this abominable measure' (ibid., 334). Agricultural labourers had less chance of organizing resistance. The farmers and gentry were firmly in control and the failure of the 1830–1 revolts, followed by hangings and transportations, had shown the futility of rioting. Farmers, if they were to have any labour force at all, were now at least forced to pay a wage on which their workers and families could subsist, while the poor were prepared to take any work and face almost any misery rather than apply for the relief that meant going into 'the house'. Official papers are full of smug, self-congratulatory little anecdotes. One witness, a farmer, contrasted the difference in attitude before and after the 1834 Act, by describing how one morning during the old dispensation 'I was up early; two men were not come; all the other men were out at work except those; when they did come, I remarked "You are very late my lads this morning, John has complained of you, you do not seem to be mended!" Sam Smith remarked, "No; if you do not like it, you must turn us away, we know that the overseer must pay us, for you are under an engagement to pay either him or us".' After the passing of the 1834 Act there was a change. 'Last spring one morning I was out, it was a little after five, during the lambing season, and I saw a man taking up roots, stript to his shirt sleeves; I asked my shepherd who it was; he said "Sir, it's a man that you never saw work before, and I never saw work before; that is Sam Smith Sir, he hates work, but I think Sam will buckle to and will become a good labourer".' (*Report of the Select Committee on the working of the Poor Law Amendment Act* (1838), 6.) At a tremendous and immeasurable cost of rural misery and suffering, the agricultural labourer was depauperized. To this extent Chadwick's theory had worked. But it was not applicable to the industrial towns of the new era.

Chadwick had assumed that there was work available if people were prepared to do it, and, in the routine of agriculture, broadly speaking this was true. But if the land could provide a fairly constant level of employment, industry could not. A trade boom sucked workers in, a depression threw them out. When the mills of Manchester or Bradford lacked orders the workers were helpless. They had been trained for one task, and there was no alternative work available. In these circumstances the offer of 'the house' was both unjust and inadequate. Unjust because men were willing and, indeed, desperately anxious to work and could find none, inadequate because no workhouse could provide accommodation for all those who technically should have been forced to enter it in order to receive relief. It was unfortunate also, for the success of the new system, that it should have been introduced into the industrial north in 1837, just as a trade depression was hitting the textile manufacturers. Again the fault was not Chadwick's. He had wanted to get the boards of guardians elected, and the administrative machinery in good working order, while trade was good. But the commissioners, Chadwick being only their secretary, insisted, against his advice, in depauperizing the agricultural south first, arguing that it was there that the abuses were most rife. As a result the opportunity of introducing the new arrangements into the industrial areas while conditions were favourable was lost. When the attempt was finally made in 1837–8 it was in the teeth of strenuous opposition from many of the mill-owners as well as the operatives. Over the years it became clear that however resolute the determination to eliminate all outdoor relief for the able-bodied the new system was only partially viable. Sometimes tasks at the workhouse, or road-making, were used as a test of necessity, sometimes part of the relief was given in kind, but outdoor relief, though no longer in the form of a grant to supplement wages, continued to be given. Nevertheless the workhouse hung as a constant threat over the heads of the workers. To go there was considered a disgrace. Hatred of the Poor Law was one factor that encouraged the Chartist movement. The administrative changes introduced by the hated statute are of less importance to the social historian, but in combining the small unit of the parish into reasonable sized unions, by providing for paid and specialized staff, and by placing control in the hands of elected boards of guardians of the poor, while giving the overall control to the three commissioners who sat in London, who kept in touch with the unions through itinerant assistant commissioners, the Act removed the major administrative weaknesses of the old Poor Law. It was now better able to serve the needs of the more closely knit society that, with better communications, was slowly replacing the older, smaller local communities.

Though the ministry had been anxious to push forward this drastic reform of the Poor Law it had to be harried into dealing with the working conditions of the new factory population, and with the deplorable sanitary state of the towns. In both these spheres there was no tradition of government interference, and when Parliament did at last interest itself in legislation for these purposes it was inaugurating still another important social revolution. It would not be true to say that in the past it had never interfered to prevent the exploitation of the worker. But such interference had been very limited and governmental concern had mainly been for the smooth running of

industry rather than the welfare of the workers. Indeed such legislation as existed was chiefly intended to protect the employer against
the demands of his workpeople.

The thin edge of the wedge was inserted with government willing-
ness to interfere to protect the health of pauper apprentices employed
in cotton mills, which was justified on the ground that their welfare
was the responsibility of the Poor Law authorities who had placed
them there. As has been said, the textile mills had a large appetite
for child labour, both to act as piecers and to sweep away the cotton
waste beneath the machines. Because the early mills were water-
driven they were often located on small streams in remote places
where there were insufficient local children. As overseers generally
were only too anxious to bind out either orphans or the children of
paupers in other parishes, in order to change their place of settlement,
the needs of the cotton manufacturers were their opportunity. In the
late eighteenth century large numbers were apprenticed in this way,
the London parishes being the great source of supply. In 1795 Samuel
Oldknow, inquiring in Clerkenwell, was told that between forty and
fifty children were available. Subsequently they were brought to his
factory at Mellor by the parish beadle. For the next few years further
children were regularly recruited in this way. The youngsters who
came to Mellor were lucky compared with many pauper apprentices.
They lived in an adequate apprentice house. They had milk porridge
and wheaten bread every day for breakfast and meat for dinner, with
fruit from the orchard in season. They received some religious instruction; there was a Sunday school and each Sunday they went to church,
neatly dressed in their best clothes. But even so their working day was
from six in the morning until seven at night. Many children fared
worse and worked longer, their treatment depending entirely upon
their master. Most of the early mills were badly ventilated because
fine spinning required a hot, humid atmosphere. Dependence upon
water power also meant irregularity of working hours; when shortage
caused a stoppage lost time was made up afterwards, sometimes to
the extent of a fifteen-hour day. Children could only be kept to their
tasks in such conditions by the use of the strap and the blow. When
poor food and dirty living conditions also prevailed the factories
became hothouses of disease. As early as 1784 a bad outbreak of fever
in Manchester drew the attention of Dr Percival to the state of the
cotton mills, which he thought were particularly harmful for young
people under fourteen. As a result of his recommendations the
Manchester magistrates refused to bind local children to any mill

where they would have to work more than ten hours a day or at night. Though this prevented the exploitation of local children, such resolutions had no power to prevent manufacturers from getting pauper apprentices from elsewhere.

It is interesting that it was often the more progressive manufacturers rather than the ministry who were most instrumental in promoting remedial legislation. Some of them at least were inspired by humane considerations. As a child John Fielden had worked in his father's small mill and later, recalling those early days, he wrote 'I shall never forget the fatigue I often felt before the day ended and the anxiety of all of us to be relieved from the unvarying and irksome toil we had gone through.' (J. Fielden, op. cit., 32.) Yet in his father's mill the hours of labour 'did not exceed ten a day winter and summer'. In many cases pity was reinforced by an awareness that over-tired children meant spoilt work. But whatever their motives the more enlightened manufacturers were unwilling to risk being undercut by more unscrupulous competitors, and were determined that improvements in conditions must be made to apply to all. Peel's first excursion into the realms of factory legislation, however, applied only to pauper apprentices and as such aroused little opposition. Its practical impact was debatable because there was no adequate machinery by which the provisions of the Act could be enforced. Its chief interest lies in the fact that it laid down what benevolent contemporaries thought were reasonable standards for children employed in factories when these children were the responsibility of the Poor Law authorities. The buildings in which they worked were to be washed down with water and quicklime twice a year and there were to be sufficient windows to ensure a 'proper supply of fresh air'. Working hours were not to be more than twelve in the twenty-four, exclusive of meal times. Work was not to start before six in the morning or continue after nine at night. For the first four years young apprentices were to be instructed for some part of every working day; they were to have an hour of religious instruction on Sundays and attend divine service at least once a month. They were also to be provided with two whole and complete suits of clothing during their apprenticeship. It was a meagre charter.

Even had it been effective, its period of usefulness would have been limited. With the adoption of the steam engine and concentration of manufacturing in the towns of the north and midlands, the need for pauper apprentices died out. There were now enough local children who could be engaged or dismissed at the mill-owners' convenience as trade boomed or slumped, whereas the apprentice, once bound, remained his responsibility until the indentures expired. Many of the so-called 'free children' first went into the mill at the age of six, seven or eight and worked there for as long as the adult workers. Once again it was a manufacturer, this time Robert Owen of New Lanark, who initiated a movement for their protection. A crank and an idealist in some ways, Owen had early realized the value of a contented and healthy labour force. When he went to New Lanark in 1814 he found what he described as 'a wretched community'. Over the years he cut excessive hours, built houses for his workers, set up a shop where sound goods could be bought at fair prices, and laboured unceasingly, by providing a sensible regime of controls and facilities for education, to instil into his workpeople standards of responsibility and respectability. Eventually his mill became a show-place, visited by tourists from all over the Continent. He took especial pains over the treatment of his child employees. He provided schools, which were run on surprisingly enlightened lines, and he allowed no child to work in the mill before the age of ten. They then worked a $10\frac{1}{2}$-hour day, exclusive of $1\frac{1}{2}$ hours for meals. No cruelty was allowed in his mill. Owen was able to prove that these reforms did not lead to bankruptcy: New Lanark was prosperous. Nevertheless he found it almost impossible to convert his fellow-manufacturers, few of whom, doubtless, were prepared to spend the time and trouble that Owen devoted to his schemes. In 1815 he enlisted the help of Sir Robert Peel in order to get legislation, based on his own experiments, to regulate the employment of free children in cotton mills.

This proposal met with bitter opposition. The arguments put forward against either fixing a minimum age or maximum hours of work for children provide a revealing insight into contemporary thinking on the subject. Modern readers may find some of them barely credible. Some of the more theoretical objections bore little resemblance to reality. The defenders of the status quo relied on three lines of argument. The first was the danger of interfering with free labour. The children under discussion were not pauper apprentices but children of parents who were free to send them to the factory or not as they pleased. They were the natural guardians of their children and to interfere was to imply that they were unfit to exercise their parental responsibilities. Surely this, it was argued, must lessen the bond between parent and child and lead to filial disrespect! When the bill was debated in the Lords, Lord Lauderdale took his stand on what he called 'the great principle of Political Economy that labour ought to be left free'. It was also argued that the children's health could not suffer from these long hours, because the work that they did was light and not in itself physically exhausting. Baines, the contemporary historian and glorifier of the cotton manufacturer, worked out to his own satisfaction how many seconds elapsed between each movement that the little piecers had to make, and by adding them together and balancing them against the working seconds he reduced by some hours the time for which they were actively employed. In the debates recorded in *Hansard* during the discussion of the bill in 1818, speaker after speaker argued that the health of the children was not adversely affected. Mr Curwen declared that he had never seen children with better looks or better health than those he had seen when visiting factories. Indeed the opponents of the bill had so much to say about their healthiness that the younger Peel was driven to remark sarcastically that as apparently they were the healthiest places in the kingdom it was clearly the duty of the legislature to set them up everywhere in order to promote the health of His Majesty's subjects! In the Lords, Liverpool argued, with commendable common sense, that if children worked 72 hours a week, 'and this was admitted by counsel at the bar, then, in spite of all the testimony that might be brought, he would assert that it was morally impossible that such labour should not have injurious effects that called for legislation'. (*Hansard*, 19 May 1818.) So nervous, however, was Parliament about the effects of legislative interference with free labour that, in spite of the contention made by the supporters of the bill that parents had no alternative to allowing their children to work these exhausting hours, because their earnings were a vital part of the family budget, all it was prepared to do was to forbid the employment of children under the age of nine and to limit the hours worked of those between nine and sixteen to twelve a day. To be fair to the opponents of this extension of the authority of the state, one should not dismiss as pure hypocrisy their contention that children employed in other manufactures worked for as long in even worse conditions. It must also be remembered that the filth of the streets, the overcrowding of the houses and the lack of educational facilities, make it arguable that conditions outside the factory were equally dangerous to health. It is little wonder that the expectation of life in the working class districts of a town like Manchester was so low.

It would be tedious, and in a study of this kind irrelevant, to give a blow-by-blow account of the protracted struggle to get decent working conditions even in the factories. Certain aspects do, however, play an important part in the social development of England and Wales. Therefore some attempt must be made to isolate them from the mass of legislation in which they were entangled. Very important in this respect is the increasing involvement of the workers themselves in the struggle for better working conditions. They were not concerned solely, or perhaps, as their critics claimed, even mainly with the plight of the children. The report of the royal commission on the employment of children in factories (1833) declared categorically: 'Although the case of the children is invariably put forward as a plea for the restriction in all the appeals to the public, it is hardly so much as mentioned in the meetings and discussions of the operatives themselves'. They too were finding the length of the working day intolerable as the new machines needed more and more concentrated attention. In the 1818 debates Peel had stated that older men, working in the hot humidity required for fine spinning, found a twelve hour day too exhausting, but during the long depression the preoccupation of the majority of adult operatives had been with wages. When trade picked up they became more and more anxious to win some curtailment for themselves. They knew that a direct claim for this kind would never be accepted in the teeth of the opposition of the economists. To fight behind the children was their only hope.

During the thirties, there were some minor attempts to introduce some amending legislation, but it was not until the publication of Ostler's famous letter on 'Yorkshire Slavery', which appeared in the *Leeds Mercury* on 16 October 1830, that the movement for reform moved into its next phase. At this time Wilberforce and his evangelical supporters were campaigning actively for the abolition of slavery. Now, because children who worked in the worsted mills had not even the meagre protection of the 1819 Act, Ostler argued passionately that philanthropy, like charity, should begin at home, writing:

> The very streets that receive the droppings of an 'Anti-Slavery Society' are every morning wet with the tears of innocent victims at the accursed shrine of avarice, who are compelled (not by the cart whip of the negro slave drivers but by the dread of the equally appalling thong or strap of the overlooker) to hasten, half dressed but not half fed, to those magazines of British Infantile Slavery—the Worsted Mills in the town and neighbourhood of Bradford!

When Michael Sadler then attempted to introduce a new bill for factory reform, the operatives were solidly behind him, demanding a ten hour day for the children in the belief that it would prove impossible to run the mills without them. An interesting social aspect of the ensuing campaign was the skill with which they, together with their middle class sympathizers, organized meetings, petitions and propaganda. In the textile towns Short Time (i.e. for the ten hour day) Committees were formed and monster petitions presented to Parliament in support first of Sadler's, and, after he had lost his seat in the 1832 election, of Lord Ashley's Ten Hour bill, when Ashley assumed responsibility for the campaign in the Commons. When the government, who were not sympathetic, appointed a royal commission to collect further evidence, as that presented by a select committee under the chairmanship of Sadler was very partisan, the Short Time Committees organized mammoth local protests in the belief that the commissioners would prove to be merely the stooges of the manufacturers. This was a misconception. Chadwick, who was one of the three appointed, was definitely nobody's tool. His recommendations pleased neither the workers nor the manufacturers in spite of the fact that he secured some alleviation for the children. In the face of their disappointment, the operatives kept their organization alive, but it was not until 1853 that an effective ten hour day for women, which in practice meant a ten hour day for all adult workers, was finally secured. An Act of 1847, which in theory had obtained this, proved to be full of loopholes and had to be amended. The Ten Hour movement, with its successful conclusion, was yet another milestone in the progress which the working classes had achieved through the mechanism of orderly protest and parliamentary pressure, even before the majority of them had secured the right to vote, though they would hardly have done so without some middle class support.

Another important outcome of this fight to secure better working conditions for women and children was the acceptance by the state of the fact that man's self-love was not necessarily God's providence and, as a corollary, that it might be its duty both to give some protection to those sections of society who could not protect themselves, and to pay some regard to the health and education of its future citizens. In 1833 the commissioners declared: 'We are therefore of the opinion that a case has been made out for the interference of the Legislature on behalf of the children employed in factories' (*Report of the Royal Commission for inquiring into the Employment of Children in Factories* (1833), 47). The 1833 Factory Act, in its final form, restricted all children under the age of thirteen to a forty-eight hour week, but ordered in addition that they should attend some school for two hours a day.

This was the first provision for compulsory schooling for any section of the population, and though, as we have seen, the schools that were available to such children were only too often appalling travesties, and though the parents had to pay the small fees demanded by them, this again was a great social milestone. The 1833 Act also gave some slight protection to what we should today describe as 'teenagers'. They were not to do night work between 8.30 p.m. and 5 a.m., and their working day of twelve hours was to be so arranged that they had a clear one and a half hours for meals. When the question of interfering with free labour had first been discussed in 1818 opponents of Peel's bill had warned the Commons that, once the dyke had been breached, there was no knowing where the flood would stop. The next inroad was in 1844 when children became half-timers, working on an average not more than six and a half hours a day in either the morning or the afternoon shift, and spending the other half at school. The same Act included women with the teenagers working a twelve hour day. Finally the securing of an effective ten hour day for all had shown how strong this flood could be.

Nor did interference with free labour stop at the textile industry. The 1833 commission had pointed out that it was no worse, and even in many ways better, than many other industries in its treatment of child workers. Perhaps the report that shook Victorian public opinion more than any other was that which told the world what was happening in the coal mines. The cotton mills had been accused of being hotbeds of immorality, though there is no evidence to prove that the people who worked in them were any more promiscuous than the rest of the population. When in 1842 it became known that in the West Riding of Yorkshire 'the men worked in a state of perfect nakedness, and that they are in this state assisted in their labours by females of all ages, from girls of six years old to women of 21, these females being themselves quite naked down to the waist' (*Report of the Royal Commission for inquiring into the Employment of Children in Manufactures: Mines* (1842), vol. xvi, 42), respectable Victorian England was horrified. It was this, almost more than the sufferings of the little trappers and haulers, that made it possible to rush the Act of 1842 through a shocked Parliament. This forbade all female labour underground, and only permitted that of boys over the age of ten. Once the process of inquiring into the conditions of children's employment had begun the flood of legislation swept on. A royal commission appointed in 1842 found that in industry after industry the length and irregularity of the hours children worked were both a dangerous hazard to health

and precluded any chance of education. Slowly, but by now inevitably, Parliament found itself more and more forced to interfere in
industrial conditions and to make that interference more and more
detailed.

This was found to be necessary because, in the early decades of
social legislation, there was so large a gap between the intentions of
Parliament and the effectiveness of the Act. This again was to be
important for future social development. There is a feeling today that
the rights of the individual are being encroached on at every turn.
This encroachment was something that Victorian society accepted
with the greatest reluctance. A man's home was his castle; a mill-
owner regarded his mill in the same way. It was a place where he was
free to do what he pleased, where his word was law. Though many
prominent manufacturers had welcomed, and even promoted, the
new Factory Acts, many had resented them bitterly as hampering their
business activities. Such men soon showed that they could drive the
proverbial coach and horses through the well-intentioned statutes.
Before 1833 their enforcement had been so poor that, to ensure less
laxity, Chadwick had recommended the payment of paid, full-time
factory inspectors. The number of mills that each had to supervise
was ridiculously large, and though they had some help from assistant
inspectors, the manufacturers were so jealous of the privacy of their
factories that the latter were not allowed to go further than the counting
house, where the records for inspection were kept. Only the inspectors
themselves were able to see what went on on the factory floor. Their
appointment was yet another important milestone in the creation of
a civilized industrial society. From 1833 the state, not content with
framing regulations, was taking administrative steps to see that they
were carried out. From the way in which unscrupulous employers
manipulated meal times, and the relay system, which the new legislation had forced them to adopt if they still wished to keep their mills
open, it became clear from the inspectors' reports that the legislation
would have to be made more precise. Too many mill-owners were
cooking the books. The result was a more detailed definition of meal
times, and of the hours between which children, and later women,
might remain in the mill. Had men had less original sin they might
not now be so enmeshed in red tape! It was the experience of the
factory inspectors that first drove home the necessity for it if social
abuses were to be stamped out effectively by Act of Parliament.

Factory legislation had one pleasing, if minor, result. It showed that
economists were not infallible and that humanitarian reforms did

not necessarily lead to national economic disaster. The economist Nassau Senior had been of the opinion that 'the whole net profit is derived from the last hour . . . if the hours of working were reduced by one hour a day (processes remaining the same) net profit would be destroyed; if they were reduced by an hour and a half even gross profit would be destroyed'. (Nassau Senior, op. cit., 12–13.) This opinion, quoted in the debates on the 1844 Act in March of that year, was widely accepted as correct. Time was to prove that though the worker benefited by a reduction in the hours of labour the axe was not laid to 'the tree of England's commercial greatness', as Sir James Graham, the Home Secretary, had prophesied. With the shortening of the working week a new era could begin for the British working class, though at first it was only the workers in the textile industries who were able to benefit from this increased leisure.

Factory reform was pushed through in the teeth of opposition. The task of cleaning up the towns, and making them healthier and pleasanter places in which to live, was also uphill work. The main obstacles to initiating any campaign for sanitary reform on a national scale were ignorance, apathy and conservatism and, sheltering behind them, vested interests in the status quo and the fear of financial commitments. By the thirties, better-class districts had undergone a certain amount of superficial improvement. Most towns had some arrangements for the main streets to be kept reasonably clean, by nineteenth-century standards, though the number of waifs who picked up a living as crossing-sweepers or shoeblacks bears witness to the degree of dirt that was accepted as normal. The introduction of gas had revolutionized street lighting, though today we should think Victorian streets dim and dingy. Many houses had the new-fangled water closet which was connected with a sewer or emptied into a cesspool. Drains carried away surface water, which no longer stood in deep stagnant puddles. In many industrial towns better-class people were moving out to pleasanter suburbs, leaving the centre of the towns to shops and warehouses. As Engels pointed out, the streets that connected the two, though often dingy, gave no hint of the sanitary horrors that lay behind them. Middle class people had no occasion to penetrate into the worst working class areas, and the few who did took it for granted that dirt and poverty were inseparable. They were equally unaware of the lurking hazards to their own health. They did not realize that inefficient drains let sewer gas seep into their own basements, that cesspools contaminated the wells from which they drew their water, that polluted rivers spread disease, and that the water with which the water companies supplied their houses was teeming with those, as yet unknown, organisms, germs. Because both ill-health and bad smells were most common in the poorer parts of the town, it was widely believed, even by medical men, that it was the smell, by tainting the atmosphere, that caused disease. People remained oblivious to the hidden dangers that did not intrude themselves upon their noses, which in any case were tolerably used to them.

In the poorer areas, where the houses were closely packed and overcrowded, the streets often undrained and the filth more apparent, the inhabitants, like their betters, took these things very much for granted. Nevertheless questioning unearthed many instances of overflowing courts, stinking middens and reeking slaughterhouses, which even a population inured to filth found almost unbearable. The movement for sanitary reform was largely the work of a comparatively small group of medical and professional men, of whom Chadwick was one of the leading spirits; it received little active support from the working population. This may have been because their energies went into the fight for better wages, embryonic trade unions, short time committees, and, for the politically minded, Chartism. Though willing to pay extra for water, if this could be piped into their dwellings, working folk often seemed most reluctant to pay more rent for a house with an extra bedroom, and remained oblivious to the advantages of ventilation, preferring a good warm fug. When in funds their money went on food and clothing. It is difficult today to realize the extent to which dirt, disease, hunger and hardship were accepted as part of the normal pattern of living by the majority of British people even a hundred and fifty years ago. Tom Grimes, the sweep's apprentice in *The Water Babies* (Charles Kingsley), was typical.

> He cried half his time, and laughed the other half. He cried when he had to climb the dark flues, rubbing his poor knees and elbows raw; and when the soot got into his eyes, which it did every day in the week; and when his master beat him, which he did every day in the week; and when he had not enough to eat, which happened every day of the week likewise. And he laughed the other half of the day, when he was tossing half pennies with the other boys, or playing leap frog over the posts.

Chadwick found this apparent indifference of urban workers to cleanliness easy to understand. He realized that it was too much to expect a man or woman, after twelve hours' toil in a factory or workshop, to face the further fatigue of carrying water from a pump perhaps two hundred yards away, or of cleaning privies or courts when neighbours were unco-operative. Whatever else he blamed the workers for, it was not the insanitary condition of those districts where they lived. What did arouse his wrath was the unscientific conservatism of the authorities and their blindness to the situation. Both his own *Sanitary Condition of the Labouring Population* (1842) and the subsequent *Report on the Sanitary Condition of Large Towns and Populous Districts* (1845) showed how completely haphazard were the arrangements of the past. Some towns, Preston was one, had no map of their sewers, and it was stated that 'it was the work of several weeks to open up the streets in order to ascertain the lines and depths of the sewers'. (*Report on the State of Large Towns . . .* , vol. 1, 25.) Often, too, Chadwick was driven to despair by the utter 'disregard of scientific principles in their construction'. In Bolton, he found 'some are square, others round; in fact they are of any shape that happens to coincide with the views of the builder; they have their junctions at right angles; and the filth, which from the badness of their form accumulates in them, is removed, as best it may, by the showers of heaven' (ibid., 259). In parts of London sewers could only be cleaned by opening them up and removing their disgusting contents and shovelling it into carts. The smell can be imagined! By 1842 such inefficiency was no longer tolerable. New techniques by then had made iron pipes cheap and durable. Experiments in Holborn and Finsbury had demonstrated the feasibility of flushing them with a regulated flow of water.

It was difficult, however, to persuade the local authorities that to abandon the old methods and substitute the new apparatus would be a long-term economy. In vain Mr Roe, the progressive civil engineer in charge of the Holborn scheme, stated that the capital outlay could be recovered in seven years because of cheaper operational costs and that the new method would prevent the escape of sewer gas. It was on the same score of inefficiency that Chadwick, that slayer of sacred cows, attacked water companies for their intermittent supplies of poor quality. As usual he had his experts to back up his argument. Thomas Hawkesley of the Trent Water Works, which by then had been in operation for fourteen years, explained that they were able to supply working class property in Nottingham with unlimited water at a penny a week and still pay 5 per cent on the original investment. When Chadwick's critics, therefore, opposed his sanitary proposals on financial grounds, affecting to regard them as mere charitable good works, he argued indignantly that, far from being an extravagance, provision of better sanitation would cut directly the large sums spent on the poor as a result of ill health, and cut them again indirectly by providing the country with a more efficient labour force. Moreover he affirmed that even if the initial outlay were not regarded as a social investment, it could still be considered to be sound business bringing in a cash return. If properly organized, manure could be sold, refuse sorted and re-used, water sold at an economic price and the whole system made to pay its way; in his view businessmen were ignoring a new potentially profitable market. Sanitation was not philanthropy but good business. The private water companies, the London Commissioners of Sewers (i.e. drainage) and the local authorities all resented his strictures and rejected his innovating proposals, and their opposition made it more difficult to get any effective sanitary legislation through Parliament.

This is not the place in which to give a detailed summary of the recommendations of the *Report on Large Towns*. Nevertheless they cannot be entirely omitted, partly because they had a vital bearing on the wellbeing of urban England, and partly because of the revealing light that the opposition they provoked throws on contemporary attitudes, towards public health. In the first place they bring out the utterly unscientific approach of the past, and stress the new emphasis placed on the need to employ full-time professional officers as opposed to the traditional unpaid amateur. As the preliminary to any drainage scheme being adopted for an area this was first to be professionally surveyed and reported upon and one authority was to be responsible for sanitation, drainage, cleansing, paving, removing nuisances and obstructions, such as dams on rivers, constructing or supervising the sewer system, branch sewers and house drains in the entire area. The same authority was also to make provision for an adequate water supply both for domestic consumption and for public use. In addition the local authority, the report recommended, should have the power to regulate the width of new streets and the design of courts in order to secure adequate ventilation. It was to impose minimum conditions for cellars when used as dwellings, and to see that new houses were provided at least with privies. Though the commissioners hesitated to interfere with private property, they did go as far as to recommend that if the medical officer reported any house to be so filthy as to endanger the public health, the landlord should be forced to clean it. Recommendations were also made to ensure that the area over which this local authority was to exercise its power was physically a viable one, provided with adequate outlets for drainage. The commissioners refrained from making any proposals as to the composition of the new local health authorities, which was in essence a political decision, but they were emphatic that it must appoint and employ full-time and properly qualified officers, one of whom should be 'a medical officer properly qualified to report periodically upon the sanitary condition of the town or district'. Chadwick put great store by this recommendation.

The expense of these proposals was bound to be considerable and the commissioners were acutely aware that there was little chance of their being adopted unless this could be done without placing too great a financial burden on either the ratepayers, individual householders or landlords. The suggestion that they made to overcome this difficulty is a common method of finance today, though a novelty then. What they advocated was sanitation by a species of hire purchase. The main sewers were to be paid for out of the rates, and the cost apportioned between the properties that were benefited. Owners of property were to pay for the improvements to their own property, such as house drains, or the paving of courts, but repayments could be spread over twenty years, and so reduced to manageable proportions. This was a very necessary concession when so much working class property was in the hands of small owners; the provision made for a widow was often the possession of two or three such houses. In order to raise the necessary capital for these expensive projects the money could be borrowed, with the sanction of the national health authority, on the security of the rates, a method of financing still used.

The campaigners for public health had in these recommendations a reasonable blueprint for action. To get something like them on the statute book proved a very difficult task, showing how little general concern the public felt until the threat of a fresh outbreak of cholera gave the matter a new urgency. The Queen's Speech at the opening of Parliament in 1845, with its hope that the report would provide a basis for a measure for 'promoting the Health and Comfort of the poorer Classes of my Subjects', is an illuminating sidelight on the, as yet, almost total failure of the rest of the community to realize that public health was a seamless garment and that a pure water supply was as vital to the rich as to the poor. It took until 1848, after three years of heartbreak and frustration, for even a mangled and emasculated version of the report to become law. During that time the opposing forces of the old and the new concepts of administration were locked in bitter conflict, the one a hangover from the old local self-sufficiency, the other a looking forward to a common standard imposed from Westminster. Under cover of this dislike of 'centralization' speculators and vested interests fought a spirited and partially success-ful rearguard action. Without the House of Lords, which intervened to restore some of Chadwick's ideas which had been thrown out by the Commons, the measure that finally emerged would have been even weaker. The Public Health Act of 1848 set up, for an experimental period of five years, a central Board of Health consisting of three members, of whom Chadwick was one. Where the death rate was more than 23 per 1,000, or where 10 per cent of the ratepayers requested it, the Board was empowered first to send down an inspector and then to authorize the town council to carry out the duties imposed on it by the Act. Where there was no town council, the Board was autho-rized to set up local boards of health. Each of these local authorities was required by the Act to appoint a clerk, a treasurer, an inspector of nuisances and a surveyor and, if it wished, a medical officer of health. In future it was not to allow any houses to be built without a W.C., privy or ashpit, together with appropriate drains, so that the occupants need no longer throw their slops into the gutter. Also it could compel any house within a hundred feet of a sewer to be con-nected to it. The other basic requirement was that the local authority was made responsible for ensuring that the community was provided with an adequate water supply. This was normally done by coming to an agreement with the existing private water company as to stan-dards, etc. Beyond these minimum requirements, on which the central Board had the legal obligation to insist, local health authorities were given wider permissive powers if they liked to exercise them. They could provide parks for public recreation or municipal baths. How-ever, to prevent unwise or extravagant projects being undertaken, plans for improvement schemes, that involved borrowing money on the security of the rates had first to be passed by the central Board.

Though the 1848 Act had been designed primarily to benefit the working classes, unless they were also ratepayers they were denied any influence over its administration. This remained in the hands of the ratepayers who elected the local board of health on a franchise based on a graduated property qualification which gave the poorest rate-payers one vote and the richest six. This is not the place to evaluate the success of the Board of Health, which was not renewed in 1853, being replaced by other, less disliked, arrangements, but that it should have been created in the first place is yet another milestone in adapting urban society to the conditions of industrial England. However grudgingly, Parliament had accepted the responsibility for seeing that the urban environment did not fall below a minimum standard.

Even before the passing of the 1848 Act, towns like Manchester, Liverpool and Birmingham had been grappling energetically with the problem. There is no doubt that, deplorable as conditions were by modern standards, urban England was a much healthier place in 1851 than it had been at the turn of the century. That health should be recognized as a public responsibility, and that the expectation of life for the mass of the people should have been materially increased by the recognition that the link between poverty and ill-health could be broken, marks the beginning of a new era in the development of English society.

New, too, was the growing involvement of the central government in the problem of law and order. In one sense this had always been one of its fundamental responsibilities, along with finance and foreign policy, but its enforcement, like so much else had been left to the parish, the borough and the county. Parliament had defined the offences and named the penalties but beyond that it was left to individuals and to local officers to seize suspected persons and deliver them to the appropriate court, either Quarter Sessions or the Assizes. Each parish was responsible for the capture of the suspected criminal while he or she remained within its boundaries, but, once out of the parish, the alleged lawbreaker became the responsibility of the officers of the parish into which he had fled. The man on whom the potentially dangerous task of apprehending him fell was the parish or borough constable, who, if possible, was conspicuous by his absence. The watch, employed by many London parishes, were also anxious to avoid trouble, preferring to round up the drunkard and the prostitute than to tackle a dangerous thief. Two things resulted from this fragile net of the law-enforcers. Because the percentage of criminals caught was likely to be low, Parliament tended to impose ever-increasing penalties. For minor offences people could be whipped, either publicly or at Bridewell, or placed in the pillory. Petty offenders often had to endure a spell in the stocks on the village green. In the eighteenth century imprisonment, except for political offences, was regarded more as making sure that the accused did not escape before standing trial than as a punishment in itself, though minor offences, often against morality, might be punished with a few months in the house of correction. But in ordinary criminal cases imprisonment for long periods was not a normal punishment. Even imprisonment for the civil offence of debt was regarded not as a punishment but only to make sure that the debtor did not abscond.

The general conception of the function of justice was to protect the public by employing the strongest possible deterrent, and this was generally thought to be the death penalty. This was also the most economical way of dealing with crime from the administrative angle. The gallows and the hangman were cheap and there was no fear of that particular criminal committing that particular crime again. The first consequence of this was that whenever a particular type of crime seemed to be on the increase, or when new opportunities for new anti-social acts occurred, Parliament tended to impose the death penalty. Pickpockets could be hanged, sheep stealers could be hanged, forgers could be hanged, coiners could be hanged, even persons convicted of damaging Westminster Bridge or cutting down fruit trees could be hanged. Indeed most offences against property carried with them the death penalty. The eighteenth century held life cheap. The second consequence of the ineffective machinery for apprehending criminals was the emergence of the professional thief-taker. To encourage the general public to play its part, most legislation of this kind contained a tariff of rewards payable to anyone who was instrumental in bringing an offender to justice. This practice seems to have produced as many evils as it was intended to cure. On the credit side must be placed the formation of the semi-professional force organized by the Fieldings and, because they were based on the magistrates' court at Bow Street, later known as the Bow Street runners, but on the debit side were the activities of such men as Jonathan Wild. As a whole the system led to much corruption, whereby the strong were left alone and the weak betrayed, or even framed, for the sake of the reward. The rôle of government was confined to defining the offences and decreeing the penalties; normally the rest of the process of justice was left to the public, the local authorities and the courts.

The responsibility for public order was also largely left to the magistrates. It was only when riots reached a more than transitory and local character that the ministry evinced much interest, mainly because such disturbances tended to have political undertones and because, in the absence of any trained and organized police force, the only way of restoring order was to call in the military. In the troubled post-war years of the early nineteenth century, when King Lud was out or the hard-hit weavers were thought to be engaged in secret drilling or to be plotting social insurrection, it was almost standard procedure for the local Bench to ask that a troop of soldiers should be stationed near the centres of discontent. The government was indeed in something of a cleft stick. Ever since the days of James II Englishmen had had a deep-rooted dislike of anything that could be called a standing army in time of peace, yet, without the assistance it could give, there were times when the forces of law and order might well be overthrown. The compromise was to leave to the Lord Lieutenant or the county magistrates the decision as to when the military, or the local militia or yeomanry, should be asked for assistance. On these officials fell the sometimes perilous task of ordering a turbulent or threatening crowd to disperse within the half-hour. This was, in a sense, a formal warning that the troops would be called in to disperse it, if it refused to disperse voluntarily. It is usually known as 'reading the Riot Act', though this description is legally inaccurate. If the soldiers then fired on the crowd or charged them, they could claim to be acting under the authority of the civil power, whereas troops that fired without this formality might find themselves under attack for having acted on their own responsibility. It was not a satisfactory system as the use of the yeomanry at Peterloo was to demonstrate.

By then the employment of troops to quell discontent, the state of the prisons and the savagery of the penal code, were all coming under attack from the more radical, and more humane, men and women in public life. Public attitudes to such things were changing, and the widespread use of the death penalty for minor crimes was beginning to be recognized as defeating its own ends. Juries were reluctant to condemn a young pickpocket, who stole a silk handkerchief, to the gallows, and the difficulty of catching thieves continued with the reluctance of juries to convict them when caught was turning the chance of punishment into a lottery with more blanks than black-capped judges. Even judges were often glad to transmute the death sentence into one of transportation though, by a legal quirk, the prisoner had to be asked whether he would rather be hanged than transported! The growing use of transportation brought with it its own difficulties. After 1776 the American colonies were no longer available, and a select committee advocated the building of penitentiaries wherein the offender might be reclaimed and made more useful to society. This was very much in line with late-eighteenth-century thought and, in one form or another, lay behind much contemporary philanthropy. For a time the discovery of Australia and the transportation of prisoners to Botany Bay, and after 1840 to Van Diemen's Land, solved the immediate problem of what to do with convicted prisoners when there was no suitable prison to which they could be sent, and when they were too numerous to be hanged out of hand. Meanwhile the ideas that had given rise to the suggestion of the penitentiary began to gain ground, as more people became conscious of the misery and degradation that confinement in places like Newgate brought. In such prisons men and women alike were placed in irons unless they could pay the gaoler; without such payments they had no bedding, no firing, dirty water and little bread. During the day men and women occupied the same yards. One of the gaoler's most profitable perquisites was a right to keep the tap and sell drink to the prisoners. Everywhere there was filth and stench and typhus, enlivened only by drink and immorality. In such places no one could be reclaimed; the ignorant or the innocent could only be contaminated. It is against this background that the proposals of the reformers must be studied. Prisoners, they argued, must be saved from contamination and given time for reflection and repentance by being confined in separate cells. They must be re-introduced to industry by hard labour but should receive medical care and religious instruction. Their food was to be plain but sufficient. Today we should consider a regime harsh in which prisoners, outside the hours of their labour, faced solitary confinement, though in extenuation it must be said that many working class political prisoners, for instance those convicted of selling unstamped papers, were not cut off from books and used their enforced solitude for self-education.

Throughout the first half of the century progress towards these ideals was patchy. As early as 1778 John Howard had begun his work of exposure. In 1817 Elizabeth Fry, shocked by the state of women prisoners in Newgate, embarked on her campaign of compassion and reform. Meanwhile like-minded persons were constituting themselves into a 'Society for the Improvement of Prison Discipline'. This title has a harsh sound to modern ears because today it is easy to forget the horrors that a lack of discipline made easy, even inevitable. The reformers were arguing that without discipline within the gaol regeneration was impossible, and though the methods advocated were dictated by a strict evangelical outlook, little in accord with modern psychology, it should not be condemned unhistorically. In Newgate Elizabeth Fry had some success. Irons were to be used only for 'urgent, and absolute necessity'. Male and female prisoners were to be kept separate and the women placed under the care of female wardresses. Though the efforts of well-known persons to improve conditions in well-known prisons did at least point the way ahead, improvement over the whole country was slow and patchy. The first prison built to give effect to the new thinking on the treatment of offenders, Millbank, was not ready to receive prisoners until 1816 and remained very much an isolated experiment.

Here, as in so many other aspects of social engineering, reformers saw the need of some form of central control. Local prisons were the responsibility of the borough and the county and many of the borough prisons were not much more than lock-ups in which conditions were deplorable. Both Houses of Parliament began to show an increased interest. In 1831 a select committee of the Commons recommended that prisoners should be kept in separate cells and that the state should finance an expensive programme of prison building to meet the new requirements. In 1835 the Lords advocated the desirability of a uniform treatment of the prison population and stressed the importance of appointing inspectors to enforce it. Once again local autonomy was under attack in favour of centralization. The result of these recommendations was an Act passed in 1839 which made it possible for prisoners to be confined in separate cells. Pentonville, built in 1840, embodied the new ideas, having 520 separate cells in which to house its inmates. Many people, however, disapproved strongly of this new policy and feared that it could merely have the effect of 'feather bedding' the criminal. Vested interests in the old system, together with the expense of adopting the new, which required special premises, made many local authorities slow to follow suit. The result was an even greater lack of uniformity. Within a few years fifty-four authorities fell into line, but the City refused to be pressurized into new ways, as did many of the smaller municipal authorities. Moreover even when the new principles of management were adopted there was still little uniformity in the way in which they were applied with regard to diet, hard labour and the general harshness or leniency with which the discipline was administered. In 1833, indeed, Chadwick declared that the food in many prisons was better than the independent poor could afford. When the severity of a prison sentence came to depend more and more on the prison in which it was served, the situation was clearly unsatisfactory. It was not, however, until 1849 that still another select committee addressed itself to working out methods by which uniformity could be achieved.

By then the problem had become more pressing. An attack on the lavish use of the death penalty as a deterrent had increased the potential number of prisoners by reducing the number of hangings. A growth of population, unaccompanied by a reduction in crime, augmented this potential. The man to whom goes the honour of leading this attack against a penal code 'written in blood' was Sir Samuel Romilly. His immediate success was small. In 1808 he managed to get an Act substituting transportation for life for the death penalty for picking a pocket, and in 1812 he secured the repeal of an old Elizabethan vagrancy law, which had made it an offence punishable with death for a soldier or sailor to beg for alms without a permit from a magistrate or from his commanding officer. But other projected easements of the law, such as an Act which would have made it no longer a capital offence to steal goods worth more than 5s from a shop, were blocked by the Lords, although in practice juries rarely now convicted and, if they did, the judge usually substituted transportation. To admit this publicly by changing the law would, it was argued, open the floodgates to a new crime wave. Little more was achieved until 1823 when Peel, acting on the recommendations of an earlier select committee of the Commons, carried a succession of Acts which together got rid of the death penalty for around a hundred felonies. In 1832 more went; sheep-stealing, horse-stealing and coining false money, for instance, were no longer to be considered as capital offences. Gradually the number of felonies carrying the death sentence disappeared, until after 1838 it was reserved only for attempted murder, murder and treason. Nevertheless, because the death penalty was now reserved only for the most serious of crimes it was felt necessary to surround it with all the deterrent atmosphere possible. Tyburn Days, those macabre public holidays of mass hangings, had disappeared before the end of the eighteenth century, to the regret of Dr Johnson, but public hangings still took place outside the gaol, so that prospective murderers might be warned of the end that would await them. Before the use of the long drop, hanging was not a pleasant death to watch.

A new efficiency was also introduced into the maintenance of public order. The lawlessness of London's streets and the violence of its mobs were notorious and successive committees of the Commons in 1793, 1812, 1817, 1818 and 1822 on the best way of dealing with the problem bore witness to the concern of members. As in so many other matters, a changing society was producing a change in traditional attitudes. In 1795 Patrick Colquhoun, a London magistrate, published a treatise *On the Police of the Metropolis* in which he argued that a police force should be used to prevent crime and not merely to arrest the criminals. The obstacle in the way of constituting such a force lay in the deep-rooted prejudices of the majority. However little freedom large classes of men enjoyed in practice, the belief in the 'free-born Englishman' as opposed to the foreign-born slave was widely cherished, and it was equally widely believed that a police force would be used to destroy this liberty. Though progressive circles had come to agree with Colquhoun, it was not until 1829 that Robert Peel, having secured yet another examination of the problem by a select committee in the previous year, was able to introduce an Act for the improvement of the police in 1829. This was a limited measure. Two special justices, working under the immediate control of the secretary of state and with a tiny office in what later was to become famous as Scotland Yard, were appointed to run the new force of some 3,000 men and to be responsible for the policing of metropolitan London. The City, jealous as usual, refused to merge its responsibility for law and order with the rest of the geographical area that made up London. As might have been expected, the new force of uniformed men was intensely unpopular. Georgiana Ellis, in a letter written on 3 November 1830, declared that 'The town was in a great state of excitement all day; the cry of the mob against the police is very great' (Maud, Lady Leconfield, *Three Howard Sisters* (1955), 153), while four days later her sister Harriet, Lady Gower, wrote 'The anti-police cry is most barbarous against these unfortunate unarmed people. One was said to have been struck with knives' (ibid., 157). The climax came in 1833, when, at a meeting of Chartists in Coldbath Fields, during a struggle between the demonstrators and the police three officers were stabbed, one fatally, and a coroner's jury brought in a verdict of justifiable homicide.

Gradually public hostility died down as the advantages of a system of maintaining order through a disciplined force controlled by the civil power, rather than having to call on the military after an ugly situation had got out of hand, became apparent. Also, whatever their deficiencies the new police were both more efficient and less corrupt than the old thief-takers, and the 'Bobby' or 'Peeler' became an accepted part of the London scene. The success of the experiment led to a royal commission charged, among other police matters, with examining how this method of safeguarding the community could be extended to other parts of the country. Once again the obstacle was the fetish of local autonomy. Many towns had organized some sort of a paid watch and in 1835 the Municipal Corporations Act had allowed them to appoint a watch committee and hire paid watchmen, but there was nothing in the shape of a uniform system. As a result of the recommendations of the commission, a new Act in 1839 conferred on the counties the right to raise and pay a county constabulary under a chief constable if they considered that their existing and traditional machinery for keeping the peace was insufficient. In the same year the City of London reorganized its old policing arrangements along the same lines as that of the metropolitan police force. The new provisions for dealing with the age-old problems of crime and disorder were only adopted slowly, as the counties without such a force found themselves the happy hunting grounds for criminals chased from better-policed areas. By 1853 only twenty-two counties had adopted the permissive legislation of 1839 in its entirety. As with the state of the prisons, by the mid-century there was still no uniformity in the handling of public order and the prevention of crime. Nevertheless, as in so much else, a beginning had been made and the lines of future development laid down.

This was also true of other aspects of social reform. What had been accomplished so far was limited, both in scope, because many sides of the national life were still untouched by the reformer's probing finger, and in the degree to which even what had been attempted had been pushed. So far only the conditions of work of women, teenagers and children, had been legally improved in the manufacture of textiles. Beyond a little tinkering with children's employment in the great mass of industries which employed them, and the abuses of which the public was only made aware by a commission which started its investigations in 1842, only coal mining had come under regulation. A tentative beginning had been made to improve the environment in towns, but here again only those towns with an abnormally high death rate had been forced by law to carry out minimum improvements. Nevertheless there was an increasing awareness of the value of human life, which showed itself as the connecting thread between all the various attempts to adjust society to the new material conditions of a country where industry was supplanting agriculture and the town the countryside. Pushed by a combination of realism and normal fervour the community, in the form of the state, was being driven to accept more and more responsibility for its individual members. There was to be a standard below which no human being was to be allowed to fall, though this, by modern standards, was incredibly low. Harsh though the Poor Law was, death by starvation was no longer the unavoidable fate of the most unfortunate. In the inhuman world of employment the state accepted the duty of interference to secure a minimum of leisure and even education for the children. In the towns the better-off were forced to contribute through the rates to provide a better environment for those who could not provide it for themselves. The state even tried, through permissive legislation, to achieve for all its members more security of person and of property, not by the older methods of the rope and the whip, but by a preventive police and more civilized prisons. Self-help was still the ideal, and a bracing private charity compounded of moral earnestness and a sense of responsibility on the part of the better-off towards their poorer neighbours had still an important part to play in softening the harshness of life for some of the vast majority for whom the state, as yet, accepted no responsibility, or of whose needs it was unaware. Much more remained to be done in civilizing society, in recognizing that human dignity was an attribute of all members of society, whatever their class and circumstances, and in accepting that there were many reforms that only the state, acting for the community as a whole, could carry through. Nevertheless to the men and women of 1776 what had already been done by the state to curb the few in the interests of the many would have seemed a revolutionary break with the world of Adam Smith.

Figures

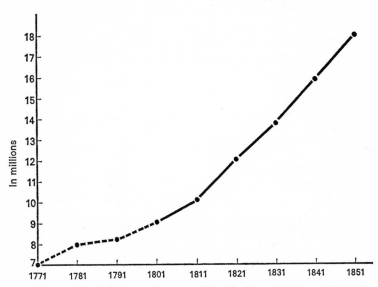

Figure 1 Growth of the population of England and Wales, 1771–1851

There are no official statistics before the census of 1801 and therefore the estimates for the preceding decades are liable to a margin of error, though this is unlikely to be sufficiently large to alter the general appearance of the curve.

On the graph the unofficial curve is marked - - - - - - and the official decades based on the census by ———.

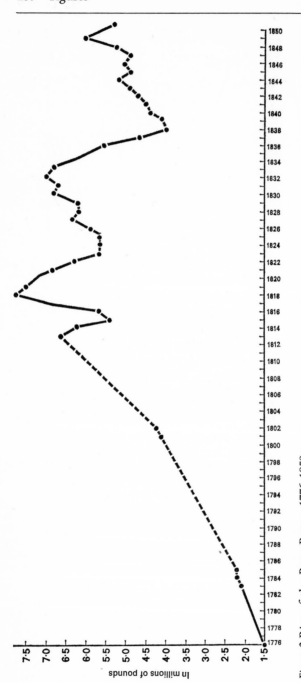

Figure 2 Rise of the Poor Rates, 1776–1850

Here again there is a lack of official statistics for many of the early years. There is therefore likely to be considerable distortion between 1785 and 1802–3 and again between 1803 and 1813. It is clear that between these dates the amount raised in rates for the relief of the poor was increasing, but in view of the fluctuations later, due to changes in the population, economic depression and the price of grain, it is hardly probable that the real situation can be represented by a steady upward curve. If sufficient data were available the Poor Rates are much more likely to be seen to have climbed upwards in a series of fluctuations from year to year. It must also be remembered that these figures are averages and as such often present a misleading picture. For instance, Clapham has pointed out (*An Economic History of Modern Britain,* vol. 1, 363) that although the amount spent on poor relief in 1830–1 averaged 9s 9d per head of the population, a county such as Sussex spent

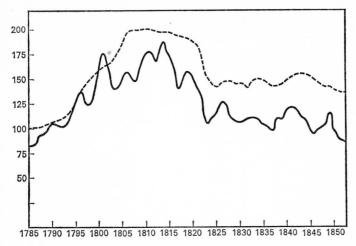

Figure 3 English agricultural earnings, 1785–1850

General course of English agricultural earnings (after Bowley) ————. Working class cost of living index (after Silberling) ––––––––. *Note.* Such estimates tend to vary according to the way in which the cost of living index is constructed and can never provide more than a rough, and often controversial, guide to a very general situation. Both wages and prices tend to vary according to local circumstances. Moreover of late years historians have been fiercely divided as to the general standard of the working class in the early Industrial Revolution.

(Bowley, A. L., *Wages in the United Kingdom in the Nineteenth Century,* 1900, and Silberling, N.J., 'British prices and business cycles, 1779-1850', *Review of Economic Statistics,* 1923.)

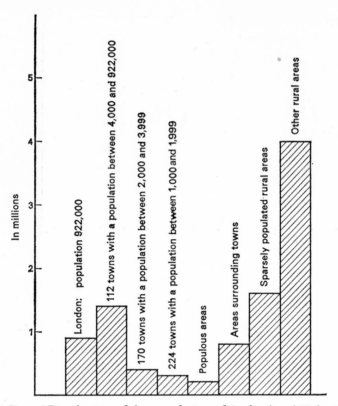

Figure 4 Distribution of the population of England and Wales in 1801

These figures are based on an article by Thomas A. Welton in the *Journal of the Statistical Society*, LXIII. The points to be noticed are the disproportionate size of London and the great predominance of population in the rural areas.

Suggestions
for Further Reading

So much has been written on every aspect of English society during the so-called 'Industrial Revolution' that it is difficult to make a brief selection of those books most likely to be useful to readers who wish to delve deeper into the period covered by this volume without leaving them overwhelmed by too large a choice. I have tried therefore to divide my suggestions for further reading into those books which deal with the period under review in a more general sense, and those which deal mainly with a particular aspect, though obviously in many cases there is a varying amount of overlap. As many of the books listed below contain good bibliographies, those who want to read more widely on any particular topic should have no difficulty in doing so with their help.

GENERAL SURVEY

This section can usefully be divided into those books whose stress is mainly on the economic and social aspects of the period, and those books which, while not excluding such factors, are equally, if not more, concerned with religion, politics and what can be described as the general climate of thinking of the age.

In the first group, S. G. Checkland, *The Rise of Industrial Society in England, 1815–1885* (Longmans, 1964 and St Martin, 1965) and Harold Perkin, *The Origins of Modern English Society 1780–1880* (Routledge & Kegan Paul and University of Toronto Press, 1969) are to be highly recommended to serious students.

In the second group, serious students will find the period very fully covered in E. L. Woodward, *The Age of Reform, 1815–1870* (Oxford University Press, 1938) or, if they prefer a more chronological treatment, in E. Halévy, *A History of the English People in the Nineteenth Century*: vol. 1, *England in 1815*; vol. 2, *The Liberal Awakening*; vol. 3, *The Triumph of Reform* (re-issued by Benn, 1964–5 and Barnes & Noble, 1961). Readers who want something shorter in this category will find Asa Briggs, *The*

Making of Modern England, 1784–1867: The Age of Improvement (Longmans and Harper Torch Books, 1959) excellent. R. S. White, *Life in Regency England* (Batsford, 1963) and *From Waterloo to Peterloo* (Heinemann, 1957) provide graphic pictures of pre-Victorian English society. For the Victorian era, G. M. Young's penetrating *Portrait of an Age* (Oxford University Press, 1936), G. Kitson Clark, *The Making of Victorian England* (Methuen and Harvard University Press, 1962) and *An Expanding Society: Britain 1830–1900* (Cambridge University Press, 1967) explore the more general aspects of nineteenth-century English society. *Early Victorian England*, 2 vols. ed. G. M. Young (Oxford University Press, 1934) is a mine of information on the various aspects of Victorian life.

Easily accessible contemporary material
Collections of select documents:

Bland, A. E., Brown, P. A. and Tawney, R. H., *English Economic History: Select Documents* (Bell, 1914).

Cole, G. D. H. and Filson, A. W., *English Working Class Movements* (Macmillan and St Martin, 1951).

Gash, N., *The Age of Peel* (Arnold, 1968 and St Martin, 1969).

Nicholls, D., *Church and State in Britain since 1820* (Routledge & Kegan Paul, 1967 and Humanities, 1968).

Pike, E. Royston, *Hard Times: Human Documents of the Industrial Revolution* (Allen & Unwin and Praeger, 1966).

Rose, M. E., *The English Poor Law, 1760–1930* (David & Charles, 1971).

All the above provide useful extracts from contemporary sources, including government reports, statutes, etc. Novels also give vivid pictures of Victorian society. Nevertheless neither official papers nor novels should be read uncritically. Material is not necessarily unbiased because it is contemporary, as any reader of the modern Press is well aware. Chadwick and his colleagues concentrated on those aspects of society which, in their opinion, were in most need of reform, while happier aspects were ignored. Among the novelists Charles Dickens saw society in terms of black and white and condemned much of what he saw, while social abuses left Jane Austen unmoved. Her readers are made aware of a hundred delicate social nuances in middle class and genteel society but, if they confined themselves to her pages, they could well remain ignorant of the fact that England was in the throes of an Industrial Revolution. On the other hand, one reads the Brontës' novels, particularly *Shirley*, and Mrs Gaskell for pictures of northern industrial society, Emily Eden's delightful novels, *The*

Semi Detached House and *The Semi Attached Couple* (reprinted in Gollancz Classics, 1961) for those of upper class life, just as one reads Trollope *par excellence* for the background of the cathedral town and the country gentry and Disraeli for the world of politics with excursions, as in *Sybil*, into that of social problems. For sporting England the reader must turn to Surtees and his creation Jorrocks, while for the undercurrents of romantic horror that marked the Regency no better guide can be found than the novels of Mrs Ratcliffe or Mary Shelley's *Frankenstein* (1818), to which the novels of Charlotte M. Yonge, with their pictures of the Christian evangelical way of life, provide a complete contrast. Later, novels by authors such as George Eliot reveal still other facets of Victorian England.

SPECIAL ASPECTS

Social and economic

Books and articles on the causes and course of the Industrial Revolution are legion, but readers who are not specializing in economic history will probably find all they are looking for in Phyllis Deane, *The First Industrial Revolution* (Cambridge University Press, 1965), which also contains a useful bibliography, or in the rather more general P. Mathias, *The First Industrial Nation: an Economic History of Britain 1700–1914* (Methuen and Scribners, 1969). For a more specialized approach, H. Perkin, *The Age of the Railway* (Panther, 1970) combines economic and social history in a stimulating analysis. For purposes of reference rather than sustained reading, Sir John Clapham, *The Economic History of Britain*, vol. 1, *The Railway Age*, contains a great deal of information (Cambridge University Press, 1926; 2nd edition, 1950).

Urban England

Invaluable contemporary material is to be found in Edwin Chadwick, *Report on the Sanitary Condition of the Labouring Population of Great Britain*, 1842. There is a modern edition with an excellent introduction by M. W. Flinn (Edinburgh University Press and Aldine, 1965), but the references in my text are to the 1842 edition. Much of this report is concerned with rural housing and sanitation as well as with urban conditions. Closely linked with its findings but urban in its concentration is *The Second Report of the Commissioners for Inquiring into the State of Large Towns and Populous Districts*, 1854, from which I have also quoted extensively. Useful modern studies are Asa Briggs, *Victorian Cities* (Odhams, 1963 and Harper

& Row, 1965), H. J. Dyos, ed., *The Study of Urban History* (Arnold and St Martin, 1968) and J. K. Kellett, *The Impact of Railways on Victorian Cities* (Routledge & Kegan Paul and University of Toronto Press, 1969).

Rural England

Bovill, E. W., *The England of Nimrod and Surtees, 1815–54* (Oxford University Press, 1959).
Hobsbawm, E. J., and Rudé, G., *Captain Swing* (Lawrence & Wishart and Pantheon, 1969).
Mingay, G. E. and Chambers, J. D., *The Agricultural Revolution, 1750–1880* (Batsford and Schocken, 1966).
Mingay, G. E., *Landed Society in the Eighteenth Century* (Routledge & Kegan Paul and University of Toronto Press, 1963).
Thompson, F. M. L., *Landed Society in the Nineteenth Century* (Routledge & Kegan Paul and University of Toronto Press, 1963).

Religion and the Climate of Opinion: Upper and Middle Classes

Brown, F. K., *Fathers of the Victorians: the Age of Wilberforce* (Cambridge University Press, 1961).
Chadwick, Owen, *The Victorian Church, part 1, 1829–59* (Black and Oxford University Press, 1966).
Houghton, F. W., *The Victorian Frame of Mind, 1830–1870* (Yale University Press).
Inglis, K. S., *The Churches and the Working Class in Victorian England* (Routledge & Kegan Paul and University of Toronto Press, 1963).
Jaeger, M., *Before Victoria* (Chatto & Windus and Fernhill, 1956).
Reader, M. J., *Professional Men: The Rise of the Professional Classes in Nineteenth Century England* (Weidenfeld & Nicolson, 1966).
Rosenbaum, R. A., *Earnest Victorians* (Heinemann, 1962).

Religion and the Climate of Opinion: Working Class

Briggs, Asa, *Chartist Studies* (Macmillan and St Martin 1969).
Duncan, B., *The Handloom Weavers* (Cambridge University Press, 1969).
Engels, F., *The Condition of the Working Class in England in 1844*. There are several translations and editions available, of which the most modern is by W. O. Henderson and W. H. Chaloner (Blackwell, 1958 and Stanford University Press, 1968).

Hammond, J. L. and B., *The Town Labourer, 1760–1832* (Longmans, 1917, reprinted 1966, and Anchor Doubleday, 1968).

Hammond, J. L. and B., *The Village Labourer, 1760–1832* (Longmans, 1919, reprinted 1966 and Harper Torch Books, 1970).

Hammond, J. L. and B., *The Skilled Labourer, 1760–1832* (Longmans, 1919 and Harper Torch Books, 1970).
> These three books have been reprinted at various times and have made an important contribution to social history. They are written with passionate sympathy, but modern historians do not accept all their conclusions without reservations.

Hollis, Patricia, *The Pauper Press: A Study in Working Class Radicalism of the 1830's* (Oxford University Press, 1970).

Read, Donald, *Peterloo: the Massacre and its Background* (Manchester University Press and Kelley, 1958).

Thompson, E. P., *The Making of the English Working Class* (Gollancz, 1963 and Pantheon, 1964). An exhaustive study written with working class sympathies.

Walmsley, R., *Peterloo: the Case Re-opened* (Manchester University Press, 1969).

Webb, S. and B., *The History of Trade Unions* (Longmans and Kelley, 1950).

Politics and the Constitution

Consult Asa Briggs, E. Halévy and E. L. Woodward for the general background and, for the effect of the Reform Act of 1832, Norman Gash, *Politics in the Age of Peel* (Longmans and Humanities, 1950; later edition 1964).

Social Reform

Blaug, M., 'The myth of the old Poor Law and the making of the New', *Journal of Economic History*, 1963 and 'The new Poor Law re-examined', *Journal of Economic History*, 1964.

Eden, Sir Frederick, *The State of the Poor* (1797). There is an abridged edition edited by A. G. Rogers (Routledge & Kegan Paul, 1938 and Blom, 1969) and a facsimile reprint (Cass, 1966).

Finer, S. E., *The Life and Times of Sir Edwin Chadwick* (Methuen, 1952 and Barnes & Noble, 1970).

Lewis, R. A., *Edwin Chadwick and the Public Health Movement, 1832–54* (Longmans and Kelley, 1952).

Marshall, D. J., *The Old Poor Law, 1795–1834* (Longmans, 1968).

Poynter, J. R., *Society and Pauperism: Ideas on Poor Relief, 1795–1834* (Rout-
  ledge & Kegan Paul and University of Toronto Press, 1969).
Roberts, F. D., *The Victorian Origin of the Welfare State, 1830–55* (Yale
  University Press, 1960).
Thomas, M. W., *The Factory Movement* (Macmillan, 1948).

Index